Multilingual Selves and Motivations for Learning Languages other than English in Asian Contexts

PSYCHOLOGY OF LANGUAGE LEARNING AND TEACHING
Series Editors: Sarah Mercer, *Universität Graz, Austria* and Stephen Ryan, *Waseda University, Japan*

This international, interdisciplinary book series explores the exciting, emerging field of Psychology of Language Learning and Teaching. It is a series that aims to bring together works which address a diverse range of psychological constructs from a multitude of empirical and theoretical perspectives, but always with a clear focus on their applications within the domain of language learning and teaching. The field is one that integrates various areas of research that have been traditionally discussed as distinct entities, such as motivation, identity, beliefs, strategies and self-regulation, and it also explores other less familiar concepts for a language education audience, such as emotions, the self and positive psychology approaches. In theoretical terms, the new field represents a dynamic interface between psychology and foreign language education and books in the series draw on work from diverse branches of psychology, while remaining determinedly focused on their pedagogic value. In methodological terms, sociocultural and complexity perspectives have drawn attention to the relationships between individuals and their social worlds, leading to a field now marked by methodological pluralism. In view of this, books encompassing quantitative, qualitative and mixed methods studies are all welcomed.

All books in this series are externally peer-reviewed.

Full details of all the books in this series and of all our other publications can be found on http://www.multilingual-matters.com, or by writing to Multilingual Matters, St Nicholas House, 31-34 High Street, Bristol, BS1 2AW, UK.

PSYCHOLOGY OF LANGUAGE LEARNING AND TEACHING: 24

Multilingual Selves and Motivations for Learning Languages other than English in Asian Contexts

Edited by
Anas Hajar and Syed Abdul Manan

MULTILINGUAL MATTERS
Bristol • Jackson

DOI https://doi.org/10.21832/HAJAR7229
Library of Congress Cataloging in Publication Data
A catalog record for this book is available from the Library of Congress.
Names: Hajar, Anas, editor. | Manan, Syed Abdul, editor.
Title: Multilingual Selves and Motivations for Learning Languages other
   than English in Asian Contexts/Edited by Anas Hajar and Syed Abdul Manan.
Description: Bristol; Jackson: Multilingual Matters, [2024] | Series:
   Psychology of Language Learning and Teaching: 24 | Includes
   bibliographical references and index. | Summary: 'This book focuses on
   individuals learning languages other than English in a range of
   under-researched Asian contexts. The chapters explore learners'
   motivational trajectories, multilingual identities and
   conceptualisations of the "ideal multilingual self"' – Provided by publisher.
Identifiers: LCCN 2024002661 (print) | LCCN 2024002662 (ebook) | ISBN
   9781800417229 (hardback) | ISBN 9781800417212 (paperback) | ISBN
   9781800417243 (epub) | ISBN 9781800417236 (pdf)
Subjects: LCSH: Language and languages – Study and teaching – Asia. |
   Motivation in education. | Multilingualism – Social aspects. | LCGFT: Essays.
Classification: LCC P53.48 .M85 2024 (print) | LCC P53.48 (ebook) | DDC
   418.0071/05 – dc23/eng/20240302
LC record available at https://lccn.loc.gov/2024002661
LC ebook record available at https://lccn.loc.gov/2024002662

British Library Cataloguing in Publication Data
A catalogue entry for this book is available from the British Library.

ISBN-13: 978-1-80041-722-9 (hbk)
ISBN-13: 978-1-80041-721-2 (pbk)

Multilingual Matters
UK: St Nicholas House, 31-34 High Street, Bristol, BS1 2AW, UK.
USA: Ingram, Jackson, TN, USA.

Website: https://www.multilingual-matters.com
X: Multi_Ling_Mat
Facebook: https://www.facebook.com/multilingualmatters
Blog: https://www.channelviewpublications.wordpress.com

Copyright © 2024 Anas Hajar, Syed Abdul Manan and the authors of individual chapters.

All rights reserved. No part of this work may be reproduced in any form or by any means without permission in writing from the publisher.

The policy of Multilingual Matters/Channel View Publications is to use papers that are natural, renewable and recyclable products, made from wood grown in sustainable forests. In the manufacturing process of our books, and to further support our policy, preference is given to printers that have FSC and PEFC Chain of Custody certification. The FSC and/or PEFC logos will appear on those books where full certification has been granted to the printer concerned.

Typeset by Riverside Publishing Solutions.

Contents

Figures and Tables	vii
Contributors	ix
Acknowledgements	xv
Abbreviations	xvii
Foreword	xix
Xuesong (Andy) Gao	

1	Introduction *Anas Hajar and Syed Abdul Manan*	1
2	Language Learning Motivation and the Multilingual Turn *Alastair Henry*	13
3	Negotiating Agentive Selves in Arabic Learning: A Case Study of Arabic Learners at a Chinese University *Ning An and Yongyan Zheng*	34
4	The Construction of Ought-To Multilingual Selves and their Roles in Shaping Chinese Language Learners' LOTE Motivation *Tianyi Wang*	53
5	Japanese Learners' LOTE Motivation and Persistence in Learning: Focusing on the Influence of English *Chika Takahashi*	71
6	Exploring International Students' Experiences of Learning Japanese in Japan through Multimodal Language Learning Histories *Tae Umino*	89
7	Identity, Investment and Language Learning Strategies: Voices of Undergraduate Students Learning Korean in Kazakhstan *Anas Hajar and Syed Abdul Manan*	108
8	Indonesian Students' Mental Images of Portugal and their L2 Motivation *Raan Hann Tan and Larisa Nikitina*	126

9   Multilingual Language Profiles, Perceptions and Motivations
    within the Context of Majoring in a Foreign Language
    in Malaysia   143
    Stefanie Pillai and Roshidah Hassan

10 Understanding Pakistani University Students' Motivations for
    Learning Chinese in Pakistan: A Bourdieusian Perspective   173
    *Muhammad Yasir Khan, Liaquat Ali Channa and
    Muhammad Mohsin Khan*

11 Understanding Challenges, Strategy Use and the Ideal
    Multilingual Self of Internally Displaced Syrians on the
    Syria–Turkey Border   192
    Anas Hajar

12 L2 Selves as a Source of Emotional Discomfort:
    A Self-Discrepancy Perspective   209
    Yeji Han

13 Current Understandings and Future Directions in L2
    Motivation Research   230
    Amy S. Thompson

    Index   236

Figures and Tables

Figures

4.1	Participants' ought-to multilingual selves	65
6.1	Soyeon's (Korean) slide showing Hiragana to represent the Japanese language	95
6.2	Ubin's (Korean) slide showing the place (Fukuoka) where he decided to study Japanese	95
6.3	Xuyang's (Chinese) slide showing his anxiety and the pressure on him to speak Japanese	96
6.4	Jianguo's (Chinese) slide showing the resources he used to learn Japanese	96
6.5	Qingqing's (Chinese) slide showing the changes in her Japanese skills	96
6.6	Sora's (Korean) slide showing how her motivation for learning Japanese developed	97
6.7	Sora's (Korean) slide showing how she used the lyrics of anime songs to learn Japanese	98
6.8	Maki's (Japanese) slide showing the notification of passing the EIKEN test	99
6.9	Maki's (Japanese) slide showing changes in her image of English	100
6.10	International students' reasons for learning Japanese, at different school ages	101
6.11	Japanese national students' reasons for learning English, at different school ages	102
8.1	Students' images of Portugal	134
9.1	First languages of respondents	151
9.2	Number of languages respondents know and use	153
9.3	Word cloud representing the perceptions of the respondents towards their language majors prior to studying it	154
11.1	The final thematic map	198

Tables

3.1	Participant demographics	38
3.2	A conceptual framework of the current study	39
3.3	Arabic learners' construction of MASs in a dialogically spatial–temporal continuum	48
5.1	The interviewees	75
5.2	Timeline of interviews	76
5.3	Summary of the interviewees' LOTE learning and motivation	85
6.1	Types of visual images appearing in the MLLHs of ISs and JSs	95
6.2	Percentage of students falling into the four main types of MLLHs	97
6.3	Students' reasons for learning their FLs	101
8.1	Categories of images, their favourability (MV) and salience (SI)	134
8.2	Findings concerning language learners' L2 motivation	137
8.3	Reasons for learning Portuguese	139
9.1	Respondents' language major and ethnicity	149
9.2	Language major and perceptions of being multilinguals: Total responses, percentages, scores and mean scores	155
9.3	Perceptions about language major and speakers: Total responses, percentages, scores and mean scores	156
9.4	Motivations to learn language major: Total responses, percentages, scores and mean scores	159
9.5	Perceptions about learning/knowing a foreign language: Total responses, percentages, scores and mean scores	161
10.1	Participant demographics	178
11.1	Demographic data of the participants	197
12.1	Component correlations of L2 dejection	219
12.2	Component correlations of L2 anxiety	219
12.3	Descriptive statistics of upper and lower quartiles of the ideal L2 self discrepancy (distance * plausibility) and the ought-to L2 self discrepancy (distance * plausibility) on the subconstructs of L2 dejection and L2 anxiety	220

Contributors

Ning An is a PhD candidate in applied linguistics at Fudan University, China, and a visiting postgraduate research student at the University of Auckland, New Zealand. Her research interests include multilingual education (especially pedagogical translanguaging, LOTE teaching and learning etc.), and language-in-education policy and planning. Her recent publications have appeared in *Current Issues in Language Planning* (SSCI), *Círculo de Lingüística Aplicada a la Comunicación* (SSCI), *Foreign Language Teaching and Research* (CSSCI), and *Foreign Language Education* (CSSCI). She is a member of the Hamburg–Fudan–Macquarie New Generation Literacies Network.

Liaquat Ali Channa holds a PhD in language and literacy education with a specialization in TESOL and World Language Education from the University of Georgia, USA. He is a Fulbright alumnus. He currently serves as a professor in the Department of English at Balochistan University of IT, Engineering & Management Sciences (BUITEMS), Quetta, Pakistan. He is also a research affiliate at the Mittal South Asia Institute at Harvard University. His research interests include English medium instruction; bilingual and multilingual education; language policy and planning; and educational linguistics.

Xuesong (Andy) Gao is Professor of Language and Literacy Education in the School of Education, University of New South Wales, Australia. His research interests include language learner autonomy, language education policy and language teacher education. He is the editor-in-chief for *International Review of Applied Linguistics in Language Teaching*, an executive editor for *Teaching and Teacher Education*, a principal associate editor for *The Asia-Pacific Education Researcher*, and a section editor for *SAGE Open* (Education Section). He is also Series Editor for the English Language Education Series published by Springer.

Anas Hajar is a graduate of Warwick University in England, holding a PhD in language education. He worked as a postdoctoral research and teaching fellow at the University of Warwick, Coventry, and at

Canterbury Christ Church University in England and as an assistant professor at the Chinese University of Hong Kong in Hong Kong SAR. He is currently an associate professor of multilingual education at Nazarbayev University in Kazakhstan. He is particularly interested in motivational issues in language learning and intercultural engagement. He also works in the areas of internationalization and education abroad, language learning strategies and shadow education.

Yeji Han is Senior Lecturer in Korean and Linguistics at York St John University, UK, where she teaches Korean language and applied linguistics courses. Prior to her current position, she taught applied linguistics and the Korean language in Canada, the USA and Vietnam. She has worked with learners of Korean language for her research on motivation and L2 selves. Her research can be found in *IRAL, Innovation in Language Learning and Teaching*, and the *Journal of Language, Identity and Education*, among other journals. On top of L2 selves and motivation, she is currently working on research projects on foreign language enjoyment, on telecollaboration, and on translanguaging in Korean-pop fandom communication among learners of Korean language.

Roshidah Hassan, PhD, is an associate professor in the Department of Asian and European Languages, Faculty of Languages and Linguistics, Universiti Malaya, where she teaches on the Bachelor of French Languages and Linguistics and the Master of Arts (Linguistics) programmes. Her areas of research include phonetics and phonology, ethnolinguistics and language acquisition. She is co-editor (with Patricia Nora Riget) of *Foreign Language: Teaching and Learning in the Malaysian Context* (University of Malaya Press, 2020).

Alastair Henry is Professor of Language Education at University West, Sweden. His research involves the psychology of language learning and teaching. In addition to motivation, his work has focused on teacher identities, digital technology and language choices in contexts of migration. He was the principal investigator for the Motivational Teaching in Swedish Secondary English (MoTiSSE) project. He is co-editor (with Zoltan Dörnyei and Peter MacIntyre) of *Motivational Dynamics in Language Learning* (Multilingual Matters, 2015), and co-author (with Zoltan Dörnyei and Christine Muir) of *Motivational Currents in Language Learning: Frameworks for Focused Interventions* (Routledge, 2016).

Muhammad Mohsin Khan holds a Masters in English literature and language. He is currently a lecturer in the Department of English, Balochistan University of Information Technology & Management

Sciences (BUITEMS), Quetta, Pakistan. His research interests include language policy and planning, applied linguistics and critical discourse analysis.

Muhammad Yasir Khan is a lecturer in linguistics at Balochistan University of Information Technology & Management Sciences (BUITEMS), Quetta, Pakistan. He is currently pursuing his PhD at the Graduate School of Education (GSE) at Nazarbayev University, Astana, Kazakhstan. His research interests include language policy and planning, curriculum and instruction, and bi/multilingual education.

Syed Abdul Manan holds a PhD in applied linguistics. He is currently an associate professor in the multilingual education program in the Graduate School of Education, Nazarbayev University Nur-Sultan (Astana) Kazakhstan. His work on sociolinguistics, language policy and planning, bi/multilingual Education, World Englishes and linguistic landscape has been published in a range of impact factor journals, including *Language and Education, Language Policy, World Englishes, Language Problems and Language Planning, International Journal of Multilingualism* and *International Journal of Bilingual Education and Bilingualism*.

Larisa Nikitina, PhD, is a senior lecturer in the Department of Asian and European Languages, Faculty of Languages and Linguistics, Universiti Malaya. Her research interests centre around the psychological and emotional factors involved in learning an additional language.

Stefanie Pillai, PhD, is a professor in the Department of English Language, Faculty of Languages and Linguistics, Universiti Malaya. Her main areas of research are varieties of English, in particular Malaysian English, as well as language use in multilingual contexts. The latter includes language education, language policy and endangered languages in Malaysia. Her research on, and documentation of, Melaka Portuguese led to the development of materials with community representatives to encourage the use of this endangered language. She has recently co-edited (with Hanafi Hussin and Roshidah Hassan) *Selected Research on Orang Asli Communities* (University of Malaya Press, 2022).

Chika Takahashi is an associate professor at Ehime University, Japan. She holds a PhD in second language studies from the University of Hawai'i at Mānoa, and her research interests include L2 motivation, L2 self-instruction and research methods. She is particularly interested in motivation to learn multiple languages that may sometimes extend beyond formal education and how that can be captured in empirical studies. She has recently published articles in *The Language Learning Journal* and *Studies in Second Language Learning and Teaching*, and is the author of *Motivation to Learn Multiple Languages in Japan: A Longitudinal Perspective* (Multilingual Matters, 2023).

Raan Hann Tan, PhD, is a research fellow at the Institute of Malaysian and International Studies (IKMAS), Universiti Kebangsaan Malaysia (UKM). Her research interests include multilingualism, ethnic and religious minorities, kinship, social organization, music, food and identities.

Amy S. Thompson is Professor of Applied Linguistics and Department Chair of World Languages, Literatures, and Linguistics at West Virginia University, USA. Her primary research interests involve individual differences in second language acquisition and their interaction with multilingualism. She is the author of *The Role of Context in Language Teachers' Self Development and Motivation: Perspectives from Multilingual Settings* (Multilingual Matters, 2021) and co-editor (with Ursula Lanvers and Martin East) of *Language Learning in Anglophone Countries: Challenges, Practices, Ways Forward* (Palgrave MacMillan, 2020). Her work has been published in a range of applied linguistics journals.

Tae Umino received her PhD in applied linguistics from the UCL Institute of Education, University of London and is a professor at the Institute of Japan Studies, Tokyo University of Foreign Studies. Her research currently focuses on self-instruction, out-of-class L2 learning, L2 learning in study-abroad and the use of visuals in narrative inquiry. She is co-author (with Phil Benson) of a chapter entitled 'Study-abroad in Pictures: Photographs as Data in Life-story Research' in Paula Kalaja and Silvia Melo-Pfeifer's (eds) *Visualising Multilingual Lives: More Than Words* (Multilingual Matters, 2019) and has published articles in journals such as *System* and *The Modern Language Journal*.

Tianyi Wang is a lecturer in education in the School of Education, University of Sheffield. She completed her PhD in the Faculty of Education, University of Cambridge. Her main research interest resides in language learning motivation, motivational intervention and multilingualism. She has also worked as a research associate for the Education Reform and Innovation Research team at the University of Cambridge and focused on education reform and teacher agency before becoming a lecturer at the University of Sheffield. Her publications include articles in *Language Teaching Research*, *Teaching and Teacher Education* and *International Journal of Multilingualism*

Yongyan Zheng is Professor of Applied Linguistics at Fudan University, China, where she teaches English academic writing and applied linguistics. Her research interests include second-language development, bilingual and multilingual education, and academic literacy practices. Her recent publications have appeared in *Current Issues in Language Planning*, the *International Journal of Multilingualism*, *Language Awareness*, *Language Policy*, the *Journal of Multilingual and Multicultural Development*, the *Journal of Scholarly Publishing*, *System* and *The Modern Language Journal*. She is the Editor of *Language, Culture and Curriculum*, and the Co-Editor-in-Chief of *System*. She is a co-founder of the Hamburg–Fudan–Macquarie New Generation Literacies Network.

Acknowledgements

We would like to thank the series editors Professor Sarah Mercer and Professor Stephen Ryan for their guidance and support. We would also like to thank the contributors for their patience and engagement throughout the writing and editing process. Our profound gratitude is extended to the energetic and supportive Multilingual Matters family for their recommendations throughout the preparation of this volume. Last but not least, we thank our families, colleagues and friends for their encouragement and support.

The work described in this volume was partially supported by a grant (grant number 20122022FD4117) from Nazarbayev University Graduate School of Education, Astana, Kazakhstan.

Abbreviations

AMTB	Attitude/Motivation Test Battery
CEFR	*Common European Framework of Reference for Languages*
CMV	Composite mean value
CFA	Confirmatory factor analysis
DMM	Dynamic Model of Multilingualism
EFL	English as a foreign language
GDA	Gwadar Development Authority
GPA	Grade point average
IELTS	International English Language Testing System
L2MSS	L2 Motivational Self System
LLHs	Language learning histories
LLSs	Language learning strategies
LOTEs	Languages other than English
MASs	Multilingual agentive selves
MEXT	Ministry of Education, Culture, Sports, Science and Technology
MFLS	Modified free-list salience
MLLHs	Multimodal language learning histories
MOE	Ministry of Education
MS	Mean score
MV	Mean value
NGO	Non-governmental organisation
NPRMs	Near peer role models
NUML	National University of Modern Languages
PCA	Principal component analysis
PPLI	Perceived positive language interaction
RMSEA	Root mean square error of approximation
SD	Standard deviation
SI	Salience index
SLA	Second language acquisition
TL	Target language
TOEFL	Test of English as a Foreign Language
TOPIK	Test of Proficiency in Korean

Foreword

Xuesong (Andy) Gao

It is exciting to see an edited volume on multilingual selves and motivations for learning languages other than English (LOTEs) in Asian contexts. Asia is well known for enthusiastically embracing English as the language of status, and this phenomenon plays a critical role in sustaining the global dominance of the English language. However, little is known about the region's potential as a major player in promoting LOTE education, or about its critical contribution to the promotion of multilingualism and multiculturalism (Gao & Zheng, 2019).

In many contexts, there has been a decline in LOTE learning and teaching in the age of the global spread of English, which is contributing to a waning interest in other languages. The number of school pupils in England taking at least one modern language to age 16 declined from 439,805 in 2015 to 300,422 in 2023 (Collen, 2023), while the number of Danish secondary school students graduating with three modern languages dropped from 40% in 2000 to 4% in 2016 (Gao & Zheng, 2019). The Modern Language Association in the United States has similarly reported that foreign language enrolment at American colleges dropped from 9.1% of students in 2006 to 7.5% in 2016, causing universities to close their modern language programmes. Seismic political events such as Brexit have added uncertainty to the future of LOTE education globally. In contrast, we have seen that governments in the Asia–Pacific region, including the Chinese government, have increased investment in teaching and learning LOTEs. Although these developments are unlikely to challenge the dominance of English language education, they have drawn attention to LOTE learning and teaching in the region.

In the past few years, I have had the opportunity to engage with LOTE learning and teaching research in Greater China (a region including Mainland China, Hong Kong, Macau and Taiwan) and co-edited with Professor Yongyan Zheng at Fudan University, China a special issue of the *Journal of Multilingual and Multicultural Development* on the topic (Gao & Zheng, 2019). I also reviewed a research monograph on Japanese language learners' motivation to learn multiple languages (Takahashi, 2023) for the *Asia Pacific Journal of*

Education (Guo & Gao, 2023). Both publications focused on specific regions in Asia (i.e. Greater China and Japan). This edited volume is the first I am aware of to explore language learners' motivation for LOTE learning in a variety of Asian contexts. It is a collection of quality research from colleagues I respect highly and whose work I engage with in my own research. I believe that readers will find Alastair Henry's chapter (Chapter 2) on language learning motivation and the multilingual turn highly informative as it expertly captures how language learning motivation researchers can best respond to the multilingual turn in the study of second language acquisition.

The volume has many commendable features, but I would like to highlight the inclusion of diverse Asian contexts as its most significant and unique feature. In the past, China and Japan have received disproportionate attention in LOTE education research and, for this reason, each context has two chapters in the volume. This fact notwithstanding, the volume also includes studies in an impressive range of Asian contexts that have traditionally been underrepresented in the literature, including Indonesia, Kazakhstan, Malaysia, Pakistan, Syria and Vietnam. It is, for example, truly amazing to read Hajar's chapter (Chapter 11) on internally displaced Syrians talking about their motivation to learn Turkish. Turkish is presented as a target language being learned by internally displaced Syrians under highly challenging conditions. It is also enlightening to hear Indonesian students describing their mental images of Portugal and their motivation to learn Portuguese in Tan and Nikitina's chapter (Chapter 8). The volume also addresses a number of languages that have attracted less attention in the research. For instance, it includes a chapter (Chapter 3 by An & Zheng) reporting on a case study of Arabic learners at a Chinese university. The Korean language is the subject of two chapters (Chapter 7 by Hajar & Manan on LOTE learners in Kazakhstan and Chapter 12 by Han on learners in Vietnam).

The chapters in the volume will surely enrich our understanding of language learning motivation, as research in this area has been dominated by the rise of English as a global lingua franca. This edited volume can be regarded as a collective effort to develop our critical understanding of language learning motivation through empirical findings and conceptual insights from studies on LOTE learning motivation in a variety of Asian contexts.

I feel honoured, and I am also truly humbled, to have the opportunity to participate in this exciting project. I congratulate Dr Anas Hajar and Dr Syed Abdul Manan on producing this highly significant volume that reflects a collective will to pursue LOTE education research in Asia. I truly hope that more research on LOTE education in Asia will follow to show that the region is a powerhouse for LOTE education.

References

Collen, I. (2023) *Language Trends 2023: Language Teaching in Primary and Secondary Schools in England*. British Council. https://www.britishcouncil.org/sites/default/files/language_trends_england_2023.pdf.

Gao, X. and Zheng, Y. (2019) Multilingualism and higher education in Greater China. *Journal of Multilingual and Multicultural Development* 40 (7), 555–561. https://doi.org/10.1080/01434632.2019.1571073.

Gu, J. and Gao, X. (2023) *Motivation to Learn Multiple Languages in Japan: A Longitudinal Perspective* by Chika Takahashi, Bristol, Multilingual Matters, 2023, 211pp., £89.95 (hardback), ISBN 9781800414839; £15.00 (e-book), LCCN 2022033937. [Book review.] *Asia Pacific Journal of Education*, 1–3. https://doi.org/10.1080/02188791.2023.2224632.

Takahashi, C. (2023) *Motivation to Learn Multiple Languages in Japan: A Longitudinal Perspective*. Multilingual Matters.

1 Introduction

Anas Hajar and Syed Abdul Manan

Why a New Volume on Language Learning Motivation?

In the field of second language acquisition (SLA), motivation is regarded as the primary impetus to initiate second language (L2) learning and sustain it. As expressed by Corder's (1967: 164) oft-cited words: 'given motivation, it is inevitable that a human being will learn a second language if they are exposed to the language data'. The implication of Corder's words is that a deeper understanding of motivation can lead to better language learning outcomes; indeed, motivation tends to be perceived as the mantle of the 'holy grail' (Ryan, 2020: 169). L2 learning motivation research has thus become a vibrant field since its inception in Gardner and Lambert's (1959) seminal paper, 'Motivational Variables in Second Language Acquisition', published in the *Canadian Journal of Psychology*. The vibrancy and maturity of L2 motivation can be marked by the first handbook devoted to this research domain (Lamb *et al.*, 2020).

Nevertheless, previous research on L2 motivation has had a longstanding monolingual bias, primarily due to its disproportionate focus on global English, which has often been positioned as 'a preferred, indeed obligatory, additional language' (Duff, 2017: 598) and hence research on English language motivation has surpassed the study of languages other than English (LOTEs). Henry (2010: 151) highlighted this point more than a decade ago, indicating that 'research into L2 motivation … has, in theoretical terms, largely concerned itself with situations where monolingual learners are engaged in learning a single L2', in particular English. Elsewhere, Henry (2017) points out that the global English bias is intensified by the questionable certainty of the theoretical paradigms in L2 motivation – including Gardner's (2001) Socio-Educational Model and Dörnyei's (2009) L2 Motivational Self System – because they have been constructed according to a monolingual logic where the pursuit is mainly to explain individuals' motivations to learn English. Empirically, in their systematic and comprehensive survey of L2 motivation research from 2005 to 2014 (N = 416), Boo *et al.* (2015) have demonstrated the imbalance between research in English and LOTE learning, reporting that 72.67% of the empirical studies have examined the motivation to study English. Such monolingual bias in L2 motivation research generates 'a reductionist picture' because insufficient attention has been paid to the motivational profiles of learners of LOTEs, including immigrants residing in non-English-speaking countries (Dörnyei & Al-Hoorie, 2017: 456).

Although L2 motivation researchers may be accused of embracing 'a no difference assumption' (Henry & Thorsen, 2018: 349), recent years have seen some shift from the traditionally skewed focus on English to LOTEs, or concomitantly examining English and LOTE motivation (Takahashi, 2023). This can be evidenced by the two special issues of *The Modern Language Journal* edited by Ushioda and Dörnyei (2017) and Duff and Byrnes (2019), where several articles focus on the 'multilingual turn' in SLA and individuals' motivations to learn LOTEs. Ushioda and Dörnyei (2017: 452), for instance, point out that the continued bias towards global English should not persist, emphasising that L2 motivation researchers' mission is to 'take a critical look at this largely uncharted area of motivation to learn languages other than English (LOTEs) in the current era of globalisation and multiculturalism' to understand the possibilities of motivational interactions or interferences when individuals are engaged in learning LOTEs in parallel with L2 English. Learning LOTEs can help individuals interact effectively in a multicultural and multilingual future workplace, making it a valuable social, economic and cultural asset (Quinto *et al.*, 2023).

As multilingualism is the norm for a large section of the population in many societies (May, 2014; Ortega, 2014), the importance of investigating the motivation to learn LOTEs has been increasingly apparent in published articles in top-tier journals such as the *International Journal of Multilingualism,* the *Journal of Multilingual and Multicultural Development* and *The Modern Language Journal*. Nevertheless, edited collections and monographs on L2 motivation have predominantly centred on the study of English, including those directly addressing motivation in Asian language learning contexts (e.g. Apple *et al.*, 2017; Hennebry-Leung & Gao, 2023). Hennebry-Leung and Gao (2023) point out that English is the most strategic foreign language in Asian contexts, due to its dominant position in economic development, transportation, popular culture (e.g. pop songs and movies) and societal modernisation. It has long been regarded in most Asian contexts as the language for 'a good education and a good job', as well as 'for attaining the better life' (Young & Igcalinos, 2019: 172). Related concerns are the way neoliberalism promotes English as an essential artefact for fostering the ideologies of individualism and competition in both educational and non-educational settings, such as the workplace (Manan & Hajar, 2022). However, by definition, SLA concerns the learning of any 'additional language, including second, foreign, indigenous, minority, or heritage languages' (Douglas Fir Group, 2016: 19).

In Apple *et al.*'s (2017) edited volume, Lopez and Gonzales' chapter (Lopez & Gonzales, 2017) stands out as the first apparent example of LOTEs in Asian context-based L2 motivation studies. The researchers quantitatively examined 640 Filipino university students' motivation to learn one of the LOTEs – namely, Mandarin, French, Japanese or Spanish. They also investigated the correlation between the learning motivation of LOTE students and their critical thinking motivation. The study found that there were differences in the level and type of motivation between male and female students, as well as between female students studying various languages. Significantly, female students learning Mandarin demonstrate greater inclination towards integrative motivation, while female students learning French showed the highest instrumental orientation. Another clear exception is Takahashi's 2023 monograph, *Motivation to Learn Multiple Languages in Japan*, which qualitatively documents the multilingual motivational trajectories of two Japanese learners of English and LOTEs (e.g. French and German) in Japan as they successfully but differently negotiated context and agency over nine years while they progressed from high school to the world of work. Takahashi's (2023) study reveals how language learners in English and LOTEs are not successful because they are like 'an idealised monolingual native speaker' (Cook, 2016: 11) but rather by virtue of being able to 'function in more than one language vis-à-vis whatever life demands a person faces, by circumstance or choice' (Ortega, 2019: 25). Takahashi (2023) acknowledges the limitations of her longitudinal study by focusing only on the dynamic language learning experiences of two participants in Japan, calling for in-depth examinations of multilingual learners' motivations for learning LOTEs in other under-researched contexts because most previous studies of LOTEs were conducted in European and Anglophone contexts.

By representing a multilingual and multicultural world, this edited volume is one of the first to examine the motivational trajectories and multilingual identities of learners of LOTEs (e.g. Arabic, Chinese, French, German, Japanese, Korean, Portuguese and Turkish) across eight Asian contexts (China, Japan, Kazakhstan, Indonesia, Malaysia, Pakistan, Syria and Vietnam). Several chapters of this volume underline individuals' holistic linguistic repertoires and strategic language learning efforts to accomplish their ideal end states and desired identities. This volume may be regarded as a response to Ortega's (2019: 33) call for expanding the nascent engagement of SLA with multilingualism beyond the elite, familiar, European model: 'SLA knowledge is almost exclusively based on contexts located in the 36% countries (N = 78) that are classified by the World Bank as high income'. Similarly, May (2019: 124) correctly remarks that while LOTE learning motivation has become a burgeoning line of inquiry, SLA research is confined to a narrow slice of the diverse experiences of multilingual learning, that of 'outliers – initially monolingual adult language learners, elite and often college-based, who are learning an additional language sequentially and discretely'. Therefore, one of the significant contributions of this volume is to report scholarship on LOTEs from relatively under-researched contexts such as Indonesia, Pakistan, Syria and Vietnam. Syria, for instance, has suffered from the prolonged quagmire of unresolved civil war since 2011.

This volume also aims to align with the 'multilingual turn' in SLA that offers a critical alternative conceptualisation of languages, learners and language learning. It perceives languages as an integrated, crosslingual, dynamic and multimodal semiotic system, and indeed, as translocal and mobile resources owned by those who use them to engage in practice within a contact zone (May, 2014; Thompson, 2020). In this sense, learners may be viewed as individuals of a multilingual society with unique, complex, heterogenous and dynamic identities such as 'students', 'immigrants', 'actors', 'university lecturers' etc. The concept of 'the ideal multilingual self' (Henry, 2017; Ushioda, 2017) has thus been proposed to capture an individual's aspirations to become multilingual in the future. Related to this, Mercer (2014: 160) underlines the complexity of self that encapsulates 'a range of self-related cognitions, beliefs, emotions, motives, roles, relationships, memories, dreams and goals, as well as expressions of who you feel you are not'.

Who is this Book for?

Those who might find this book useful include:

- *Policymakers.* Since there has so far been so little research done to address the realities of motivational trajectories and multilingual identities of individuals learning languages other than English (LOTEs) in Asia, this book provides insights into these realities for those responsible for implementing educational policies.
- *Thesis writers.* This volume provides a valuable source of information on language learning motivations and language identities. It advances suggestions for further research which could be especially useful for thesis writers from a wide range of contexts worldwide.
- *Students and their teachers/private tutors.* This volume provides a large bank of wide-ranging information and evidence that can be used to help university students attending courses on individual differences in SLA. Furthermore, it informs teachers/private tutors about the practices of students learning English and LOTEs across different settings, especially in Asia.
- *Researchers* (especially those in the field of language learning motivation). Researchers wishing to keep abreast of the latest developments in this area in the hope of stimulating further research

will benefit from reading this book. Most studies draw on empirical data and deploy various research instruments that suit their respective contexts: we hope, therefore, that future researchers working in this area will utilise and adapt the same tools for their research.

Organisation of the Volume

The volume comprises 13 chapters written by contributors working in various global contexts. Chapter 1 states the rationale, aims and theoretical context of the volume. It provides a brief overview of how a focus on the motivation to learn LOTEs has gained increasing attention in SLA research – which is moving in more multilingually-attuned directions – and how this in turn has encouraged people to be/become multilingual and develop an ideal multilingual self. In Chapter 2, 'Language Learning Motivation and the Multilingual Turn', Alastair Henry explores ways in which a self-concept referencing future multilingualism can emerge through the process of cross-linguistic interaction. With a focus on the functional relevance of the working self-concept, Henry describes four self-concepts that can emerge from the experience of learning an additional language or languages, and which can direct learning behaviours in particular ways. These are, respectively, a *monolingual self*, a *contentedly bilingual self*, an *ideal multilingual self* and an *ought-to multilingual self*. Henry provides illustrations from his previous qualitative work for each of these high-order self-concepts. After reviewing quantitative findings demonstrating the motivational properties of multilingual selves, the chapter ends by reflecting on the challenges involved in L2 motivation research to make a multilingual turn.

In Chapter 3, 'Negotiating Agentive Selves in Arabic Learning: A Case Study of Arabic Learners at a Chinese University', Ning An and Yongyan Zheng investigate how a group of Chinese learners crafted their multilingual agentive selves (MASs) when they chose to learn Arabic as a less commonly taught language in China's English-dominated policy context. Drawing on narrative accounts and semi-structured interviews, the findings reveal how the participants' agentive selves were multi-faceted and fluid, and their actions both perpetuated and transformed their language learning habits, practices and living in their imagined future. Furthermore, the participants' agentive selves were simultaneously facilitated and constrained by multi-dimensional structural factors, such as limited learning resources and an unbalanced credit system.

The trajectories of Chinese learners' ought-to multilingual selves while learning German as a LOTE in a Chinese university are examined in Chapter 4, 'The Construction of Ought-To Multilingual Selves and their Roles in Shaping Chinese Language Learners' LOTE Motivation'. Tianyi Wang, in conducting three rounds of interviews over three years, found that while her participants' ought-to selves in the initial stages of learning were mainly associated with their fear of losing their linguistic advantage of English, they gradually developed more context-specific and individualised reasons to be multilingual, attributable to the accumulation of participants' multilingual experience. Wang's study demonstrates the importance of recognising the role of ought-to multilingual selves in developing language learners' persistence with LOTE learning.

In Chapter 5, 'Japanese Learners' LOTE Motivation and Persistence in Learning: Focusing on the Influence of English', Chika Takahashi reports on a multiple-case study of three Japanese students learning Korean or German as a LOTE at a national university's faculty of law and letters in rural Japan. Takahashi finds that although her participants equally perceive English as a global language, their LOTE learning motivation trajectories follow different paths, particularly after the end of the compulsory language learning period – two persisted in LOTE learning but the third did not. Nevertheless, the study shows that all of them appreciate the nature of LOTE courses being compulsory at university.

In Chapter 6, 'Exploring International Students' Experiences of Learning Japanese in Japan through Multimodal Language Learning Histories', Tae Umino analyses digitally produced multimodal language learning histories (MLLHs) to understand the language learning experiences of two groups of university students in Japan: one was international students learning Japanese, and the other was Japanese students learning English. The study found that international students used images of resources more frequently than Japanese students, who preferred to use images of people to describe their actions and emotions. This finding is ascribed to international students' strongly intrinsic orientations, describing their Japanese learning experiences in terms of their interest in Japanese pop culture. In contrast, Japanese students tend to describe extrinsic orientation and motivational changes using images of people. This study confirms that learners' motivational orientation is influenced by the context of their target language, highlighting the potential to use multimodal data to study second or foreign language learning experiences.

Chapter 7, 'Identity, Investment and Language Learning Strategies: Voices of Undergraduate Students Learning Korean in Kazakhstan', examines a group of Kazakhstani students' experiences of learning Korean as L4 or L5. Anas Hajar and Syed Abdul Manan reveal that most participants are influenced by the Korean Wave, and their interest in K-pop and K-drama represented their main motives to start learning Korean. The participants also gradually recognise the academic and economic benefits of learning Korean – namely well-paid occupations and opportunities for studying abroad in Korea. The study emphasises the modelling effect of *near peer role models* (NPRMs) for learning LOTEs, along with the importance of exploring language learners' development of their intercultural/global citizenship identity while learning LOTEs.

In Chapter 8, 'Indonesian Students' Mental Images of Portugal and their L2 Motivation', Raan Hann Tan and Larisa Nikitina investigate 48 Indonesian university students' mental images of Portugal and their motivation to learn Portuguese as an additional language in Indonesia. The participants show a positive attitude to Portugal attributable to the influence of important Portuguese figures and the linguistic impact of Portuguese on the Indonesian language. In addition, the participants refer to the cultural, economic and personal gains of learning Portuguese. Tan and Nikitina conclude their study by underlying the importance of integrating specific activities inside the classroom that can enhance language learners' positive mental images towards the target language and its culture.

In Chapter 9, 'Multilingual Language Profiles, Perceptions and Motivations within the Context of Majoring in a Foreign Language in Malaysia', Stefanie Pillai and Roshidah Hassan draw on a questionnaire survey to analyse the multilingual profiles of 83 respondents from four undergraduate programmes in foreign languages and linguistics, majoring in four foreign language undergraduate programmes at a public university in Malaysia. The study discusses how these respondents perceive themselves as multilinguals vis-à-vis the languages they already know and use, and their motivations for pursuing a LOTE degree programme. The study shows a sense of the utilitarian use of their language major (e.g. for travel and work opportunities) and a socially driven sense of motivation, such as communicating with locals and the use of language for networking purposes. Taken together, the multilingual profiles, the respondents' perceptions about their language majors and the inclusion of the new language as part of their multilingual repertoire, along with the perception of themselves as fluent users of these languages, can be linked to their motivation for learning these languages.

In Chapter 10, 'Understanding Pakistani University Students' Motivations for Learning Chinese in Pakistan: A Bourdieusian Perspective', Muhammad Yasir Khan, Liaquat Ali Channa and Muhammad Mohsin Khan employ qualitative interviews to explore the Pakistani university students' motives to learn the Chinese language. The study suggests that university students regard the Chinese language as a means to improve their socioeconomic status due to growing Chinese investments in Pakistan. As well as its promised employability, students learn the Chinese language to pursue higher education opportunities in China. In Bourdieusian terms, participants perceived the Chinese language as an alternative capital that is acquiring currency in the field.

By conferring institutional recognition, academic capital can be given a monetary value, allowing for the establishment of conversion rates between cultural and economic capital (Bourdieu, 2010).

Little research has explored individuals' multilingual selves when learning LOTEs in conflict-affected situations. To this end, Anas Hajar, in Chapter 11, reports on a qualitative study of the experiences of a group of internally displaced Syrians learning Turkish as an L3 or L4 in Afrin, located on the Syria–Turkey border. The study finds that the driving force behind the participants' desire to learn Turkish ranges from improving their curriculum vitae and securing a job in the Afrin area to reasons associated with achieving their ideal selves by imagining themselves working/studying at a Turkish university and becoming integrated into the Turkish community in future. The participants act agentively, recognising that attending Turkish private tutoring courses with low-qualified tutors is insufficient to improve their Turkish language proficiency. Hajar stresses the importance of exploring the nexus between motivation for learning/teaching LOTEs and peacebuilding, as well as conducting research on private tutoring in languages, particularly in LOTEs.

In Chapter 12, 'L2 Selves as a Source of Emotional Discomfort: A Self-Discrepancy Perspective', Yeji Han offers a quantitative investigation of the emotional experiences of 533 Vietnamese students enrolled in an undergraduate degree programme in Korean language and culture in Hanoi, Vietnam. Han finds that students who perceived their ideal and ought-to L2 self as being more distant and less plausible, had experienced dejection and anxiety more intensely than those who perceived the lower discrepancies. The study provides a new perspective on emotional experiences in L2 motivation research, which may hold promise for future research in other LOTEs contexts.

In the concluding chapter, Chapter 13, 'Current Understandings and Future Directions in L2 Motivation Research', Amy Thompson addresses 'ways forward' for language learning motivation research, highlighting aspects that are often under-researched: multilingualism, LOTEs and contexts, interwoven with other complexities.

Finally, we are delighted to be able to include a Foreword by Professor Xuesong (Andy) Gao, who shares his views on the timely publication of this volume in relation to exploring the ways in which multilingualism/plurilingualism can constitute a way to understand individuals' motivations to learn LOTEs.

Conclusion

Asia is widely recognised for its enthusiastic adoption of English as the language of power and its important role in maintaining the global dominance of English. Hence, English learning motivation is a highly researched topic in L2 acquisition in Asia, as evidenced by the expanding number of published books, journal issues, articles, doctoral theses, conference papers and institutional research reports on this research domain. However, not much attention has been given to Asia's potential to become a significant promoter of LOTE education, and its critical contribution to the promotion of multilingualism and multiculturalism (Gu & Gao, 2023).

This volume stands out from many publications on L2 motivation in that it is the first to explore the learning of LOTEs across different Asian contexts, including China, Japan, Kazakhstan, Indonesia, Malaysia, Pakistan, Syria and Vietnam. It highlights the significance of SLA research in serving all multilingual individuals, not just the privileged ones, by encouraging language researchers to conduct empirical studies in non-affluent geographies including '[g]rass-roots multilingualism and the multilingualism of marginalized and minoritized communities' (Ortega, 2019: 32). The volume comprises 13 chapters that showcase how LOTE learners reflect on the value of languages, comprehend the implications of language learning on their evolving identities, and appreciate cultural practices and values associated with different languages. These insights significantly enhance learners' motivation to learn LOTEs.

The empirical studies included in this volume move forward the discussion of how to construct learners' LOTE and multilingual selves in the language classroom and develop realistic goals for their LOTE learning, taking into account the mediating role of language learning context (Mercer, 2016; Thompson, 2021). Mercer (2016: 13), for instance, remarkably points out that context is not monolithic but refers to 'multiple levels of contexts stretching from micro-level interactional contexts to macro-level cultures'. In certain Asian countries such as Indonesia, Syria and Vietnam, people may have more limited exposure to individuals from different cultural and linguistic backgrounds than in countries like China, Japan, Kazakhstan and Malaysia. This is because people in the latter countries tend to travel abroad more frequently to gain exposure to languages other than their own. Additionally, they may have more opportunities to interact with international students and resources that enable them to broaden their experiences and develop their language identities.

While context inevitably shapes individuals' language learning experiences, it has an *influential* rather than a *determining* impact on their persistence in multiple language learning and the strategies they use to achieve the ideal multilingual self (Hajar, 2019). In this sense, both learner agency and context are essential in language learning; learners can create their own micro-contexts in difficult circumstances for successful language learning: 'In short, there is no doubt that context matters in SLA, yet what matters just as much is the individual agency of L2 learners, inherently part of and actively shaping the developing contexts of learning, input and interaction in which they are situated' (Ushioda, 2014: 189).

In today's globalised yet multicultural and multilingual world, language learning occurs in various contexts, each with unique challenges. As such, a number of language researchers (e.g. Gregersen & Mercer, 2022; Henry, 2023) emphasise the need to shed light on the psychological factors that underlie efforts made by language learners. Henry (2023: 197), for instance, suggests that teachers of LOTEs and researchers of language development should recognise the danger of attributing the lack of multilingual aspirations in their students or research participants to personal shortcomings or failures, rather than the structures that shape them. This is because many students raised in monolingual environments may struggle to imagine a future involving multilingualism, which could hinder their ability to envision an ideal multilingual self or an ideal L2 self.

This volume, which is the first on LOTE learning in different Asian contexts, also presents the results of various studies that can inspire readers to consider the educational system and pinpoint areas for improvement in terms of teaching and learning multiple languages, apart from English. However, it has some limitations. In particular, the volume only covers the experiences of language learners who learned LOTEs in eight Asian regions, and the study participants were adult learners of LOTEs. Therefore, further research is required to investigate the experiences of individuals, particularly young children, who are learning LOTEs in other Asian settings to provide a comprehensive understanding of the dynamics and context sensitivity of their future aspirations, taking into consideration their previous language learning experiences and linguistic repertoires.

References

Apple, M.T., Da Silva, D. and Fellner, T. (eds) (2017) *L2 Selves and Motivations in Asian Contexts*. Multilingual Matters.

Boo, Z., Dörnyei, Z. and Ryan, S. (2015) L2 motivation research 2005–2014: Understanding a publication surge and a changing landscape. *System* 55, 145–157.

Bourdieu, P. (2010) The forms of capital (1986). In I. Szeman and T. Kaposy (eds) *Cultural Theory: An Anthology* (pp. 81–93). Wiley.

Cook, V. (2016) Premises of multicompetence. In V. Cook and Li, Wei (eds) *The Cambridge Handbook of Linguistic Multicompetence* (pp. 1–25). Cambridge University Press.

Corder, S.P. (1967) The significance of learners' errors. *International Review of Applied Linguistics* 5 (2/3), 161–169.

Dörnyei, Z. (2009) The L2 motivational self system. In Z. Dörnyei and E. Ushioda (eds) *Motivation, Language Identity and the L2 Self* (pp. 9–42). Multilingual Matters.

Dörnyei, Z. and Al-Hoorie, A.H. (2017) The motivational foundation of learning languages other than global English: Theoretical issues and research directions. *The Modern Language Journal* 101 (3), 455–468.

Douglas Fir Group (2016) A transdisciplinary framework for SLA in a multilingual world. *The Modern Language Journal* 100 (S1), 19–47.

Duff, P.A. (2017) Commentary: Motivation for learning languages other than English in an English-dominant world. *The Modern Language Journal* 101 (3), 597–607.

Duff, P.A. and Byrnes, H. (2019) SLA across disciplinary borders: Introduction to the special issue. *The Modern Language Journal*, 103 (Supplement 2019), 3–5.

Gardner, R.C. (2001) Integrative motivation and second language acquisition. In Z. Dörnyei and R. Schmidt (eds) *Motivation and Language Acquisition* (pp. 1–19). University of Hawai'i Press.

Gardner, R.C. and Lambert, W.E. (1959) Motivational variables in second language acquisition. *Canadian Journal of Psychology* 13, 266–272.

Gregersen, T. and Mercer, S. (eds) (2022) *The Routledge Handbook of the Psychology of Language Learning and Teaching*. Routledge.

Gu, J. and Gao, X. (2023) Motivation to Learn Multiple Languages in Japan: A Longitudinal Perspective by Chika Takahashi, Bristol, Multilingual Matters, 2023, 211pp., £89.95 (hardback), ISBN 9781800414839; £15.00 (e-book), LCCN 2022033937. [Book review]. *Asia Pacific Journal of Education*. https://doi.org/10.1080/02188791.2023.2224632.

Hajar, A. (2019) *International Students' Challenges, Strategies and Future Vision: A Socio-Dynamic Perspective*. Multilingual Matters.

Hennebry-Leung, M. and Gao, X.A. (2023) *Language Learning Motivation in a Multilingual Chinese Context*. Routledge.

Henry, A. (2010) Contexts of possibility in simultaneous language learning: Using the L2 Motivational Self System to assess the impact of global English. *Journal of Multilingual and Multicultural Development* 31 (2), 149–162.

Henry, A. (2017) L2 motivation and multilingual identities. *The Modern Language Journal* 101 (3), 548–565.

Henry, A. (2023) Multilingualism and persistence in multiple language learning. *The Modern Language Journal* 107 (1), 183–201.

Henry, A. and Thorsen, C. (2018) Teacher–student relationships and L2 motivation. *The Modern Language Journal* 102 (1), 218–241.

Lamb, M., Csizér, K., Henry, A. and Ryan. S. (eds) (2020) *Palgrave Macmillan Handbook of Motivation for Language Learning*. Palgrave Macmillan.

Lopez, M.Y. and Gonzales, R.D.L.C. (2017) Examining the relationship between foreign language learning motivation and critical thinking motivation: The case of Filipino foreign language learners. In M.T. Apple, D.D. Silva and T. Fellner (eds) *L2 Selves and Motivations in Asian Contexts* (pp. 94–118). Multilingual Matters.

Manan, S.A. and Hajar, A. (2022) 'Disinvestment' in learners' multilingual identities: English learning, imagined identities, and neoliberal subjecthood in Pakistan. *Journal of Language, Identity & Education*, 1–16. https://doi.org/10.1080/15348458.2022.2083623.

May, S. (2014) *The Multilingual Turn: Implications for SLA, TESOL and Bilingual Education*. Routledge.

May, S. (2019) Negotiating the multilingual turn in SLA. *The Modern Language Journal* 103 (S1), 122–129.

Mercer, S. (2014) The self from a complexity perspective. In S. Mercer and M. Williams (eds) *Multiple Perspectives on the Self in SLA* (pp. 160–177). Multilingual Matters.

Mercer, S. (2016) The contexts within me: L2 self as a complex dynamic system. In J. King (ed.) *The Dynamic Interplay between Context and the Language Learner* (pp. 11–28). Palgrave Macmillan.

Ortega, L. (2014) *Understanding Second Language Acquisition*. Routledge.

Ortega, L. (2019) SLA and the study of equitable multilingualism. *The Modern Language Journal* 103 (Supplement), 23–38.

Quinto, E.J.M., Ong, A.K.S., Valiente, L.F.L., Olleres, L.J.B., Pinugu, J.N.J., Gaerlan, M.J.M. and Castillo, J.C.D. (2023) Exploring the motivations and emotions of Filipino learners of languages other than English: A structural equation modelling approach.

International Journal of Multilingualism, 1–21. https://doi.org/10.1080/14790718. 2023.2224010.

Ryan, S. (2020) Motivation and individual differences. In M. Lamb, K. Csizér, A. Henry and S. Ryan (eds) *Palgrave Macmillan Handbook of Motivation for Language Learning* (pp. 163–182). Palgrave Macmillan.

Takahashi, C. (2023) *Motivation to Learn Multiple Languages in Japan: A Longitudinal Perspective*. Multilingual Matters.

Thompson, A.S. (2020) My many selves are still me: Motivation and multilingualism. *Studies in Second Language Learning and Teaching* 10 (1), 159–176.

Thompson, A.S. (2021) *The Role of Context in Language Teachers' Self Development and Motivation: Perspectives from Multilingual Settings*. Multilingual Matters.

Ushioda, E. (2014) Motivational perspectives on the self in SLA: A developmental view. In S. Mercer and M. Williams (eds) *Multiple Perspectives on the Self in SLA* (pp. 127–141). Multilingual Matters.

Ushioda, E. (2017) The impact of global English on motivation to learn other languages: Toward an ideal multilingual self. *The Modern Language Journal* 101 (3), 469–482.

Ushioda, E. and Dörnyei, Z. (2017) Beyond global English: Motivation to learn languages in a multicultural world: Introduction to the special issue. *The Modern Language Journal* 101 (3), 451–454.

Young, C. and Igcalinos, T. (2019) Language-in-education policy development in the Philippines. In A. Kirkpatrick and A.J. Liddicoat (eds) *The Routledge International Handbook of Language Education Policy in Asia* (pp. 165–184). Routledge.

2 Language Learning Motivation and the Multilingual Turn

Alastair Henry

> Perhaps a more profound and complete reframing for SLA in the 21st century is needed, one that targets a deeper renewal of disciplinary goals and harnesses the unique benefits of studying bi/multilingualism and late learning, all while making transdisciplinary connections of relevance. I have come to think of this encompassing reframing as a bi/multilingual turn in SLA.
> (Ortega, 2019: 123)

The Multilingual Turn in SLA

If the beginnings of a 'multilingual turn' in second language acquisition (SLA) can be traced to a series of high-profile publications from the middle of the last decade (e.g. Conteh & Meier, 2014; May, 2014), its roots are far deeper (Melo-Pfeifer, 2018). As far back as the 1990s, Cook identified a need to re-think the interests and aims of SLA. Rather than examining contrasts between native and non-native language use, Cook argued that the appropriate disciplinary goal for SLA was the investigation of language learning/acquisition later in life, and where the focus would be on 'multi-competence' rather than L2 deficiencies (Cook, 1991, 1992). Challenging the view that L2-users' language systems represent 'imperfect' versions of those of native speakers, he argued that when learning/acquisition takes place beyond childhood, varying cognitive systems are implicated, and that multi-competence involves the *whole* mind. When investigating multilingual acquisition, this means that researchers would need to traverse the broader disciplinary spectra of applied linguistics, and its associated fields (Cook & Li, 2016).

While bi/multilingualism has increasingly become recognized as the norm in global societies (Aronin, 2017), and while multilingualism has generated significant attention in SLA (as evidenced by the number of journals that have had special issues on multilingualism), Ortega (2018: 65) has argued that 'a multilingual turn has yet to fully change the disciplinary ethos of SLA'. To embrace the notion of multi-competence, she contends, more is required than simply shifting perspectives. Rather, a reconceptualization of language learning in adult life is needed (Ortega, 2018). Ultimately, the degree to which SLA will be transformed by a multilingual turn will depend, Ortega (2019) argues, on the preparedness of researchers to embrace transdisciplinarity:

> I believe it is the ability for SLA researchers to invest in future positive reframings of the late-learned, bi/multilingual nature of L2 acquisition that will most radically impact on the field's continued and growing transdisciplinary relevance in the 21st century. Moreover, I predict it will take a bi/multilingual turn in SLA, one of similar depth and magnitude as the earlier social turn experienced (Block, 2003), for these reframings to flourish. (Ortega, 2019: 122)

The social turn (Block, 2003; Firth & Wagner, 1997; Norton, 2000) shifted SLA in new directions. Through engagements with poststructuralist and social systems (Bourdieu, 1977; Lave & Wenger, 1991), it introduced new ways of thinking, and theorizing that could shed light on language use in social interactions. With learning sometimes taking a 'back seat' role (Ellis, 2021: 198), the social turn provided a complementary direction to cognitive linguistics. However, while the social turn might have had the greatest impact of the many 'turns' witnessed in recent years, it did not require the type of fundamental re-think about language *systems* and learning/acquisition *processes* that the multilingual turn implies (Melo-Pfeifer, 2018; Ortega, 2018).

Essentialist and Non-Essentialist Thinking about Language and Language Systems

Historically, the second languages in which learners develop skills have been regarded as separate entities, bounded by particular grammars. Research has studied development in relation to single target languages (TLs), and in a compartmentalized manner, isolated from the processes of growth and attrition taking place in the other languages in a person's repertoire. Rather than 'whole person' understandings of linguistic development, research has provided fragmented insights into aspects of processes that are *separate by design*. As Ortega (2018: 64) has argued, essentialist ontologies – where languages are viewed as separate entities and studied in separation from each other – have had the effect of locking SLA 'into a monolingual worldview'. For the multilingual turn to exert greater leverage, and to transform SLA in fundamental ways, essentialist ontologies need to be problematized and replaced with non-essentialist thinking about languages and the processes through which development takes place (Ortega, 2018).

In motivation research, Ushioda (2017, 2019) has championed a non-essentialist, *multi-competence* perspective. Arguing that theories of motivation and the practice of research can benefit from an inclusive and constitutive approach, she has called for research that reflects 'the more complex sociolinguistic realities of today's linguistically and culturally pluralist societies', and which 'places value on a person's capacity to operate effectively between languages' (2017: 477). However, as Ushioda (2017: 478) has made clear, language learning motivation has been slow to engage with multilingual conceptualizations of learning/acquisition: '[w]hile the multilingual turn is increasingly influencing thinking across many domains of theory, pedagogy, and research in language education, it seems that it has been slower to make inroads into our thinking about language learning motivation'.

Ontological Shifts in Motivation Research

While motivation research continues to be dominated by separationist thinking, the beginnings of a shift to non-essentialist standpoints can be witnessed in Ushioda and Dörnyei's (2017) guest-edited issue of *The Modern Language Journal* on motivation to learn languages in a multicultural world. Foregrounding the 'motivational interactions or interferences' that arise when people engage in multiple language learning (Ushioda & Dörnyei, 2017: 452), the special issue marks an important step in the direction of an inclusive, systemic and 'whole person' approach. While all the contributions 'raise awareness of the importance of understanding language learning motivation in multifaceted, multilingual ways in the diverse linguistic contexts represented by each research site' (Duff, 2017: 605), two are more firmly rooted in non-essentialist ontologies.

In the articles by Thompson (2017) and Henry (2017a), motivation is conceptualized and explored as an emergent phenomenon that arises in multilingual practices and through cross-linguistic interactions. While in Thompson's research, the focus is directed to the multilingual learner's perceptions and understandings of transfer phenomena, Henry's work focuses on the ways in which the languages in a person's repertoire are activated in processes of sense making and decoding, and how language self-concepts are brought online in working cognition.

In Thompson's study of US university students (N = 195) learning a range of languages (34 listed), it was found that higher-level multilingual students (with experience of learning an L2 and an L3) had significantly stronger ideal selves than their bilingual counterparts (who only had the experience of learning an L2) and multilingual students with lower levels of L3 proficiency. The importance of this study lies in Thompson's conceptualization of positive influences on motivation attributable to experiences arising through cross-linguistic interactions. To conceptualize the beneficial effects connected to language transfer, she used the Perceived Positive Language Interaction (PPLI) construct (Thompson, 2016). Derived from Odlin's (2008) concept of *interlingual identification* and Kellerman's (1979) work on *perceived language distance*, PPLI is operationalized as the perception of positive interactions between languages learned post-L1 and the (implicit) acknowledgement of interconnectivity between language systems (Thompson, 2017). From this multilingual standpoint, the study could shed light on 'the complex nature of motivation when more than one foreign language is involved', and how 'previous experience with other languages [can] affect students' psychological aspects of self' (Thompson, 2017: 498).

The second contribution embracing a non-essentialist ontology is Henry's (2017a) conceptual article exploring the emergence of multilingual self-guides. Also drawing on the complexity-influenced theorizing of cross-linguistic interaction – a linguistic process that includes transfer, interference, codeswitching and borrowing, and cognitive phenomena relating to the effects of multilingual development at a system level (Herdina & Jessner, 2002; Jessner, 2008) – Henry argued that, in cross-linguistic interactions, Lx self-guides could be activated in Ly learning situations. Over time, he suggested, multilingual self-guides could emerge.

Although both articles involved a development of previous work (e.g. Henry, 2014; Thompson, 2016), they can be seen as the cornerstones of an emerging body of ontologically non-essentialist research that explores motivation in contexts of multiple learning/acquisition. As the contributions to this book reveal, much of this work has involved an extension of the theorizing in Henry's (2017a) article. Revisiting this theorizing, and with the aim of enhancing conceptualizations of the functions and effects of emergent higher-order self-guides, in the sections that follow I describe and illustrate three self-guides that can emerge from the experience of learning an additional language or languages, and which can function to direct learning behaviors in particular ways. These are, respectively, a *monolingual self*, a *contentedly bilingual self* and an *ideal multilingual self*. Thereafter, I examine a fourth self-guide which can arise in contexts of multilingual learning/ use, and which references a perception of being obligated to expand one's linguistic repertoire: an *ought-to multilingual self* (Liu, 2022). First, however, I briefly discuss the self system approach to investigating L2 motivation (Dörnyei, 2005, 2009) and, thereafter, the function of the working self-concept (Markus & Nurius, 1986). I suggest that insight into the operation of the working self-concept can provide a key to understanding how higher-order self-guides can arise in language learning processes, the functions that a self-guide can have in working cognition, and the effects on the language learner's motivation.

A Self System Approach to Understanding L2 Learners' Motivation

In the 1980s and 1990s, new perspectives emerged in the science of human motivation. During this period, convergences between personality and social psychology were sought (Higgins, 1990). Emphasizing the *systemic nature* of the self, the objective was to provide holistic, integrated accounts of human functioning. For Dörnyei (2005), a self system approach that combined personality and social psychology and that was focused on the '"doing" side of personality' was closely aligned with his conceptualization of motivation for language learning:

> This new shift has resulted in an increased convergence of the concepts of personality and motivation, as both are now seen as active antecedents of behavior. The L2 Motivational Self System ... is in accordance with this new development and, I believe, it offers increased explanatory power with regard to variations in L2 learning. (Dörnyei, 2005: 118)

Beyond the convergence of personality and motivation, a self system approach had additional appeal. It provided a solution to the problem of accommodating the related constructs of *possible selves* (Markus & Nurius, 1986) and *regulatory self-guides* (Higgins, 1987) within a single, unified model. While the L2 Motivational Self System (L2MSS) (Dörnyei, 2009) encompasses the nomenclature and the regulatory mechanism of self-discrepancy theory – *ideal* and *ought self-guides* and the emotional vulnerabilities that arise from discrepancies from an actual self – most of the work that the model has generated has involved representations of future language use and the motivational effects of *possible selves*. It is therefore important to keep in mind that while self-guides (Higgins, 1987) are the established descriptors for the L2 learner's future-oriented self-concepts, the theorizing that underpins the conceptualization of the emergence and purported functions of multilingual self-guides (Henry, 2017a; Liu, 2022) is rooted in work by Markus and her associates on the dynamics of *working cognition* (e.g. Markus & Kunda, 1986; Markus & Nurius, 1986; Ruvolo & Markus, 1992).

Working Cognition and the Working Self-Concept

Refuting the singularity of human identity, cognitive science has long emphasized the multidimensionality of the self-concept (James, 1892/1948). With the recognition that people have multifaceted identities, and that not all aspects of a person's identity will be salient and operable on any single occasion, cognitive psychologists developed conceptualizations of how certain collections or groupings of self-knowledge and self-representations can be *currently* active and thus constitute the 'self-concept of the moment' (Markus & Wurf, 1987: 306). The amalgam of currently active self-conceptions has been variously referred to as the 'online', 'accessible', or 'working' self-concept (e.g. Markus & Nurius, 1986; Markus & Wurf, 1987; Markus *et al.*, 1985).

At any one time, only a *subset* of a person's overall repertoire of self-knowledge and self-conceptions will be operational in cognition. These self-concepts can be consciously invoked or subconsciously brought online by a specific cue, event or stimulus. Consequently, as Markus and Wurf (1987: 306) explain, the working self-concept 'is best viewed as a continually active, shifting array of accessible self-knowledge'. Highly sensitive to shifts in contextual circumstances, the constellation of self-conceptions in the working self-concept changes constantly from one moment to the next. However, it would be a mistake to think that the composition of a working self-concept is simply random. While the working self-concept is highly dynamic, it also demonstrates temporal consistencies (Markus & Kunda, 1986). Because people's social actions and behaviors follow generally predictable patterns – a person's preferences and the domains in which they act are not unlimited – and because there is a 'bidirectionality of influence between the self-concept and the environment' (Nurius, 1989: 290), particular 'types' of working self-concept (collections of self-knowledge and self-conceptions relevant to particular activities, practices, relationships and circumstances) become operational in frequently encountered contexts and situations.

Closely associated with working memory, the working self-concept can be understood as the person's 'functionally relevant' self-concept, as Nurius (1989) explains:

> [T]he self-concept of the moment – the working self-concept – is variable, vulnerable to influence, and constitutes the currently *functionally relevant* self-concept. The issue of functional relevance is important for practice purposes. A great diversity of self-conceptions may very well reside in long-term memory. However, it is that subset accessible to working memory that is most directly engaged in perception, interpretation, evaluation, decision-making, and response in the moment – and consequently is most functionally relevant in the moment. (Nurius, 1989: 287–288; original emphasis)

Rarely touched upon in the theoretical literature on possible selves, but highly important in applied contexts, *functional relevance* provides a key to understanding how continuity is created within a particular domain. Over time, repeated activations of particular constellations of self-conceptions have the effect that, in the circumstances in which they come online, continuity is created. It is in this way that domain-specific self-concepts can demonstrate the same combination of malleability and consistency that is characteristic of the self (Markus & Kunda, 1986).

Possible Selves and the 'Functionally Relevant' Self-Concept in Language Learning

Possible selves are highly personalized representations of a person's goals, desires and fears. They function as motivators and regulators of behavior (Markus & Nurius, 1986; Ruvolo & Markus, 1992). Responsive to changes in the environment, possible selves are sensitive to situations 'that communicate new or inconsistent information about the self' (Markus & Nurius, 1986: 956). In domains which implicate growth, learning and personal development, possible selves are the most dynamic constituents in the working self-concept (Markus & Kunda, 1986). When a person is deeply committed to a practice or relationship where time and resources have been invested, possible selves can be highly effective in directing behavior:

> Some [possible selves] are extremely well-articulated and elaborated with detail garnered during years of observing and cataloguing one's own and others' reactions in a particular domain. Examples include the 'physician self', for the weary medical resident, the 'presidential self' for the dedicated up-and-coming political candidate, or darker visions such as the 'down-and-out self' for the individual who used to be and fears again becoming poor, isolated, or actively abusing alcohol. (Nurius, 1989: 289)

In any domain, there is rarely a single possible self that is operable. As well as the 'ideal selves that we would very much like to become', the working self-concept can also contain 'the selves we could become, and the selves we are afraid of becoming' (Markus & Nurius, 1986: 954). To take 'the weary medical resident' in Nurius' (1989) example, we can imagine how the working concept (activated during the lonely hours of a night shift) can potentially contain other, contrasting, possible selves, such as a 'general practitioner self' or a 'medical researcher self' (less prestigious professional roles, but with less demanding working conditions). For the 'dedicated up-and-coming political candidate', the working self-concept might at times include possible selves referencing less ambitious (but perhaps more likely) futures, such as a 'loyal confederate self' or a 'cabinet minister self'.

With nearly two decades of research examining the nature, content and effects of possible selves in language learning domains, we have seen many examples of the types of current and future selves that can be generated. While these selves resonate with the possible selves identified in related fields (see, for example, Henderson *et al.*, 2018), language learning differs from other areas in which development is implicated in an important respect. At the point where a learning process begins, the person engaged in learning already speaks at least one language (and frequently more than one). Further, during a learning trajectory, people can be involved in the acquisition of a new additional language. Thus, for a language learner, the working self-concept can contain possible selves that relate not only to the target language but also to *other languages* that the student knows or is learning, and that can be activated as part of the learning process (e.g. when triggered by cross-linguistic interactions). Importantly, higher-order self-conceptions that are related to, but which transcend, language-specific selves, can emerge from interactions between possible selves that are brought online in cross-linguistic interactions (Henry, 2017a).

The Emergence of Higher-Order Self-Guides

As explained previously in this chapter, in processes of cross-linguistic interaction, language learning self-concepts can become active in working cognition. Consequently, the working self-concept that is operational in L*y* learning situations can also contain self-guides that relate to the L*x* (Henry, 2017a). When an L*x* self-guide is activated in an L*y* learning context, varying effects are possible. To a large degree, outcomes will depend on the influence that the 'imported' self-guide has on the constellation of self-concepts in the currently active working self-concept (Henry, 2010, 2011).

In research into the self, an important area of inquiry has involved conflicts between a person's self-concepts and the question: 'What happens when two self-conceptions are incompatible?' (Markus & Wurf, 1987: 304). However, work has mostly focused on the global self-concept. Less is known about interactions in the working self-concept. From related research into self-concept dynamics (e.g. Nowak *et al.*, 2005) and developmental processes within the dialogical self (Hermans, 2013, 2019), we can understand how interactions between two self-conceptions (complementary or antagonistic) can lead to the emergence of a new self-conception with higher-order functions, and which can provide coherence and continuity within a particular domain. As demonstrated in dialogical self theory, two (or more) competing or collaborating self-concepts can be 'brought together to form adaptive and productive combinations' (Hermans, 2019: 37). With the emergence of a new self-concept that complements, subsumes or amalgamates preexisting self-concepts, stability is brought to the identity system and directions for future development are provided (Hermans, 2013, 2019).

In the working self-concept of a person learning an additional language(s), interactions of this sort can take place. When in L*y* learning situations, the intrusion of the L*x* self is nondisruptive, it can function to complement the L*y* self. Conditions are created in which a self-concept referencing future multilingualism can emerge. A possible self that emerges in such conditions can be understood as an *ideal multilingual self*. However, if relations are antagonistic, and the newly included L*x* self functions as a counterpoint to the L*y* self, the equilibrium of the working self-concept can be disrupted and altered in a manner where cognitive resources are channelled in directions other than L*y* development. In such circumstances, higher-order self-concepts that reference bilingualism can emerge (Henry, 2017a).

Over time, characteristic adaptations following L*x* intrusions can affect the strength of L*y* selves. In cases where L*y* and L*x* selves coexist unproblematically within a working self-concept activated in L*y* learning contexts, and where an emergent ideal multilingual self more frequently becomes part of the 'self-concept of the moment' (Markus & Wurf, 1987: 306), the motivational power of the ideal L*y* self stands to be enhanced. This is because the L*y* self and the higher-order multilingual self can direct energy in a similar direction. Becoming proficient in the L*y* is both an end in itself *and* part of the process of becoming someone who is multilingual. However, in cases where there is antagonism, and where an emergent self-guide favouring bilingualism can become more frequently active within the working self-concept, energy for L*y* learning can be hard to sustain. With a higher-order self-concept that favors bilingualism (i.e. L1 + L*x*), motivational power attaching to an ideal L*y* self can be weakened (Henry, 2017a).

Drawing on data from my own research and work by one of my students, in the sections that follow I present three examples that illustrate the processes described above. However, before looking more specifically at the *contentedly bilingual self* and the *ideal multilingual self* – higher-order self-guides hypothesized to emerge in conditions of multiple language learning – I begin by considering how, through similar processes, a *monolingual self* can emerge.

A monolingual self

In a teacher education degree project, a student of mine used ethnographic methods to investigate motivation to learn and communicate in English at an agricultural college in a rural part of Sweden (Egonson, 2018). Observing lessons, and interviewing a number of the students at this upper secondary institution, Egonson's findings revealed how the study participants could see no need to learn English and had no ambitions to use English beyond the classroom. As part of his research, Egonson provided his participants with six picture cards. Five of the images – a coastal archipelago, a remote wilderness area, a village, a farm and an apartment block in a city area – were from Sweden.

The sixth image was a street scene from New York. Having given the students time to study the images, Egonson then invited them to select a picture and to talk about the feelings that it evoked, and what they imagined life would be like in this location. The cards most frequently selected were the pictures of recognizable scenes (the village and the farm). Thereafter, students were invited to select and talk about another picture from those that remained. Here, the scenes most frequently selected depicted Swedish landscapes (the archipelago and the wilderness). None of the students chose the picture of New York. When Egonson drew attention to this picture, few could say anything about it, or about the emotions it generated. Reflecting on the activity, Egonson suggested that 'no one was interested in the picture of New York, because they do not imagine their future selves to be a part of what the picture represents; globalism with English as its lingua franca' (Egonson, 2018: 38).

In observations of classroom interactions, Egonson noticed how the students were reluctant to communicate in English and, when they did, how they would often exaggerate Swedish prosody and intonation patterns. This, he concluded, appeared to stem from 'low self-esteem' and 'issues of identity' in relation to English (2018: 37). Exploring these observations in subsequent interviews, Egonson discovered how these students never experienced situations of fluent production, and that everything they said in English was mediated through Swedish. As one student, Kenny, explained: 'at our last school the skilled students were always gaming ... then they were really good at English ... but they just switch ... they just think in Swedish and speak English. I have to translate every word' (2018: 55).

In Egonson's study, the lack of an ideal L2 self can be traced not only to the inability to visualize a future that included English: as the findings clearly show, the students' local identities (articulated through the choice of images of rural life)[1] were connected to a monolingual identity (evident in their resistance to speaking English where exaggerated Swedish accents highlighted perceived inadequacies). While a *monolingual self* and its effects on learning behaviors have not been examined in motivation research, from a different epistemological stance Kramsch (2009) has provided an insightful take on how monolingual self-concepts can arise:

> For young people who are seeking to define their linguistic identity and their position in the world, the language class is often the first time they are consciously and explicitly confronted with the relationship between their language, their thoughts, and their bodies. Engaging with a different language sensitizes them to the significance of their own and of language in general. Those who just sit out the language class as a boring but necessary step towards graduation find themselves vindicated in their monolingual selves. Later, they will say with pride, 'I have had six years of French and I can't even order a cup of coffee in French.' Others will

start having thoughts they never had in their mother tongue. *The experience of the foreign always implies a reconsideration of the familiar.* (Kramsch, 2009: 4–5; emphasis added)

The notion that 'the experience of the foreign always implies a reconsideration of the familiar' can aptly explain the functional dynamics in the working self-concepts of the students in Egonson's study. As we can understand from the '6 pictures' activity, in a working self-concept operational at this time, a monolingual self assumes a dominant presence. Guiding behavior that favors the known over the unknown, it precludes entry of a self-concept referencing future use of English (and which could potentially have been brought online by fantasizing about being in New York).

This is similarly the case in the interview with Kenny. He recognizes that while other students at his former school could shift seamlessly between languages, this was never possible for him. Reflecting on the psycholinguistic dominance of Swedish in situations when he attempted to understand and communicate in English, we can understand how in the working self-concept activated in English lessons, a monolingual self assumes a dominant role. As in the '6 pictures' activity, the monolingual self dominates to a degree such that entry of a self-concept referencing future use of English is essentially precluded.

A contentedly bilingual self

Returning to Kramsch (2009), and her notion that 'the experience of the foreign always implies a reconsideration of the familiar', we can understand how, for the students in Egonson's (2018) study, a monolingual self emerges through experiences with English. Of course, for these students, there are no situations where encounters with a third language are likely to take place. However, for other young people in Sweden, secondary and upper education can involve the learning of two additional languages: English and another foreign language. For many, learning a second foreign language (usually, French, German or Spanish) can be unappealing.[2] For students who are only studying a second foreign language because it is an educational requirement, or because it can improve their grade point average (GPA), similar processes can take place in the working self-concept that becomes operational in L3 contexts.

In my article in the special issue of *The Modern Language Journal* (Henry, 2017a), I described an identity that was 'founded on the person's indifference to multilingual competence' (2017a: 553). Referencing a desire to 'insulate themselves' from other languages (The Douglas Fir Group, 2016: 26), I suggested that a *contentedly bilingual self* could arise in situations where the L2 self is robust but where the L3 self is weak and can be negatively compared with the L2 self. In such circumstances, the

L2 self can be an intrusive presence in a working self-concept operational in L3 learning contexts. Interactions between the L2 and L3 selves can be antagonistic. As the respective selves vie for limited cognitive resources, the L2 self can often come out on top (see also Henry, 2010, 2011).

The nature and emergence of a contentedly bilingual self is aptly illustrated in an interview I carried out in a study examining the impact of English on motivation to learn an additional foreign language. In this study (Henry, 2011) one of the participants (Oscar) reflected on the experience of learning Spanish as a second foreign language, and how, when working with Spanish texts and vocabulary, the sense of being a proficient speaker of English could frequently come to mind:

> I was actually quite OK at Spanish. Er I thought that it was so-so enjoyable but I also thought that it was troublesome learning three different languages. I thought that [pause] no I thought that it became too much. And it was also that I was really interested in English so that er, if we were to read some text, I thought instead like damn, no it would be much better to read this in English I thought, like I want to read it in English instead of Spanish and so my knowledge of Spanish suffered somewhat as a result. (Henry, 2011: 252)

> I don't think English would have been [pause] felt so enjoyable if I had not taken another language because learning Spanish meant that I wanted to learn even more English than before actually because er it made me realize that English is a much more enjoyable language than both Swedish and Spanish. (Henry, 2011: 253)

Immediately following this excerpt (but not included in the article), Oscar continued to describe the relationship between the two languages:

> Oscar: So, I think actually that Spanish was nevertheless useful. But for me it was useful, to the degree that I studied it, and that it has helped me. But if I was to continue with it, I don't think that I would have had great use of it.
>
> AH: So it gave you the opportunity to see the possibilities of English?
>
> Oscar: Yes, exactly. Exactly. It gave me a further a further eye for English. As long as I have got English. And the better I am in English, the better it feels.

As these excerpts reveal, Oscar had a strong affinity with English. He had a dream of going to the USA to study business administration, and he could describe images of a life lived in the US. In Spanish lessons it appeared that English was a consistent psycholinguistic presence. For example, he created vocabulary lists where a Spanish word was not only translated into Swedish (his L1) but also into English: 'I always made three columns. First I would take Spanish then Swedish and then English' (Henry, 2011: 252). In these circumstances, where a highly developed and fully elaborated ideal L2 (English) appears as a more-or-less permanent constituent of a working self-concept operational in L3 (Spanish) lessons, we can understand how a *contentedly bilingual self* can emerge.

Of course, there can be situations when a person can develop a *contentedly bilingual self* without ever having attempted to learn an L3. Possible selves are socially constructed and influenced by social norms (Markus & Cross, 1990). In Sweden and the Nordic countries – where English is ubiquitous in social discourse – a perspective common among students learning L3s is that 'it is enough with English' (e.g. Rosén, 2017). When there is antipathy to L3 learning, when attitudes to English are overwhelmingly positive, and when competence is generally high, circumstances conducive to the development of a *contentedly bilingual self* can arise (Henry, 2012).

An ideal multilingual self

As suggested in the *Modern Language Journal* article (Henry, 2017a), an ideal multilingual self can emerge when interactions between ideal Lx and ideal Ly selves are mutually complementary. When this happens, motivation is generated not only by the desire to become a proficient speaker of the Lx and the Ly, but also by the desire to become a person who is multilingual (Henry, 2017a). To exemplify the processes hypothesized to take place in the working self-concept in situations where an ideal multilingual self might emerge, I again draw on the study from the previous example (Henry, 2011), this time focusing on another participant (Anton).

In secondary school, Anton had learnt French. At the time of our interviews (in upper secondary school) he was learning Russian. For Anton, the possibilities for self-expression in languages not commonly chosen by peers were alluring. He actively sought opportunities to use his multilingual skills and to develop and express an emergent multilingual identity. As I observed, 'in addition to classroom activities and internet contact with friends in other countries, he also creates opportunities for the expression of his plurilingual identity in real-time interaction with peers' (Henry, 2011: 245).

As an attempt to access the processes hypothesized to take place in the working self-concept, the research design included an activity where participants were presented with a vignette portraying a situation involving a challenging L3 text. In this vignette, a student verbalizes comparisons that they make with English: *'this would have been so much better if it had been in English. This stuff that we are doing now would have been so much easier if it had been in English'* (Henry, 2011: 243).

When presented with the vignette, and asked if it captured an experience he could recognize, Anton provided the following response:

Anton: Yes, it is, but I go on and do it anyway. I completely refuse not to read a text. Instead I read it and in this way try to learn.

AH: So it doesn't trouble you then, this type of thought, when you compare with English? You get over it and read it anyway?

Anton: Yes, it's like so you get a text, ah-ha, it would have been much easier in English, well who cares? I read it anyway, I don't really care if it had been much easier in English.

Elicited through the vignette, we can see how the activation of English in cross-linguistic processing, and the triggering of the English self-concept in working cognition, do not appear to have negative consequences (cf. the situation for Oscar). Illustrated in the many examples of code-switching that Anton provided in the interviews – talking about how he would shift between languages in interactions with friends, and describing imaginary dialogues played out in his mind – in the working self-concept operational in L*y* situations, relationships between the various language selves are non-hierarchical, and interactions do not involve subordination.[3] In such circumstances, a self-guide referencing multilingual situations, multilingual practices and multilingual values can emerge.

A multilingual self-guide prefaced on obligation

In the preceding examples, the perspectives on the self that are embodied within a *monolingual self*, a *contentedly bilingual self* and an *ideal multilingual self* relate to the individual's *own* viewpoint. However, for a self-guide that involves the perception of a *need* to be/become multilingual, the perspective on the self is one that is voiced by a social other. When motivation for L2 learning is conceptualized as a self-system or, as Henry and Liu (2023) have recently argued, as a *self-regulatory system*, there is a need to identify the range of meaningful others who can voice a perspective on the self. Using Horney's (1946) words, this involves identifying the various others who constitute the self's 'inner audiences'.

As Higgins (2019) has made clear, the sense in which a person becomes a meaningful other is a situational accomplishment. Although self-guides will initially develop through a child's interactions with its caregivers, not all self-guides will originate within a close dyadic relationship:

There are a variety of other life experiences that influence the development of self-regulation. In addition to parents, a wide range of significant others (e.g., other family members; teachers; social, political, and religious figures; and fictional characters) are important in molding the self-guides that individuals adopt. (Moretti & Higgins, 1999: 211)

Seen this way, the range of others whose perspectives and expectations have the potential to influence an individual's sense of self can be far wider than the people with whom they may be closely related. In a self-regulatory system conceptualization of L2 motivation (Henry & Liu, 2023), the range of social others who can express a view on the self will therefore extend beyond those in close proximity to the individual, and can encompass various social constellations as well as society at large. In fact, the range of represented others who can hold a view on the self can be considerable. As Markus and Cross (1990: 585) have made clear, in the self-system 'others are the larger "society" in its various forms'. Consequently, the fourth multilingual self-concept – the *ought-to multilingual self* (Liu, 2022) – can be understood as arising through socialization processes, and from normative standards that generate perceptions of obligation, duty, need and conformity (Higgins, 1987, 1990).[4]

As Higgins *et al*. (1986: 5) have explained, an ought self can be understood as 'a normative, socially prescribed self that involves individuals' beliefs about what others believe they ought to be like'. Investigating motivation for language learning in multilingual South Africa, Coetzee-Van Rooy (2014) has argued that in social settings where multilingualism is the norm, people can develop ought language selves. In such settings, motivation can be generated by the perception of needing to conform to prevailing norms, directing people to believe 'that if they are not multilingual in this society, they do not "fit in", because well-integrated citizens in this society are multilingual' (Coetzee-Van Rooy, 2014: 124). Reflecting how normative expectations can function in a similar way, findings from Henry's (2023) case study at a school where the learning of multiple languages was actively promoted revealed how the school environment both shaped and was shaped by multilingual identities. At this school, a culture that valued multilingualism functioned to generate expectations among students that they should learn at least one foreign language over and above English (and ideally more). As students and teachers could observe, being enrolled at the school brought with it a sense of being obligated to become multilingual (Henry, 2023: 105–107):

> Joel (teacher): I think also that it is expected of the students that they [learn languages], and that they expect it of each other, and also of themselves. It's part of the school's culture that you do this. From the time that they are in grade six or grade seven, they start saying, 'is it next year that you get to choose your language, and which languages can you learn?' They are already aware of

	this when they come here to this school, that it's something you do. /.../ It's part of being here, when you are at our school, and it's ... in the brickwork.
Gino (student):	[It is] a school with many cultures and many people from different countries, both teachers and students. And that's why, I think, you can become very inspired by others, by the social environment around you.
Maja (student):	There's a psychology behind the whole thing. That you want to learn more languages so that you can, like, melt in.

In a study investigating the motivational profiles of university students in China who were engaged in the simultaneous learning of English and an additional foreign language, and which examined the personal and contextual factors that contributed to the configuration of motivation profiles, Liu (2022) found evidence of an *ought-to multilingual self*. This, she argued, could be understood as the product of interactions between language ideology at the macro level (an instrumentalist view of language), the learner's immediate social and linguistic environment (the social capital of English), and learner internal factors (an identity as either an English or a language major). Drawing on qualitative and quantitative data (see next section), Liu (2022) argued that the ought-to multilingual self could be understood as a self-guide with higher-order qualities akin to that of the ideal multilingual self:

> Similar to ideal multilingual self, the ought-to multilingual self is a higher-order motivational self-guide in the sense that it is language-general. That is, such need to expand the linguistic repertoire is not driven by the desire to learn a specific language, but rather by the need to remedy the loss of competitive edge associated with English. (Liu, 2022: 251)

Validation and Support from Quantitative Studies

Even though research into motivation that derives from a desire to become multilingual has only recently begun to accumulate, findings suggest that self-concepts that reference multilingual accomplishments can have positive effects on language learning motivation. In a study by Henry and Thorsen (2018) with secondary students in Sweden learning English (L2) and French, German or Spanish (L3), a latent variable capturing the ideal multilingual self was found to have an indirect but strong effect on the ideal L3 self and intended effort. In two recent studies with university students in China learning French or German as a minor (Liu, 2022), and a foreign language as a major (Wang, 2022), similar results were found. In Liu's longitudinal study, the ideal multilingual self had enduring direct and indirect effects on intended effort to learn French or German. In Wang's study, the ideal multilingual self was found to have an indirect effect on effort in foreign language learning. Replicating Henry and Thorsen's (2018) findings, both studies showed how the effect of the ideal multilingual self was mediated through the ideal FL (foreign language) self, with certain direct effects also found.

In Liu's (2022) study, additional effects of an ought-to multilingual self were also examined. As we have seen, the ought-to multilingual self can be conceptualized as a self-guide that refers to a learner's perception of a pressure or obligation to expand their linguistic repertoire (Liu, 2022). Analyses showed how the ought-to multilingual self had an indirect effect on intended effort to learn the L2, and a direct effect on intended effort to learn the L3. As a higher-order multilingual self-guide, the ought-to multilingual self functioned to provide an additional source of motivation that could support multiple language learning.

Conclusion

As the studies reviewed in this chapter suggest, a multilingual turn in motivation research could be on the horizon. Whether or not motivation researchers have a particular interest in studying motivation in multilingual contexts, or the motivational processes connected to multiple language learning, the shift away from a monolingual worldview means that ignoring the other languages in a learner's repertoire can be problematic. As Ortega (2018) has made clear, a standpoint that a target language 'can be studied in isolation from the other language(s) of a speaker' will mean that findings can 'remain unhelpfully compartmentalized' (2018: 72). With a growing trend to apply theories and models from mainstream motivation science in L2 settings (Lamb *et al.*, 2019), compartmentalization seems likely to continue. In the absence of careful adaptations to particular contexts of language learning, and the circumstances of individual learners, the application of mainstream constructs runs the risk of ignoring one of the distinguishing factors that makes language learning unique: the presence and effects of *other languages* in a learner's repertoire.

However, the greatest obstacle standing in the way of a multilingual turn in motivation research – and which may prove to be the most difficult to overcome – remains a continued favoring of essentializing ontologies. While the special issue of *The Modern Language Journal* broke new ground in many ways, the framing of the issue's primary objective – inquiry into *languages other than English* – is rooted in essentialist and Anglocentric views of language. If the investigation of motivation in multilingual circumstances is to gain momentum, and if a multilingual turn in motivation scholarship is to come about, a key challenge will involve the development of research designs where non-separationist perspectives form departure points. The conceptualization of multilingual self-concepts and the higher-order functions attributed to them is one way in which non-essentialist perspectives can inform contemporary motivation research and can help shift the field in a multilingual direction.

Notes

(1) In an L2 context, MacIntyre *et al*. (2017) have conceptualized a 'Rooted L2 Self' that is defined by connections to place and speakers of the L2.
(2) The antipathy to learning an additional language beyond English can be gauged by the fact that the Swedish government introduced an enhancement to the upper secondary grade point average. For students who gain a passing grade in a second foreign language at CEFR levels A2.2 and B1.1, the GPA is boosted significantly (Henry, 2017b).
(3) In the original article (Henry, 2011) I point to a process described by Markus and Kunda (1986) whereby a challenge that is made to an important self-concept can be countered by the recruitment of protective self-knowledge (e.g. positive views of the self as perseverant, and self-conceptions both as an emerging Ly speaker and multilingual individual).
(4) In addition to an ought-to self-guide, in a self-regulatory system other types of social standard can emphasize conformity and obligation (Higgins, 1990). As Higgins (1990) has made clear, standards for self-appraisal also pertain to the individuals who comprise the settings, contexts and social situations in which actions take place. Through processes of social control, 'participants in a context press for obedience to their rules, which may or may not be the same as an individual's chronic guides' (Higgins, 1990: 313). In social settings where multilingual practices are common, normative guides and social context standards can also create a sense of being obligated to be/become multilingual. For a full discussion of the functions of self-regulatory systems, and the effects of normative guides and social context standards that emphasize conformity to social and societal norms, see Henry and Liu (2023).

References

Aronin, L. (2017) Conceptualizations of multilingualism. *Critical Multilingualism Studies* 5 (1), 174–207.
Block, D. (2003) *The Social Turn in Second Language Acquisition*. Georgetown University Press.
Bourdieu, P. (1977) The economics of linguistic exchanges. *Social Science Information* 16 (6), 645–668.
Coetzee-Van Rooy, S. (2014) Explaining the ordinary magic of stable African multilingualism in the Vaal triangle region in South Africa. *Journal of Multilingual and Multicultural Development* 35 (2), 121–138.
Conteh, J. and Meier, G. (eds) (2014) *The Multilingual Turn in Languages Education: Opportunities and Challenges*. Multilingual Matters.
Cook, V. (1991) The poverty-of-the-stimulus argument and multi-competence. *Second Language Research* 7 (2), 103–117.
Cook, V.J. (1992) Evidence for multicompetence. *Language Learning* 42 (4), 557–591.
Cook, V. and Li, W. (eds) (2016) *The Cambridge Handbook of Linguistic Multi-Competence*. Cambridge University Press.

Dörnyei, Z. (2005) *The Psychology of the Language Learner: Individual Differences in Second Language Acquisition.* Lawrence Erlbaum.

Dörnyei, Z. (2009) The L2 motivational self system. In Z. Dörnyei and E. Ushioda (eds) *Motivation, Language Identity and the L2 Self* (pp. 9–42). Multilingual Matters.

Duff, P.A. (2017) Commentary: Motivation for learning languages other than English in an English dominant world. *The Modern Language Journal* 101 (3), 597–607.

Egonson, M. (2018) How to raise willingness to communicate in heterogenous students of English: A case study on WTC and investment in a Swedish upper secondary land management school. Unpublished B Ed thesis, University West (Sweden).

Ellis, R. (2021) A short history of SLA: Where have we come from and where are we going? *Language Teaching* 54 (2), 190–205.

Firth, A. and Wagner, J. (1997) On discourse, communication, and (some) fundamental concepts in SLA research. *The Modern Language Journal* 81 (3), 285–300.

Henderson, H., Stevenson, J. and Bathmaker, A.M. (2018) *Possible Selves in Higher Education.* Routledge.

Henry, A. (2010) Contexts of possibility in simultaneous language learning: Using the L2 motivational self system to assess the impact of global English. *Journal of Multilingual and Multicultural Development* 31 (2), 149–162.

Henry, A. (2011) Examining the impact of L2 English on L3 selves: A case study. *International Journal of Multilingualism* 8 (3), 235–255.

Henry, A. (2012) *L3 Motivation.* Gothenburg University Press.

Henry, A. (2014) The motivational effects of crosslinguistic awareness: Developing third language pedagogies to address the negative impact of the L2 on the L3 self-concept. *Innovation in Language Learning and Teaching* 8 (1), 1–19.

Henry, A. (2017a) L2 motivation and multilingual identities. *The Modern Language Journal* 101 (3), 548–565.

Henry, A. (2017b) Rewarding foreign language learning: Effects of the Swedish grade point average enhancement initiative on students' motivation to learn French. *The Language Learning Journal* 45 (3), 301–315.

Henry, A. (2023) Learner–environment adaptations in multiple language learning: Casing the ideal multilingual self as a system functioning in context. *International Journal of Multilingualism* 20 (2), 97–114.

Henry, A. and Thorsen, C. (2018) The ideal multilingual self: Validity, influences on motivation, and role in a multilingual education. *International Journal of Multilingualism* 15 (4), 349–364.

Henry, A. and Liu, M. (2023) Can L2 motivation be modelled as a self-system? A critical assessment. *System* 119 (December 2023) 103158, 1–13.

Herdina, P. and Jessner, U. (2002) *A Dynamic Model of Multilingualism: Perspectives of Change in Psycholinguistics.* Multilingual Matters.

Hermans, H.J.M. (2013) The dialogical self in education: Introduction. *Journal of Constructivist Psychology* 26 (2), 81–89.

Hermans, H.J.M. (2019) Dialogical self theory in a boundary-crossing society. In H. Alma and I. ter Avest (eds) *Moral and Spiritual Leadership in an Age of Plural Moralities* (pp. 28–47). Routledge.

Higgins, E.T. (1987) Self-discrepancy: A theory relating self and affect. *Psychological Review* 94 (3), 319.

Higgins, E.T. (1990) Personality, social psychology, and person–situation relations: Standards and knowledge activation as a common language. In L.A. Pervein (ed.) *Handbook of Personality: Theory and Research* (pp. 301–308). Routledge.

Higgins, E.T. (2019) *Shared Reality.* Oxford University Press.

Higgins, E.T., Bond, R.N., Klein, R. and Strauman, T. (1986) Self-discrepancies and emotional vulnerability: How magnitude, accessibility, and type of discrepancy influence affect. *Journal of Personality and Social Psychology* 51 (1), 5.

Horney, K. (1946) *Our Inner Conflicts: A Constructive Theory of Neurosis*. Routledge & Kegan Paul.
James, W. (1892/1948) *Psychology: Briefer Course*. World Publishing Co.
Jessner, U. (2008) A DST model of multilingualism and the role of metalinguistic awareness. *The Modern Language Journal* 92 (2), 270–283.
Kellerman, E. (1979) Transfer and non-transfer: Where are we now? *Studies in Second Language Acquisition* 2 (1), 37–57.
Kramsch, C. (2009) *The Multilingual Subject*. Oxford University Press.
Lamb, M., Csizér, K., Henry, A. and Ryan, S. (2019) Introduction. In M. Lamb, K. Csizér, A. Henry and S. Ryan (eds) *The Palgrave Handbook of Motivation for Language Learning* (pp. 1–17). Palgrave Macmillan.
Lave, J. and Wenger, E. (1991) *Situated Learning: Legitimate Peripheral Participation*. Cambridge University Press.
Liu, M. (2022) Multilingual future self-guides: A mixed-methods study of learners of multiple foreign languages in China. Unpublished PhD thesis, University of Cambridge.
MacIntyre, P.D., Baker, S.C. and Sparling, H. (2017) Heritage passions, heritage convictions, and the rooted L2 self: Music and Gaelic language learning in Cape Breton, Nova Scotia. *The Modern Language Journal* 101 (3), 501–516.
Markus, H.R. and Kunda, Z. (1986) Stability and malleability of the self-concept. *Journal of Personality and Social Psychology* 51 (4), 858–866.
Markus, H.R. and Nurius, P. (1986) Possible selves. *American Psychologist* 41 (9), 954–969.
Markus, H.R. and Wurf, E. (1987) The dynamic self-concept: A social psychological perspective. *Annual Review of Psychology* 38, 299–337.
Markus, H.R. and Cross, S. (1990) The interpersonal self. In L.A. Pervin (ed.) *Handbook of Personality: Theory and Research* (pp. 576–609). Routledge.
May, S. (ed.) (2014) *The Multilingual Turn: Implications for SLA, TESOL, and Bilingual Education*. Routledge.
Melo-Pfeifer, S. (2018) The multilingual turn in foreign language education. In A. Bonnet and P. Siemund (eds) *Foreign Language Education in Multilingual Classrooms* (pp. 191–212). John Benjamins.
Moretti, M.M. and Higgins, E.T. (1999) Own versus other standpoints in self-regulation: Developmental antecedents and functional consequences. *Review of General Psychology* 3 (3), 188–223.
Norton, B. (2000) *Identity and Language Learning: Gender, Ethnicity and Educational Change*. Longman.
Nowak, A., Vallacher, R.R. and Zochowski, M. (2005) The emergence of personality: Dynamic foundations of individual variation. *Developmental Review* 25 (3–4), 351–385.
Nurius, P.S. (1989) The self-concept: A social–cognitive update. *Social Casework* 70 (5), 285–294.
Odlin, T. (2008) Cross-linguistic influence. In C. Doughty and M. Long (eds) *The Handbook of Second Language Acquisition* (pp. 436–486). Wiley–Blackwell.
Ortega, L. (2018) Ontologies of language, second language acquisition, and world Englishes. *World Englishes* 37 (1), 64–79.
Ortega, L. (2019) SLA for the 21st century: Disciplinary progress, transdisciplinary relevance, and the bi/multilingual turn. In D. Macedo (ed.) *Decolonizing Foreign Language Education: The Misteaching of English and other Colonial Languages* (pp. 111–130). Routledge.
Rosén, C. (2017) Hur kan vi stärka de främmande språkens ställning i Sverige? En undersökning bland språklärare inom projektet "Rikare med språk". *Lingua* 2, 9–15.
Ruvolo, A.P. and Markus, H.R. (1992) Possible selves and performance: The power of self-relevant imagery. *Social Cognition* 10 (1), 95.
The Douglas Fir Group (2016) A transdisciplinary framework for SLA in a multilingual world. *The Modern Language Journal* 100 (S1), 19–47.

Thompson, A.S. (2016) How do multilinguals conceptualize interactions among languages studied? Operationalizing Perceived Positive Language Interaction (PPLI). In L. Ortega, A. Tyler and M. Uno (eds) *The Usage-based Study of Language Learning and Multilingualism* (pp. 91–111). Georgetown University Press.

Thompson, A.S. (2017) Language learning motivation in the United States: An examination of language choice and multilingualism. *The Modern Language Journal* 101 (3), 483–500.

Ushioda, E. (2017) The impact of global English on motivation to learn other languages: Toward an ideal multilingual self. *The Modern Language Journal* 101 (3), 469–482.

Ushioda, E. (2019) Motivation and multilingualism. In D. Singleton and L. Aronin (eds) *Twelve Lectures on Multilingualism* (pp. 179–211). Multilingual Matters.

Ushioda, E. and Dörnyei, Z. (2017) Beyond global English: Motivation to learn languages in a multicultural world: Introduction to the special issue. *The Modern Language Journal* 101 (3), 451–454.

Wang, L. (2022) Motivation and motivational dynamics of Chinese students learning languages other than English as college majors. Unpublished PhD thesis, University of Nottingham.

3 Negotiating Agentive Selves in Arabic Learning: A Case Study of Arabic Learners at a Chinese University

Ning An and Yongyan Zheng

With the multilingual turn in applied linguistics (May, 2014) that aims to counterbalance the long-lasting monolingual ideologies and English dominance, the learning and teaching of languages other than English (LOTEs) have received growing scholarly attention and have enjoyed increasing interest in applied linguistics (e.g. Gao & Zheng, 2019; Han *et al.*, 2019). Compared to the prolific findings on the teaching and learning of global English, the way in which multilingual learners act and develop in the LOTE learning process needs more research attention, especially in non-western contexts such as Asian countries experiencing increasing popularity of LOTE education.

In the field of foreign language education research, the motivation of multilingual learners has always been a hot topic, and various perspectives have been taken in exploring this issue, including but not limited to the construction of the ideal multilingual self (e.g. Henry, 2017; Ushioda, 2017; Zheng *et al.*, 2019, 2020), identity (e.g. Gearing & Roger, 2018; Liao *et al.*, 2020) and investment (e.g. Norton, 2013; Norton & Toohey, 2011). The present study seeks to blend the notions of multilingual self and agency, both of which are dynamic in nature, through the concepts of time and space, by adopting the perspective of the agentive self as socioculturally engendered, historically contingent and dialogically negotiated, to explore how and why multilingual learners choose to learn a specific LOTE language in an English-dominant context.

In the Chinese context in particular, as a response to the Belt and Road Initiative[1] (henceforth B&R), China's Ministry of Education (MOE) proposed a plan to 'Develop Educational Cooperation along the B&R'[2] in 2016, which was followed by a large-scale LOTE education reform in Chinese universities to rectify the long-standing imbalance between English and LOTEs (see An & Zheng, 2022, for more details). Arabic is gaining popularity within foreign-language education in China despite various limitations and a lack of resources. As such, this study focuses on a group of Arabic learners in an elective LOTE program at a Chinese university, and investigates how and why these multilingual learners choose to learn Arabic, confronting multiple challenges by looking at the dynamic and fluid trajectory of their constructions of agentive selves. The study seeks to demonstrate how LOTE learners navigate language learning in an English-dominant context with limited learning resources, and illuminates the long-term development of multilingual teaching and learning in Chinese tertiary education and larger contexts in Asia.

Agentive Selves and Agency in a Dialogically Spatial–Temporal Continuum

During the past two decades, multilingual learners have received growing attention in terms of their language learning motivation (e.g. Boo *et al.*, 2015; Dörnyei, 2000; Huang *et al.*, 2021; Ushioda & Dörnyei, 2017). Various studies have demonstrated that the construction of the multilingual self plays a significant guiding role in the foreign language learning process of multilingual learners (e.g. Henry & Thorsen, 2018; Liu, 2020; Orcasitas-Vicandi & Perales-Fernandez-de-Gamboa, 2023). Agency in foreign language learning is also highly notable because it relates closely to multilingual learners' choices and actions in choosing a foreign language (e.g. An & Zheng, 2022; Liddicoat & Taylor-Leech, 2021; Miller, 2012). Given that the motivational-self approach to multilingual learning usually probes into the reasons behind the learners' decisions, little is known about how learners take action, especially when they need to overcome challenges and address difficulties. This study intends to link the multilingual self and agency – the two main bodies of research on foreign language learning motivation – to explore how the self-image prompts actual actions taken by multilingual learners.

Agency in language learning can be defined as learners' socioculturally mediated capacity to undertake self-conscious, reflective actions to learn certain languages (Ahearn, 2001; An & Zheng, 2022; Zhao, 2011), which is often regarded as a significant element or even as the 'central construct' (Van Lier, 2008: 179) in language learners' learning processes (Miller, 2012). Goller (2017) concludes that agency demonstrates its full complexity only if the flow of time, as well as relational and structural aspects, are taken into consideration (see Emirbayer & Mische, 1998). This study, therefore, sees the agency of multilingual learners as a dialogical spatial–temporal continuum to demonstrate the dynamic and relational construction mediated across time and space, which is consistent with the properties of agentive selfhood (e.g. An & Zheng, 2022; Liddicoat, 2020; Vitanova, 2018; Zhao & Baldauf, 2012). Agency becomes particularly significant when learners encounter significant challenges in their language learning. Unlike learning global English, which tends to receive full support from the structural dimension of educational and institutional systems, LOTE learning generally receives less environmental support (Ushioda & Dörnyei, 2017). Given the difficulties and limitations confronted during the Arabic learning process in the current project, the ways in which LOTE Arabic learners exert their full agency to advance their language learning remain unexplored.

The concept of 'self' is regarded as an active agent that develops in the process of social experience and activities (Martin *et al.*, 2010: 119). It also exists as a dialogical spatial–temporal construct according to the notion of agentive selfhood (see Martin *et al.*, 2010). Mead (1938, 2002) argues that *perspective* is 'an orientation to an environment that is associated with acting within that environment' (Martin *et al*, 2010: 119), and the psychological and sociocultural world is perspectival in that all phenomena including selves 'emerge in the relation of organisms to their environments' (Martin *et al.*, 2010: 119). Therefore, in reality, the *self* is regarded as perspectival, dependent and reflective, relating to all individuals, relationships, and the environment. From the temporal dimension, the self is considered as 'a source of both the achieved wisdom of the past and the agentive cultivation of the future' (Martin *et al.*, 2010: 124); from the relational dimension, the self arises in both the perspectives of oneself and of others, 'especially in the common perspective of a group' (Mead, 2002: 174); from the spatial dimension, the self is not only related to social harmony but also to social conflict, which indicates the relationship between agentive self and the promoting and/or inhibiting factors within a social structure (e.g. An & Zheng, 2022; Martin *et al.*, 2010: 127).

The current study intends to blend the notion of multilingual self and agency to explore further how multilingual learners are self-motivated to take different agentive actions in the process of foreign language learning. Adopting the perspective that agentive selves are (1) socioculturally engendered, (2) historically contingent and (3) dialogically negotiated, this study, situated in a LOTE Arabic program at a Chinese university, seeks to explore how and why learners choose to learn Arabic and craft their multilingual agentive selves (MASs) despite the dominance of English and various structural limitations. The following overarching research question guides the present study:

> How do the Arabic learners construct their multilingual agentive selves temporally (past–present–future) and spatially (relating to structural factors)?

The Study

Research site

The current study is part of a classroom ethnography undertaken between 2019 and 2023. It was carried out in a public university situated in Shanghai, China. The focal university is among the top 10 universities in China and ranks among the top 100 in the world university rankings.[3], offering 70 undergraduate degree programs across the arts, humanities, sciences and medicine. Following the plan for 'Developing Educational Cooperation along the Belt & Road' proposed by Ministry of Education (MOE) of China, a Multilingual Teaching Center was established in 2016 which offers a set of elective courses in more than 10 modern foreign languages to undergraduates university-wide, including Danish, French, German, Japanese, Korean, Modern Hebrew, Portuguese, Spanish and Swedish. (see also An & Zheng, 2022). The center began to offer Arabic courses in the fall of 2018, and now three levels of course are available to undergraduates with varying proficiency: namely, Arabic I for beginners, Arabic II for intermediate learners, and Arabic III for advanced learners. Arabic I is open to undergraduates from different disciplines in the focal university. Eighteen sessions are offered each semester, with each session lasting for about 120 minutes. The teacher of the Arabic courses is an Arabic-major lecturer with more than 10 years Arabic teaching experience at the tertiary level. The main objective of Arabic I is to teach the essential knowledge of the Arabic language in terms of orthography, pronunciation and grammar, and to develop learners' basic communicative skills in Arabic.

Participants

The study recruited 21 undergraduate students (hereafter referred to as P1–P21) who registered for Arabic I at the focal university. They were of various disciplinary backgrounds. They had Chinese as their mother tongue, and English as their L2 with proficiency at approximate B2 level in the *CEFR*.[4] Most of them had no knowledge of the Arabic language before they took the course, with three of them knowing a little Arabic due to their family or religious backgrounds, but with minimal proficiency. All the participants recruited in the classroom ethnography had signed the consent form to guarantee their rights to continue or quit their participation in the research, as well as the privacy of their personal information. Table 3.1 provides detailed information about the 21 participants.

Data collection

Data sources mainly come from the participants' narrative accounts and the follow-up semi-structured interviews with them, collected in

Table 3.1 Participant demographics

Participant number	Gender	Major of study
P1	Female	Museology
P2	Female	Nursing
P3	Female	International Politics
P4	Male	International Politics
P5	Male	Chinese
P6	Female	Physics
P7	Male	Physics
P8	Male	Physics
P9	Male	French
P10	Male	Physics
P11	Female	Journalism
P12	Male	International Politics
P13	Female	Pharmacy
P14	Male	Philosophy
P15	Female	International Politics
P16	Male	Biology
P17	Female	Nursing
P18	Female	International Politics
P19	Female	Russian
P20	Male	International Politics
P21	Female	Anthropology

2019–2021 and based on classroom ethnography. Narrative accounts efficiently capture the personal and human dimensions of the individuals (Clandinin & Connelly, 2004), and can reveal the lived language learning experience and particular perspective of the focal participants regarding the current study. Each participant was asked to write a narrative account, involving their individual motivation to learn Arabic, and their perceptions of the Arabic language and related cultures. The narrative accounts were written in Chinese, with each piece being around 1000–1500 Chinese characters on average. In addition, a semi-structured interview with each participant was conducted to complement the retrospective narratives and to explore more about their educational backgrounds, language proficiency and personal values relating to certain contexts according to their retrospective narratives (see also Liao *et al.*, 2020). Each interview was undertaken in the form of a face-to-face conversation between one of the authors and a single participant. Interviews were conducted in Chinese and lasted approximately 30 minutes. The full interviews were audio-recorded and field notes were taken during the process.

Table 3.2 A conceptual framework of the current study

Multilingual agentive self	in the past	agentive actions (e.g. self-learning)
		historical/sociocultural/dialogical factors
	at present	agentive actions (e.g. choose/decide to learn Arabic)
		historical/sociocultural/dialogical factors
	as imagined	agentive actions (e.g. continue to learn; quit)
		historical/sociocultural/dialogical factors

Data analysis

The narrative accounts and transcribed interview sources were analysed using deductive and inductive approaches facilitated by NVivo 12.0 (Merriam, 2009). First, we coded all the data in terms of the temporal dimension of multilingual agentive self (MAS) *in the past, at present* and *as imagined*. Second, we paid attention to the data reflecting the specific agentive actions that the participants took in the learning process – for example, 'choose/choice', 'decide/decision', 'continue', and so forth. Third, we re-analyzed the entire dataset, and selected content that indicated the facilitating/inhibiting factors the learners confronted at different stages of their Arabic learning process – for instance, 'the orthographic feature of Arabic attracted me a lot', 'Arabic is quite related to my own academic study', 'I have got enough credits for foreign language courses', 'I have limited time and effort for the elective courses' – with reference to the 3-tier conceptualization of agentive self, *historically, socioculturally* and *dialogically*. Table 3.2 illustrates how the agentive selves of these Arabic learners were conceptualized as a dialogical spatial–temporal continuum, which is the core theoretical and analytical framework of the current study.

Findings

The findings of this study demonstrate that the MASs of these Arabic learners derive from the past, present and future in a dialogical continuum mediated by various environmental factors. For these Arabic learners, the construction of multilingual selves interacts and mutually promotes their agentive actions to learn Arabic, despite the challenges and restrictions that may be caused by various structural factors – for example, the dominance of English, unbalanced credit structures of foreign language curriculum, lack of resources for Arabic teaching and learning, and absence of uniform criteria for Arabic proficiency assessment.

In the past: Tracing back my roots and pursuing my interests

The findings illustrate that the MASs of these Arabic learners are usually affected by family or religious factors or by their particular perceptions of Arabic embedded in their past experiences.

Excerpt 1

I was born into an ethnic Hui family in Shanghai, but lived with Han Chinese afterwards. However, lots of elements in my daily life still remind me of my heritage, such as the Qur'an in Arabic that I inherited from my grandma, and the chanting in Arabic at some special festivals. My original goal to learn Arabic was to trace back my roots. ... After looking up my genealogy, I found that some of my ancestors were truly Arabs, which aroused my greatest interest to see what it [Arabic] was like. (P21, narrative account)

As shown in Excerpt 1, participant P21 was immersed in an ethnic Hui family in southeast China. Compared with the Han as the majority ethnic group in China, the Hui, as one of the 56 ethnic groups recognized by China, have a distinct connection with Islamic culture and customs. The Hui people in China refers to Chinese-speaking adherents of Islam, who predominantly speak Chinese and maintain some Arabic and Persian expressions (Gladney, 1996, 2004). The ethnic elements in P21's family prompted her to learn Arabic and to explore more about her roots. This suggests that her past experiences that were closely related to the Arabic language and culture constructed her ethnic self as a Hui member, which led her to exert agentive actions (to register in the Arabic course) to promote the development of her multilingual self.

Among the 21 participants recruited in the current study, eight were from Hui families, which have a distinct connection with Islamic culture and Arabic elements. The narrative accounts and interviews from the eight focal students show that they began to gain familiarity with Arabic in their early childhood, which is quite different from the experiences of other participants without any family- or religion-related backgrounds in Arabic. It may be seen that their early knowledge of Arabic embedded in their past made a significant impact on their construction of agentive selves to become a 'qualified' Arabic user, and therefore encouraged or even pushed them to take agentive actions to learn Arabic once access to elective Arabic curricula in the focal university became available.

Excerpt 2

The original motivation for Arabic learning came from my enthusiasm for this language because I have special feelings towards the Arabic language. I got connected with this language since I was born due to the religious beliefs of my family and me. Led by my mother, I stepped into the world of Arabic language with Chinese characteristics ... The rhythm of the Qur'an aroused my great interest in learning Arabic. I often imitated the recordings and practiced reading aloud but, with a lack of systematic guidance, there were big problems with my Arabic pronunciation. (P12, narrative account)

P12 (Excerpt 2) is an Arabic learner, and is a Muslim with a specific religious background. As mentioned in his narrative account, there was a strong connection between him and Arabic because of the religious beliefs shared by himself and his family. The 'special feelings towards the Arabic language' aroused great enthusiasm in him towards the Arabic language, and helped him to build up the MAS to be a proficient Arabic user.

However, Arabic is still regarded as a less commonly used LOTE language in China, and the resources and opportunities for Arabic learning are not as plentiful as those for learning global English and other more popular LOTEs such as Japanese, German or French, amongst others (An & Zheng, 2022). As P12 and several other participants noted, there was a profound lack of resources and opportunities to acquire Arabic in a systematic way before they registered for the Arabic I course offered at the focal university. For example, P12 exercised strong agency to learn and practice Arabic by himself while confronting great difficulty in improving his Arabic pronunciation, and he was very frustrated about having no access to any professional guidance or supervision in this regard. When he enrolled in the Arabic curriculum at the focal university, he greatly valued the resources and continued to exert strong agency (of learning Arabic) to consolidate the construction of his MAS.

Excerpt 3

Learning Arabic, for me, has been an unexpected surprise. I became quite interested in current news when I was in senior high school, and that was the time when I was attracted by issues regarding the Middle East. (P1, narrative account)

I have had a longing and curiosity about Arabic culture and customs. Classical literature such as Tales from the Thousand and One Nights, The Alchemist, and Arabic music. Many interesting things and various opportunities led me to the Arabic language, and showed a new world to me. (P5, narrative account)

Excerpt 3 portrays two Arabic learners holding strong personal interests and motivation to learn about Arabic culture in their past, but with little influence from family or religious factors as in the previous excerpts. As P1 and P5 state, their great interest in Arabic culture and history prompted them to exert their agency to actively explore the Arabic language, and established the connection between the Arabic language and themselves, and therefore helped to construct their agentive selves as Arabic learners in the future.

At present: Be competitive and be enriched

Most Arabic learners in the university in question do not come from specific family or religious backgrounds that are closely related to Arabic elements in their past experiences. As such, they are more likely to become voluntary learners with different motivations and agency regarding their current status or circumstances.

Excerpt 4

After I was enrolled in the university, it was surprising to find that we were offered courses on Arabic, so I did not hesitate for a second to register in the course. It has been proved that it is one of the most wonderful decisions I have made. (P1, narrative account)

In another course about ancient civilization, the lecturer often gave introductions to different languages such as Arabic, Persian. Looking at the waving symbols on the blackboard, I felt excited for no reason. As an undergraduate student majoring in Chinese, the grammar and morphology of Arabic were totally new to me, and it really attracted me a lot. That is the main reason for my choice of the Arabic I course. (P5, narrative account)

Echoing Excerpt 3, Excerpt 4 demonstrates P1 and P5 with great interest in Arabic in the past (see Excerpt 3), and consequently deciding to register for the Arabic course when they were offered this Arabic program. As P1 mentioned, access to the Arabic course was an 'unexpected surprise', which enabled them to take agentive actions by actively choosing the course, and hence their multilingual selves as Arabic learners gradually developed during the learning process.

Excerpt 5

I major in International Relations, focusing on conflict solutions. Hence learning Arabic helps me better understand the religious and political conflicts with culture in the Arabic world. (P15, narrative account)

My major (International Politics) is a key reason for taking the Arabic class. (P12, narrative account).

Excerpt 5 shows one of the key promoting factors for these Arabic learners in the sociocultural dimension: namely, the strong connection between Arabic and the learners' own disciplines. It was found that 13 out of the 21 Arabic learners in the current study explicitly identified positive interactions between Arabic learning and their disciplinary studies, such as International Relations (P15) and International Politics (P12). These Arabic learners usually had aspirations regarding the mutual enhancement of Arabic learning by their disciplinary studies, and vice versa, before they decided to choose the Arabic course. They gained great benefits from the Arabic learning experience during their disciplinary studies. These gains seem to validate their choice of learning Arabic and lead to stronger agency in Arabic learning at the current stage and into the future.

Excerpt 6

The reason for my Arabic learning is that, in the module Introduction to International Relations, our professor, who is the Dean of our department, mentioned that the Arabic language and culture are spreading very fast in the world today. Also, our country needs more people who can speak Arabic because of the Belt and Road Initiative. (P18, narrative account)

Excerpt 6 reflects the characterization of a typical participant learning Arabic mainly due to the promoting effects of structural factors. As shown in her narrative account, P18 was inspired by an influential professor from her discipline remarking about the significance of Arabic, which encouraged her to register for the Arabic course to achieve a better learning and understanding of Arabic. Her commitment and actions taken when learning Arabic may be regarded as an outcome of the dialogical interaction between herself and others (e.g. the professor), which strengthened her construction of agentive selves to achieve more at a personal level.

Excerpt 7

I find everything really interesting. I, together with my classmates, often preview the Arabic alphabet for the next lesson, and ask the Arabic teacher to correct our pronunciation; the teacher introduces the wonder and charm of the Arab States, such as the special cuisine, the special writing system of Arabic; my classmate displays interesting cartoons in Arabic; the excellent classmate shares the corresponding rules between International Phonetic Alphabet and Arabic alphabets; I see Arabic, on restaurant signs, in the introduction displayed in the museum ... all of these are small changes for me, but amount to the most significant gains and knowledge I get from the Arabic course. (P2, narrative account)

As indicated in Excerpt 7, P2 was attracted and influenced by the Arabic teacher, by peers in the Arabic class, and by Arabic elements in the environment outside the class. The changes she made and the improvement she perceived in the Arabic course effectively elevated her awareness of the presence of the Arabic language in her daily surroundings. This experience seems to feed back to her willingness to further her Arabic learning, promoting the development of her multilingual self. In other words, the agentive self construction of the Arabic learner P2 can be dialogically negotiated through structural factors, such as scaffolding from the Arabic teacher, cooperation with peers, achievements and changes obtained in the Arabic course, that can make effects on P2's Arabic learning trajectory in the short or long term.

In the future: Continue or quit future Arabic learning

With intensive learning of Arabic for one or two semesters in the focal university, it has been found that the MASs of these participants were also fluid and dynamic. Their prospects or visions in the near or far future, as well as the promoting or inhibiting structural factors, have a great influence on their agentive actions with regard to Arabic learning in the future. Among the 21 Arabic learners, eight of them continued to learn Arabic, either by registering in follow-up Arabic courses or via other means such as self-learning; four of them enrolled in academic programs closely relating to Arabic, such as a postgraduate program of international politics; seven of them may be prohibited by various limitations – for example, heavy academic work in their own disciplines, limited learning resources, saturated credits on foreign language courses etc.; and two of them quit Arabic learning because of their career development in other areas.

Excerpt 8

Interviewer: Do you think that you are a multilingual now?

P14: Not yet. If I can learn Arabic well then I will be really multilingual. But for now, my Arabic is still at a low proficiency. I think it is an opportunity for me to become multilingual. I hold a positive attitude towards the multilingual trends and I believe language is the reflection of the underpinning logic and culture. If we can know more about certain languages, we will get benefits for personal development. (P14, semi-structured interview)

According to the one-on-one semi-structured interview with these Arabic learners, all 21 participants embraced the multilingual turn and envisioned themselves to be multilingual in the future, which aligned with their construction of MASs. As a representative Arabic learner, P14 (Excerpt 14) held a positive attitude towards the multilingual trend in such a globalized society, and they perceived the choice of learning Arabic as an effective route to becoming cosmopolitan members in the imagined future, and therefore they continued to learn Arabic to voice their MASs in the long run. In this sense, the construction of the multilingual self and the agentive choice to learn the language co-shape each other.

Excerpt 9

During the learning process, any new knowledge obtained deepened my interest in Arabic, and increased my aspiration to learn Arabic. I think that is the magic and charm of Arabic. (P1, narrative account)

As an active participant in the Arabic course, P1's construction of multilingual self (Excerpt 9) pushed her to become an agentive Arabic learner, and the benefits and enjoyment she obtained from the language learning experience enhanced her motivation to learn Arabic in the future. According to the informal interview with P1 afterwards, she chose to register for Arabic II for intermediate learners the following semester to continue her Arabic learning. P1's case indicates that the positive experience of Arabic learning triggers a new cycle of sustainable exploration of the Arabic language and culture in the future, which further strengthens her agentive self construction as a high-proficiency Arabic learner.

Excerpt 10

Interviewer: What proficiency level do you expect to achieve in Arabic learning?

P11: In the long term, I may try to get a translation certificate. Because for non-specialist Arabic learners, there is no access to the grading test like the College English Test. (P11, semi-structured interview)

In Excerpt 10, P11 was not sure what proficiency level she could aspire to attain, so she could only conceive of a vague goal to 'get a translation certificate'. However, we can see that the absence of uniform criteria for Arabic proficiency assessment, especially for non-specialist learners, is a key inhibiting factor for these learners' Arabic learning process and agentive self construction in the sociocultural dimension.

In the Chinese context, insufficient support for non-specialist Arabic learning is probably related to the marginal status of Arabic as well as some other LOTEs, compared with the dominant position of global English in the foreign language education structure at tertiary level. Therefore Arabic, as a less commonly taught language, receives little support or resources in the current foreign language education system (An & Zheng, 2022).

Excerpt 11

Interviewer: Will you continue to learn Arabic II for higher proficiency learners?

P10: Maybe I will audit instead of registering in the class, because I have got enough credits as a fourth-year undergraduate student. (P10, semi-structured interview)

Excerpt 11 reveals another common challenge confronted by most of the Arabic learners in the current study. In the focal university, undergraduate students are required to obtain 8 credits in foreign language courses (each 16-week course for 2 credits), but a minimum of 6 out of the 8 credits should be obtained from College English courses, i.e. they are supposed to take four different language courses to complete the 8 credits. The unbalanced credit structure of foreign language curricula, as well as the relatively marginal status of Arabic in the focal university, restricts these recruited participants from continuing their involvement in Arabic learning, changes their learning path of foreign languages, and therefore hinders the development of their MASs.

It should be noted that a new Learning Certificate Program was recently implemented in the focal university, which may remedy the limitations brought about by the unbalanced credit structure in foreign language curricula. The Learning Certificate Program was carried out by the focal university as *Xuecheng* Scheme (学程计划) in 2019 as a response to the Chinese MOE's call for interdisciplinary curricular design, involving 24 faculties offering 71 elective sub-programs. Regarding Arabic courses, the Multilingual Teaching Center launched the 'Learning Certificate Program for Arabic' in the fall of 2022, including seven courses (Arabic I, II, III, Arabic Grammar, Arabic and Islamic Culture, Intermediate-level Practice and Advanced-level Practice). Undergraduate students who obtain 16 credits from at least five courses can apply for a Learning Certificate of Completion awarded by the focal university. As the Arabic teacher mentioned in an informal interview with the authors:

> I just sensed that the new *Xuecheng* Scheme was an opportunity for the Arabic program. If the students are willing to spend some credits on Arabic learning, I shall try to provide them with some sort of official certification. They can also gain a sense of accomplishment. It doesn't hurt to have a try, right? (Arabic teacher, informal interview)

The official certification of the Arabic program may counter-balance the limited credit structure to a certain extent. It may provide a sense of accomplishment to the Arabic learners, and support their career and personal development that echoes their prospects in the future. The *Xuecheng* Scheme, as well as the learning certificate of Arabic, may be considered a key facilitating factor to the construction of the MASs of Arabic learners.

Excerpt 12

Learning Arabic has changed the way I see language learning. Language is more than a tool; it's also an opportunity for me to know another culture. When I avail myself of the opportunity, I can throw away the tinted glasses and travel freely in the vast land of Arabic culture. Then I can feel what the people are feeling, not as an observer but as a participant. (P12, narrative account)

When I was young, I always dreamed of equality and freedom. Hence, I see Muslims as my pals, since their ancestors have made great contributions to human civilization just like ours, so why should they suffer from the bitterness of war and the bullying of prejudice? Then I began to think, although I may not be able to help them out, I can at least try to let others understand their authentic and splendid culture and civilization; in this sense, maybe I can't be a world peace warrior, but I can be a guardian upholding the principle of the equality of all cultures. All in all, on this basis, I decided that I should master their language: Arabic. (P14, semi-structured interview)

In Excerpt 12, participants P12 and P14 expressed that the Arabic learning experience in the focal university has greatly affected their perception of language learning, Arabic history and culture, and even ethical issues. With knowledge of the Arabic language, they have become aware of their agentive selves in the future as 'participants' of the multilingual world, and 'guardians' of the equality and freedom of all cultures and peoples, especially those of marginalized status. During the Arabic learning process, P12 and P14 defined and redefined their agentive selves by negotiating with sociocultural factors, and uplifting their multilingual selves, transcending Arabic learners to a higher level relating to broader cultural and ethical issues. This finding illustrates well the dynamic and interactive features of multilingual learners' agentive selves.

Discussion and Conclusions

Contextualized in a LOTE Arabic program of a top-tier comprehensive university in China, this study focuses on a group of multilingual learners registered on Arabic courses, to explore how their MASs are crafted and developed in a dialogical temporal–spatial continuum.

In this study, we portray the fluid landscape of the Arabic learners' MASs construction in different dimensions, as displayed in Table 3.3. Their agentive selves as Arabic learners/users were initially constructed in their past lives, and usually negotiated with historical or sociocultural factors such as family and/or religious backgrounds, personal interest or curiosity about Arabic culture and history. They then chose to take part in the Arabic program to start formal Arabic learning when they were offered the elective Arabic courses in the focal university, during which process they were encouraged and supported by a range of structural factors, including ease of access to Arabic courses, mutual promotion of Arabic learning and their own disciplinary studies, help from their

Table 3.3 Arabic learners' construction of MASs in a dialogically spatial–temporal continuum

Multilingual agentive self	in the past	agentive actions	* to make a decesion to learn Arabic * to learn and practice Arabic by himself/herself * to explore the news, history and culture of Arabic
		historical and sociocultural structural factors	+ Hui family background + religious belief + strong interest in the Arabic language and culture − lack of resources and guidance to learn Arabic
	at present	agentive actions	* to register for the *Arabic I* course * to interact with the teacher and peers in the Arabic class * to hold positive attitudes towards the changes
		sociocultural and dialogical structural factors	+ accessibe Arabic curriculum university-wide + recommendation and encouragement from influential people + mutual promotion with the majors of the Arabic learners + sense of fulfillment and enjoyment during the Arabic learning process
	as imagined	agentive actions	* to continued to learn Arabic * to perceive the changes in views of language learning and values * to struggle to find new ways for Arabic learning * to decrease efforts or quit Arabic learning
		sociocultural and dialogical structural factors	+ multilingual trend + positive feedback in the learning process − unbalanced credit system in foreign language curricula − limited time and effort for Arabic learning in the long run − absence of uniform criteria for Arabic proficiency assessment

Note: *indicates the agentive actions; + indicates promoting factors; - indicates inhibiting factors.

teachers and peers, as well as great progress and fulfillment. Therefore, the Arabic learning process enabled them to enhance their agentive selves as Arabic learners and also as multilinguals. In the imagined future, their agentive selves were flexible and diverse, negotiating with various structural factors in sociocultural and dialogical dimensions: some learners continued their Arabic learning to strengthen their agentive selves as high-proficiency Arabic users and qualified multilinguals to fit the multilingual trend, while other learners may have divested from Arabic learning with declined agentive selves because of limitations of effort, an unbalanced credit system in foreign language curricula, and so forth; yet others still redefined their agentive selves as 'participants' in the globalized world and even as 'guardians' for the equality and freedom of marginalized groups.

In the light of previous studies that have emphasized the multilingual self as a crucial guiding role in foreign language learning (e.g. Henry, 2017; Ushioda, 2017; Zheng *et al.*, 2019, 2020), the findings of the present study further reveal that the construction of the multilingual self is closely related to the actions taken and choices made by the learners. In this sense, the present study contributes to the present research on multilingual learning motivation by highlighting *self* as an active agent that can reflect on their own histories, evaluate present learning experiences and imagine future possibilities. Thus, foreign language learning is not only about what the learners may perceive themselves to do, but more about the actions they take to achieve the perceived self-image, despite the challenges and difficulties in their immediate environment.

The current study echoes the findings of previous studies that the agentive self is not static or isolated but is a dynamic sociocultural–dialogical construct in a spatial–temporal continuum (e.g. An & Zheng, 2022; Hull & Katz, 2006; Vitanova, 2018). These Arabic learners exert their agency despite multiple structural limitations at different levels, and their constructions of agentive selves develop and interact with various historical, sociocultural and relational factors in the past, at present and in the future. One key finding is that the learners define and redefine their agentive selves through their learning experiences in relation to their personal pursuits, and even in relation to the greater good of the globalized community: for instance, the imagined selves of P12 and P14 as participants and guardians in a multilingual world. In this view, the MAS is ultimately a relational construct that emerges from the learner's spatial and temporal existence.

The findings of this study also demonstrate the significance of investigating multilingual learners' agentive selves in foreign language learning, especially for the LOTEs of relatively marginal status compared to global English. The perspective of MASs displays what actions language learners can take during their learning process, why learners choose to take these agentive actions and make certain decisions, and more importantly, how the actions taken negotiate with learners' multilingual self construction and underlying structural factors in the context. This study sheds light on further studies on motivation in foreign language education that MASs can be regarded as an anchor to investigate the mutual constitution and interaction between multilingual selves construction and multilingual learners' agency, and as a conceptual tool to illustrate the mediation between learners' agentive actions and the promoting/inhibiting factors at different levels in the spatial–temporal continuum.

This study furthermore puts forward practical implications for the improvement of language policies of foreign language education, as well as the sustainable development of LOTE teaching and learning in Chinese tertiary education and across wider contexts in Asia. According to the current study, these Arabic learners actively voice and enhance their MASs in a resource-poor environment with multiple difficulties and structural limitations – for example, the unbalanced credit structure for foreign language curricula, the marginalized status of Arabic and other LOTEs compared with English in the dominant position, the immature system for Arabic proficiency assessment, and so forth. Foreign language planners and educators at different levels of language policy and planning should pay greater attention to the existing limitations of LOTE teaching and learning, and take actions to balance the resources between education on LOTE and dominant English. Based on the detailed trajectory of the Arabic learners' MASs construction elaborated in the current study, LOTE teachers can implement and adjust their teaching regarding students' diverse and flexible agency and motivation.

Admittedly, this study only relates to one single case in a specific Arabic program at a Chinese university. However, we anticipate that this study will open up further explorations of the construction of MASs in LOTE education, with the potential not only to enrich the theoretical achievements on motivation in foreign language learning but also to promote the development of relatively marginalized LOTE education in the Asian context.

Notes

(1) The Belt and Road Initiative is a global infrastructure development strategy adopted by the Chinese government in 2013, aiming to invest in more than 150 countries and international organizations, and calling for a greater leadership role for the global affairs of China (see https://www.yidaiyilu.gov.cn for details).
(2) 'The Notification by the Ministry of Education on jointly building The Belt and Road Education Act' available at http://www.moe.gov.cn/srcsite/A20/s7068/201608/t20160811_274679.html
(3) Referring to the QS World University Rankings 2023: Top global universities (see https://www.topuniversities.com/university-rankings/world-university-rankings/2023 for details)
(4) The participants' English proficiency is assessed according to *China's Standards of English Language Ability*, which is compiled by the National Education Examinations Authority and released by the Chinese Ministry of Education in 2018. http://www.moe.gov.cn/srcsite/A19/s229/201804/t20180416_333315.html

References

Ahearn, L.M. (2001) Language and agency. *Annual Review of Anthropology* 30, 109–137.
An, N. and Zheng, Y. (2022) Language learners as invisible planners: A case study of an Arabic language program in a Chinese university. *Current Issues in Language Planning* 23 (4), 371–393.
Boo, Z., Dörnyei, Z. and Ryan, S. (2015) L2 motivation research 2005–2014: Understanding a publication surge and a changing landscape. *System* 55, 145–157.
Clandinin, D.J. and Connelly, F.M. (2004) *Narrative Inquiry: Experience and Story in Qualitative Research*. Jossey-Bass.
Dörnyei, Z. (2000) Motivation in action: Towards a process-oriented conceptualisation of student motivation. *British Journal of Educational Psychology* 70 (4), 519–538.
Emirbayer, M. and Mische, A. (1998) What is agency? *American Journal of Sociology* 103, 962–1023.
Gao, X. and Zheng, Y. (2019) Multilingualism and higher education in Greater China. *Journal of Multilingual and Multicultural Development* 40 (7), 555–561.
Gearing, N. and Roger, P. (2018) 'I'm never going to be part of it': Identity, investment and learning Korean. *Journal of Multilingual and Multicultural Development* 39 (2), 155–168.

Gladney, D.C. (1996) *Muslim Chinese: Ethnic Nationalism in the People's Republic* (2nd edn). Harvard University Asia Center.

Gladney, D.C. (2004) *Dislocating China: Reflections on Muslims, Minorities and Other Subaltern Subjects.* Hurst.

Goller, M. (2017) *Human Agency at Work: An Active Approach Towards Expertise Development.* Springer.

Han, Y., Gao, X. and Xia, U. (2019) Problematising recent developments in non-English foreign language education in Chinese universities. *Journal of Multilingual and Multicultural Development* 40 (7), 562–575.

Henry, A. (2017) L2 motivation and multilingual identities. *The Modern Language Journal* 101 (3), 548–565.

Henry, A. and Thorsen, C. (2018) The ideal multilingual self: Validity, influences on motivation, and role in a multilingual education. *International Journal of Multilingualism* 15 (4), 349–364.

Huang, T., Steinkrauss, R. and Verspoor, M. (2021) The emergence of the multilingual motivational system in Chinese learners. *System* 100, 102564.

Hull, G.A. and Katz, M.L. (2006) Crafting an agentive self: Case studies of digital storytelling. *Research in the Teaching of English* 41 (1), 43–81.

Liao, J., An, N. and Zheng, Y. (2020) What motivates L3 learners' investment and/or divestment in Arabic? Understanding learning motivation in terms of 'identity'. *Círculo de Lingüística Aplicada a la Comunicación* 84, 27–39.

Liddicoat, A.J. (2020) Language policy and planning for language maintenance: The macro and meso levels. In A. Schalley and S. Eisenchlas (eds) *Handbook of Home Language Maintenance and Development* (pp. 337–356). De Gruyter.

Liddicoat, A.J. and Taylor-Leech, K. (2021) Agency in language planning and policy. *Current Issues in Language Planning* 22 (1–2), 1–18.

Liu, M. (2020) The emotional basis of the ideal multilingual self: The case of simultaneous language learners in China. *Journal of Multilingual and Multicultural Development* 43 (7), 647–664.

Martin, J., Sugarman, J.H. and Hickinbottom, S. (2010) *Persons: Understanding Psychological Selfhood and Agency.* Springer.

May, S. (2014) *The Multilingual Turn: Implications for SLA, TESOL and Bilingual Education.* Routledge.

Mead, G.H. (1938) *The Philosophy of the Act* (C.W. Morris, ed.). University of Chicago Press.

Mead, G. H. (2002) *The Philosophy of the Present.* Prometheus. (Originally published 1932).

Merriam, B. (2009) *Qualitative Research: A Guide to Design and Implementation.* Jossey-Bass.

Miller, E.R. (2012) Agency, language learning, and multilingual spaces. *Multilingua* 31 (4), 441–468.

Norton, B. (2013) *Identity and Language Learning: Extending the Conversation* (2nd edn). Multilingual Matters.

Norton, B. and Toohey, K. (2011) Identity, language learning, and social change. *Language Teaching* 44 (4), 412–446.

Orcasitas-Vicandi, M. and Perales-Fernandez-de-Gamboa, A. (2023) Translanguaging interventions and the construction of the multilingual self through culturally sustaining pedagogies. *International Journal of Multilingualism.*

Ushioda, E. (2017) The impact of global English on motivation to learn other languages: Toward an ideal multilingual self. *The Modern Language Journal* 101 (3), 469–482.

Ushioda, E. and Dörnyei, Z. (2017) Beyond global English: Motivation to learn languages in a multicultural world. Introduction to the special issue. *Modern Language Journal* 101 (3), 451–454.

Van Lier, L. (2008) Agency in the classroom. In J.P. Lantolf and M.E. Poehner (eds) *Sociocultural Theory and the Teaching of Second Languages* (pp. 163–186). Equinox Publishing.

Vitanova, G. (2018) 'Just treat me as a teacher!' Mapping language teacher agency through gender, race, and professional discourses. *System* 79, 28–37.

Zhao, S. (2011) Actors in language planning. In E. Hinkel (ed.) *Handbook of Research in Second Language Teaching and Learning* (vol. 2, pp. 905–923). Routledge.

Zhao, S. and Baldauf, R.B. (2012) Individual agency in language planning: Chinese script reform as a case study. *Language Problems and Language Planning* 36 (1), 1–24.

Zheng, Y., Lu, X. and Ren, W. (2019) Profiling Chinese university students' motivation to learn multiple languages. *Journal of Multilingual and Multicultural Development* 40 (7), 590–604.

Zheng, Y., Lu, X. and Ren, W. (2020) Tracking the evolution of Chinese learners' multilingual motivation through a longitudinal Q methodology. *The Modern Language Journal* 104 (4), 781–803.

4 The Construction of Ought-To Multilingual Selves and their Roles in Shaping Chinese Language Learners' LOTE Motivation

Tianyi Wang

Introduction

Research in the field of language learning motivation has witnessed a multilingual turn in recent years (Ushioda & Dörnyei, 2017). In particular, there has been a burgeoning interest in conceptualising language learners' motivation for being multilingual from the perspective of the self and in investigating the construction of individuals' multilingual selves (e.g. Henry, 2016, 2017; Henry & Thorsen, 2018; Thompson, 2020; Ushioda, 2017). However, compared to research on the ideal multilingual self (e.g. Henry, 2017; Zheng *et al.*, 2020), very little research attention has been paid to the ought-to dimension of the multilingual self, despite the fact that the ought-to language self also constitutes an important part of the language self (Dörnyei, 2009). There are even fewer studies exploring the role of the ought-to multilingual self in shaping language learning motivation from a longitudinal perspective. In response to this research gap, this study conducted a longitudinal investigation into the trajectories of two Chinese learners' ought-to multilingual selves when learning a language other than English (LOTE). Three rounds of interviews were conducted during the course of three years to study the formation of the participants' ought-to multilingual selves and the role of this motivational construct in developing their LOTE motivation.

Literature Review

The multilingual self

While multilingualism is a topic that has promoted heated discussion in linguistics and language education for decades (e.g. Blackledge & Creese, 2010; Herdina & Jessner, 2002; Pavlenko, 2005), it is only in recent years that research on language learning motivation has started to abandon the monolingual bias in conceptualisation (Henry & Thorsen, 2018). The proposal of a multilingual self to theorise LOTE learning motivation is one of the most important efforts of this multilingual turn (Henry, 2017; Ushioda, 2017). As Henry (2017) has pointed out, in a multilingual mind, different languages are in constant interaction with each other. Such interplay between multiple language-specific selves can lead to the emergence of a multilingual self, which is situated at a higher level of construal. In other words, the multilingual self is more than a collection of discrete language-specific selves and emphasises the hybridity and integration of languages.

With reference to the L2 Motivational Self System (L2MSS) (Dörnyei, 2009), Henry (2017) and Ushioda (2017) specifically propose the concept of the ideal multilingual self, which addresses the motivating power derived from learners' aspirations to be multilingual in the future. According to Henry (2017), even though the ideal multilingual selves might be more abstract in individuals' visualisation compared to ideal language-specific selves, the multilingual selves can still be highly motivating. This is because these self-guides are intimately related to individual learners' personal multilingual experiences and associated feelings. Empirical studies have also substantiated the motivational power of this construct (Henry & Thorsen, 2018; Wang & Fisher, 2023) and investigated the construction of the ideal multilingual self across time and in different contexts (e.g. Liu, 2022; Wang, 2020; Zheng *et al.*, 2020). However, compared to developing research on the ideal multilingual self, limited attention has been paid to another important aspect of language selves: namely, the ought-to dimension of the multilingual selves. This is despite the fact that the ought-to language self can function as an important counterbalancing force to prevent language learners from abandoning their ideal language selves (Dörnyei, 2009) and in shaping learners' overall language learning motivation (Lanvers, 2017). This situation makes further research necessary.

The ought-to language self

The ought-to language self, according to Dörnyei's (2009) definition, represents language learners' desire to meet others' expectations or combat the fear of failing to learn the target language well. In other words, the ought-to language self is related to the external demands placed on language learners. Empirical studies have showed that the ought-to language self tends to have a less motivating power than ideal language selves (e.g. Feng & Papi, 2020; Lamb, 2011; Liu & Thompson, 2018; Taguchi *et al.*, 2009), especially in relation to autonomous learning (Lamb, 2011). However, the research results become more controversial when the dimensions of time and context are taken into account when discussing the role of the ought-to language self in language learning. While some studies argue that older language learners (e.g. university students compared to secondary school students) are less likely to be influenced by their ought-to language selves (Papi & Teimouri, 2012), other studies suggest that the ought-to language self may function as a stronger motivating force in the later stages of language learning (e.g. Jiang & Dewaele, 2015; Wang & Fisher, 2023). Other research also indicates the possibility of adult language learners being more concerned about avoiding negative outcomes (Ryan & Dörnyei, 2013). The explanations for these differences might be related to the different contexts that language learners are situated in, leading to their different reactions towards others' expectations or their own fears about the future. From this perspective, the formation of the ought-to language self and its motivational power can depend significantly on individuals' interactions with their situated contexts and their interpretations of others' expectations.

Another important issue related to the theorisation of the ought-to language self is the extent to which external influences can be internalised by individuals. Research by writers such as Lanvers (2016) and Ryan (2009) has already shown that the ideal language self and the ought-to language self may not be regarded as two separate entities but exist on a spectrum depending on the extent to which individuals internalise external influences. To theorise the internalisation process of the ought-to language self, Lanvers (2016) has integrated 'own' and 'other' differentiation into the original conceptualisation and proposed the ought-to/other self (i.e. what others expect the language learner to do) and the ought-to/own self (i.e. how the individual internalises external influences). As shown in this study, the more internalised the motivational construct, the more likely it will be that language learners are effectively motivated. This aspect of the literature demonstrates the necessity of paying attention to internalisation issues when researching the ought-to language self.

The ought-to language self in Asian contexts

Despite the controversial motivating power of the ought-to language self in the literature, existing research shows that this construct seems more prominent in some Asian contexts, such as China and Japan (e.g. Chen, 2012; Taguchi *et al.*, 2009). The underlying reason might be related to the tradition of collectivism and the influence of Confucianism in these countries, which makes language learners more likely to be influenced by family expectations and teachers' requirements (Kim, 1997). For example, Taguchi *et al.*'s (2009) research found that as families in Asia tended to look highly upon the learning of English, the ought-to English self functioned as a strong motivating force for language learners there.

In spite of insights into the distinctive features of the ought-to language self in Asian contexts, research attention has mainly focused on English learning motivation. Only a few empirical studies have touched upon the ought-to L3/LOTE self (e.g. Siridetkoon & Dewaele, 2018; Wang & Fisher, 2023) and even fewer have investigated the ought-to dimension of multilingual selves. Siridetkoon and Dewaele (2018) found that participants' ought-to L3 selves could be particularly important at the initial stage of L3 learning. This is because many language learners at this stage have not fully understood why they are learning an L3, and therefore need some external pressure to continue their exploration of the new language. This suggests the potentially important role of the ought-to self in shaping learners' motivation regarding LOTE learning and being multilingual in Asian contexts. Moreover, as Lanvers (2017) has suggested, expectations of individuals' LOTE learning could vary greatly, and may even be contradictory across contexts, which adds complexity to the construction of the ought-to dimension of language learners' LOTE and their multilingual selves. This observation, along with the fact that there has been very limited research investigating the ought-to multilingual self, makes exploration of this motivational construct in an Asian context important.

Therefore, in spite of the growing research interest in conceptualising motivation from a multilingual perspective, there is still a lack of research on the ought-to dimension of the multilingual selves. This is despite the wider recognition that the ought-to language self significantly influences the development of the ideal language self and language motivation in the long term. The present study conducted a longitudinal qualitative inquiry into the formation and effect of two Chinese learners' ought-to multilingual selves while learning German as a LOTE. In China, while English is the most widely learned foreign language, increasing emphasis has been placed on learning other foreign languages, partly in relation to the national pursuit of further economic and social development during globalisation (Gao & Zheng, 2019). However, recent research has shown that learners' motivations to learn LOTEs can be much more ambiguous than those for English in China, as learners are likely to be confused about the importance of learning a LOTE (e.g. Wang & Fisher, 2023; Wang & Zheng, 2021). From this perspective, a study investigating Chinese students' LOTE motivation can be helpful in understanding the complexity involved in LOTE learning in China. Two research questions were raised accordingly.

(1) Did these two learners develop ought-to multilingual selves during their LOTE learning? If so, what were the developmental trajectories of their ought-to multilingual selves?
(2) How did these learners' ought-to multilingual selves influence their LOTE learning?

Research Context and Participants

This study adopted a qualitative design to investigate the formation and motivating effect of two Chinese undergraduate students' ought-to multilingual selves over approximately three years. This was part of a larger longitudinal research project (from 2015 to 2020) that explored the construction of Chinese learners' motivation regarding learning a LOTE as a third language. The present study was located in the Department of English at a public university in southern China. Undergraduates who majored in English in this department were required to enrol in a two-year LOTE programme that aimed to build up their holistic linguistic competence and overall competitiveness for the future.

The two participants, Xiaoyue and Ling (pseudonyms), were selected from English majors learning German as their L3, based on their own willingness to participate and the aim of including language learners with potentially different motivational trajectories. More specifically, Xiaoyue and Ling showed different motivational patterns from the beginning. While Xiaoyue reported being 'under pressure' to learn German well, Ling suggested that she was motivated mainly by 'personal interest'. During the data collection over two years, Xiaoyue continued to feel obliged to learn German and develop multilingual competence. Comparatively, Ling's ought-to language self began to decline after the first interview and almost disappeared at the last interview. Therefore, focusing on these two students was likely to reveal different developmental trajectories of the ought-to dimension of language selves and help this study gain greater insights into the role of the ought-to multilingual self in language learning. Xiaoyue and Ling participated in this research from the beginning of their LOTE learning to one year after their graduation from the university. In this way, this research not only looked at participants' ought-to multilingual selves when required to learn a LOTE but also investigated how such selves changed when learners were given the choice of continuing or giving up their LOTE learning.

Data Collection and Analysis

Semi-structured individual interviews were used as the primary research method in the present study. As suggested by Silverman (2020), interviews can be effective in investigating individuals' attitudes, beliefs and positioning, can provide insights into their understanding of their situated contexts and elicit unexpected answers during interactions between the researcher and the participants. Since this study aimed to explore the complexity of participants' understanding of the external expectations placed on them and their sense of obligation in relation to being multilingual, this research method stood out as the most suitable approach. Specifically, the two participants were interviewed three times over the three years, the first time during the first half year of their LOTE learning, the second when they had been learning the LOTE for nearly one-and-a-half years, and the last time one year later, 10–12 months after their graduation.

Each interview started with a general discussion about the participants' recent motivation for learning the LOTE, and this was followed up by focusing specifically on their attitudes to being multilingual. The two other rounds of interviews also included a reflection on the motivational patterns that they had reported in the previous interview. Based on the participants' preference, the interview was conducted in Mandarin (the interviewees' first language), and each on average lasted 45 minutes. The author, who is qualified in Chinese-to-English translation, translated the interview excerpts used in the chapter. Backward translation was conducted to ensure the accuracy of the translated texts.

The interview data were then transcribed and coded with the help of Nvivo 11. The initial coding was conducted in a grounded way, with codes being assigned to chunks of raw data and grouped into different themes. These themes were then compared and categorised, during which the current literature was revisited (e.g. Dörnyei, 2009; Henry, 2017; Lanvers, 2016). The L2MSS and the concept of the multilingual self were adopted to guide the coding process, and the themes developed at this stage included the ideal/ought-to LOTE self, LOTE learning experience, the ideal/ought-to multilingual self, and the multilingual experience. It was during this process that participants' ought-to multilingual selves were found to play a crucial role in sustaining their motivation in the long term. This situation drove me to focus on the construction and motivating effect of the ought-to multilingual selves in this study. Lanvers' (2016) conceptualisation of the ought-to/own and ought-to/ought selves was introduced to develop a more elaborate coding scheme to understand the ought-to multilingual self.

Findings

Data analysis revealed that the two participants had developed different trajectories of ought-to multilingual selves, which led to two motivational patterns over the course of three years. In particular, the ought-to multilingual selves were found to be important in sustaining learners' LOTE and multilingual motivation, especially at the beginning of learning.

Case A: Xiaoyue

The construction of Xiaoyue's ought-to multilingual self

Xiaoyue had developed an ought-to multilingual self from the beginning of her German learning, which was gradually internalised in the course of learning. Interestingly, she had identified the necessity of being multilingual for her personal development after learning the LOTE for one year. Her ought-to multilingual self was also found to sustain her LOTE learning motivation across the three years and played an essential role when she was still unsure about the value of being multilingual.

Stage 1: The ought-to/ought multilingual self sustaining Xiaoyue's LOTE learning motivation

Based on the first interview, Xiaoyue recognised the need to become multilingual when she started to learn German. This initial ought-to multilingual self was related to her fear of losing her linguistic capital in an era when English was widely studied and used. As Xiaoyue pointed out, while being able to speak English was viewed as a distinct linguistic advantage in China in the last century, an increasing number of people have been able to speak this language in recent decades. Xiaoyue, therefore, found it necessary to develop new linguistic capital that could improve her competitiveness in the job market in the future. The following excerpt from the first interview best illustrates this situation:

> Everyone can speak English now and this language cannot be an advantage in the job market anymore. This situation upsets me, as I am an English major. (...) So, I want to learn more languages and become multilingual. If I can speak more languages and I am more sensitive to the similarities and differences between different languages and cultures, I believe that it will be easier for me to find an ideal job.

This excerpt clearly shows the ought-to dimension of Xiaoyue's multilingual self, as she felt obliged to speak more languages and become more linguistically and culturally sensitive. Notably, Xiaoyue at this time seemed to hold an instrumental attitude towards being multilingual: namely, whether it could be useful in the job market. It is also worth mentioning that Xiaoyue's understanding of 'being multilingual' was still very vague at this stage, as exemplified by another excerpt from the first interview:

> Researcher: Could you describe more about your understanding of being multilingual?
>
> Xiaoyue: Er, being able to speak more than three languages? Probably more than that. Will I be more culturally sensitive? (...) Well, being multilingual seems to be a state that is very hard to describe. But our teachers said that we should try to be multilingual, as it is important for our English majors.

It is evident from this excerpt that Xiaoyue had not fully internalised the value of being multilingual at this stage, as her recognition of the importance of 'being multilingual' was mainly related to the encouragement received from teachers. In other words, Xiaoyue's ought-to multilingual self should be understood from an ought-to/ought perspective at this time.

Xiaoyue's ought-to multilingual self at this stage was found to sustain her motivation to become multilingual, especially in the face of her doubts about the value of being multilingual for her future. Based on the first interview, although Xiaoyue's ought-to multilingual self was not the primary motivator for her LOTE learning, it pushed her to devote more effort to learning German. Xiaoyue reported, for example:

> I should admit that my fear of losing a competitive edge in the future significantly influenced my learning motivation. As suggested by our teachers, being multilingual is a possible way to enhance my competitiveness. Although it is not the main reason for me to learn German, it pushes me to work hard. Without the fear, I might have only focused on meeting course requirements when learning German.

It is evident from this excerpt that Xiaoyue's ought-to multilingual self was mainly related to teachers' encouragement and such an ought-to/ought multilingual self contributed to sustaining her LOTE motivation in the initial stages of learning German. Otherwise, Xiaoyue might have reduced the effort that she had put into learning German.

Stage 2: The ought-to/own multilingual self motivating Xiaoyue to spend effort on uninteresting learning tasks

While Xiaoyue's initial ought-to multilingual self was associated with her fear of failing to acquire linguistic capital for her future career, she gradually identified the value of being multilingual for her personal development during the process of learning. Her ought-to multilingual self also became more internalised and individualised. In the second interview, for example, Xiaoyue reported her deepened understanding of the importance of being multilingual in China, strengthening her obligation to learn a LOTE. She said, for example:

> After two years of German learning, I have become more assured that being multilingual can change my life, especially preventing me from being indistinguishable in the job market. This year, I have paid more attention to how being multilingual can change my life. During this process, I find myself more sensitive to cultural issues than my peers. I am still unsure how it can add to my competitiveness, but I firmly believe it will be useful in the future.

Therefore, by exploring the value of being multilingual, Xiaoyue accumulated multilingual experience, which broadened her cultural perspectives and concretised her understanding of how being multilingual could change her future. From this perspective, Xiaoyue's identification with the importance of being multilingual was no longer only related to external encouragement. Therefore, her ought-to multilingual self was more likely to be an ought-to/own language self at this stage.

The role of her ought-to multilingual self in Xiaoyue's LOTE motivation gradually decreased after she had identified the personal value to her of being multilingual. However, Xiaoyue's ought-to multilingual self still motivated her to learn German when the learning tasks were not interesting enough. She reported in the second interview, for example:

> Now I have fully realised the value of being multilingual for my future development; I am not pushed by fear to learn German. But learning a language can be sometimes hard and boring. The feeling of being obliged to be multilingual still stimulates me to work hard under these circumstances.

Therefore, Xiaoyue's strengthened identification with being multilingual lowered the role of her ought-to multilingual self in her motivation. However, her ought-to multilingual self still played a primary role in motivating her to undertake less enjoyable learning tasks.

Stage 3: The strengthened ought-to/own multilingual self adding to Xioayue's LOTE learning motivation

Xiaoyue's ought-to multilingual self continued to develop in the last round of interviews when she had completed her undergraduate study and begun to pursue a postgraduate degree in linguistics. According to Xiaoyue, being multilingual had now become 'a must' for her future:

> Now there is no doubt that I need to be multilingual. My course requires us to speak at least three languages. So being multilingual has become and will continue to be an integral part of my life. There is pressure but I am willing to face such pressure.

As shown in the excerpt, Xiaoyue's ought-to multilingual self had become even more strengthened and internalised by the time of the last interview, mainly because she had become a Master's student in linguistics and recognised a more individualised need to be multilingual. It is also notable that she did not resist such an ought-to multilingual self, as she realised the personal value of being multilingual. Put another way, her ought-to/own multilingual self had become internalised by this stage.

At this stage, Xiaoyue's ought-to multilingual self played a slightly stronger role in her learning of German and seemed to motivate her to learn another foreign language. According to Xiaoyue, in pursuing a Master's degree in linguistics, she felt more 'obliged' to develop multilingual competence, as exemplified in the following excerpt from the third interview:

> I am now studying Linguistics and I want to be a researcher in this area in the future. I need to speak three or even more languages and become multilingual. This is a necessity for me to become a qualified researcher in the future.

Notably, while her ought-to multilingual self had never been the main source of motivation for Xiaoyue's learning German, she regarded this motivational construct as crucial in laying the foundation for the development of her long-term LOTE and multilingual motivation. This was evident when she reflected on her LOTE motivational trajectory in her last interview. In particular, she mentioned that it was her initial fear of failing to gain a competitive edge that drove her to expend effort in learning German. During the deepening of her learning, she was able to recognise the value of being multilingual and finally made up her mind to pursue a postgraduate degree in linguistics, as demonstrated in the following excerpt from the third interview:

> Initially I was really worried about losing my linguistic advantage in the future. Such fear pushed me to put great effort into learning German when I was still uncertain about how speaking multiple languages would influence my future. Otherwise, I might have given up my German learning upon the completion of the course. I would also not have accumulated different language experiences and recognised the value of being multilingual. So looking back, it was not too bad to be driven by fear at the start of my learning German. In fact, I think that I might not have even recognised my interest in Linguistics if I had not been so persistent in learning German.

As shown in this excerpt, Xiaoyue perceived her initial ought-to multilingual self to be important for developing her learning motivation in the long term, as it prevented her from giving up learning a LOTE before fully recognising its value. From this perspective, the role of the ought-to multilingual self in her LOTE learning should not be underestimated.

Case B: Ling

The construction of Ling's ought-to multilingual self

Compared to Xiaoyue, Ling's ought-to multilingual self was less strong in the initial stages of learning German and became significantly weakened from the second interview onwards. According to her, this situation might, to some extent, have contributed to her difficulty in sustaining her LOTE motivation.

Stage 1: The ought-to/ought multilingual self in the initial stages

Similar to Xiaoyue, Ling also expressed worries regarding losing linguistic advantages in an era when being able to speak English was no longer 'a rare commodity' in the job market and she regarded being multilingual as a possible way to improve her competitiveness. However, unlike Xiaoyue, being multilingual was only one of several options for Ling to enhance her career perspective, as illustrated in the following excerpt from the first interview:

> I know clearly that speaking English is not enough for my future. Learning another foreign language might be helpful, according to our teachers. I need to learn German well and be more sensitive to linguistic and cultural issues. But this is not the only choice. I may pursue a second degree in management or finance, which can also enable me to have a very promising career.

As clearly shown in this excerpt, Ling's ought-to multilingual self was related to her fear of losing her competitive edge in the future but this motivation was not very strong in the early stages of learning. Such an ought-to multilingual self seemed to be more related to the ought-to/ought dimension of language selves, as Ling was influenced by teachers' suggestions.

Ling's ought-to multilingual self also drove her to learn German well in the initial stages. According to her, her worry about not being competitive enough in the job market was one of the most important reasons for her to put extra efforts into learning German beyond the course requirements. For example, she suggested in the first interview:

> In addition to homework, I also listen to news broadcasts in German and look for online language buddies. This is not only because of my interest in learning a new language, but also my anxiety about losing my linguistic advantage. Speaking German well can be useful for my future.

Therefore, Ling's ought-to multilingual self seemed to motivate her to spend extra effort on learning German.

Stage 2: The weakened ought-to multilingual self and decreasing LOTE learning motivation

Ling's ought-to multilingual self had become even weaker by the second interview, when she had become more determined to pursue a second degree in finance. As she pointed out, she could not clearly identify the need to be multilingual for her future development:

> Being multilingual seems to be very far away from my life and I cannot identify the explicit link between being multilingual and my future. I still feel a bit obliged to be more linguistically competent, as I need to build

up my competitiveness in the job market. However, this is not the only choice. In fact, I became more and more unsure about the value of being multilingual in China. Comparatively, a second degree in finance can significantly enhance my future.

Therefore, compared to Xiaoyue, Ling did not identify the personal value of being multilingual (e.g. the instrumental value of being multilingual in the job market) and therefore had not developed a more internalised ought-to multilingual self. With the option of pursuing another degree in finance, her ought-to multilingual self became increasingly weaker.

With the weakening of Ling's ought-to multilingual self, she became less willing to spend extra time and effort to improve her German and only worked to fulfil her teachers' requirements or learn something interesting, as illustrated by an example from the second interview:

I admit that the effort I put into learning German is not as much as last time. (...) Learning German to a high standard is no longer my goal. I will put additional effort into German learning only if I am interested in something. Probably this is because I do not feel the urgency to be multilingual any more.

As indicated in this excerpt, without her ought-to multilingual self, Ling was still willing to learn German and be multilingual, but it became harder for her to engage in less interesting learning tasks.

Stage 3: The disappearing ought-to multilingual self and LOTE learning motivation

Ling's ought-to multilingual self had almost disappeared by the last interview, when she had completed her Bachelor's study and started to apply for a postgraduate degree in finance. According to her in the third interview, there was no need to feel obliged to learn German anymore:

I do not think that speaking German and being multilingual would be of great importance for my future anymore. I only read some German news in my leisure time. My main focus will be on my postgraduate major in the future.

Hence, Ling's ought-to multilingual self showed a clear downward trajectory from the initial stage of her German learning and nearly disappeared after her graduation from college.

Along with the disappearance of her ought-to multilingual self, Ling had nearly given up her German learning and was only interested in picking up some German expressions when listening to German songs or reading German news. According to her, 'being able to speak three languages' became far removed from her life. It is, however, interesting to note that when she reflected on her German learning journey in the last interview, she again emphasised the role of the ought-to multilingual self in sustaining her motivation. The following excerpt from the third interview best illustrates this situation:

> I think that a bit more pressure might have been better for my language learning. It was not easy to see how being multilingual can exactly change my life. So my attitude towards being multilingual was that if I could be multilingual without too much effort, it would be great. However, being able to speak multiple languages would never be an easy task. Sometimes I think that if I had been under more pressure during my German learning, I might have studied it much harder and better. As such, I might also have identified the value of being multilingual, just like some of my classmates.

As shown in this excerpt, Ling still recognised the role of her ought-to self in sustaining her motivation to learn German and be more multilingual. Notably, like Xiaoyue, she pointed out the difficulty of identifying the importance of being multilingual, especially in the early stage of learning.

In short, both participants developed ought-to multilingual selves during the learning of a LOTE, mainly due to their fear of losing linguistic advantages in the future. Figure 4.1 visualises the trajectories of these learners' ought-to multilingual selves. Although this motivational construct does not seem to play a dominant role in their LOTE motivation, it contributes to their LOTE learning, particularly when the learning tasks are not sufficiently interesting.

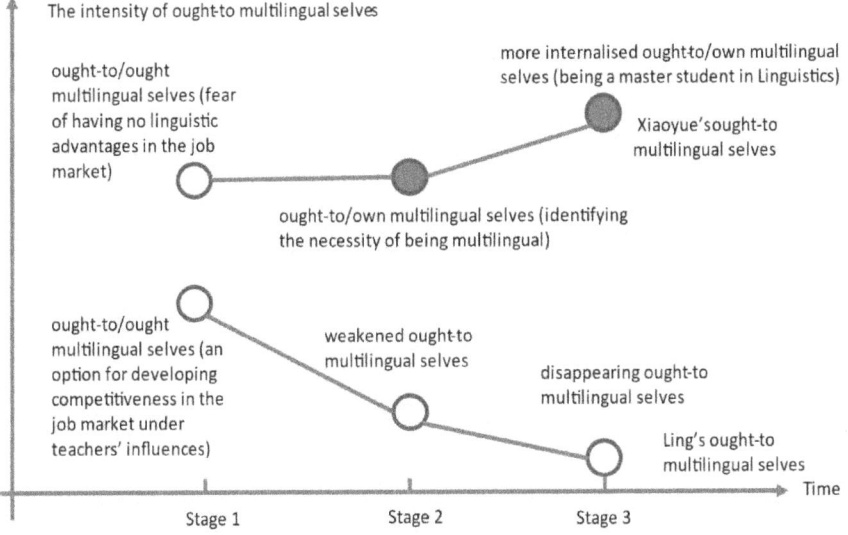

Figure 4.1 Participants' ought-to multilingual selves

A comparison between Xiaoyue's and Ling's cases further illustrates the role of the ought-to multilingual self in helping learners develop more internalised motivation, which may sustain their LOTE learning in the long term. With a stronger and more internalised ought-to multilingual self, Xiaoyue accumulated more multilingual experiences and developed a deeper understanding of how being multilingual might change her future. As revealed in the findings, this recognition benefited the development of her longer-term LOTE motivation.

Discussion

A review of the findings suggests that participants' ought-to multilingual selves, although not functioning as the most prominent motivating force in their LOTE learning, can be very important, especially in relation to sustaining LOTE motivation in the long term. In particular, learners' ought-to multilingual selves might sustain their efforts to explore their personal meaning of being multilingual, contributing to the development of the ideal multilingual self and long-term motivation. It is also notable that learners could go through an internalisation process in relation to their ought-to multilingual selves, for fear of losing their linguistic advantage, to incorporate being multilingual as an important constituent of their future lives.

Both learners' LOTE motivational trajectories revealed that the ought-to multilingual self contributed to maintaining their LOTE motivation at the beginning, when they were still unsure about the value of being multilingual in their futures. For example, in Xiaoyue's case, she paid more attention to the instrumental value of being multilingual at this time, but the information she obtained from her situated contexts regarding how multilingualism could benefit her future was limited. Therefore, her ideal multilingual self was still very vague in the initial stages. Her concern about the lack of any special linguistic capital motivated her to invest greater effort into LOTE learning. This finding echoed the results of Siridetkoon and Dewaele's (2018) study to some extent, as they also found that the ought-to dimension of language selves contributed to sustaining learners' LOTE motivation when they showed ambivalent attitudes towards the value of LOTE learning.

Although mainly related to the fear of negative outcomes (losing linguistic advantages), the ought-to multilingual self and associated motivated behaviours seemed to lay the foundation for learners to identify their personal understanding of being multilingual. As reported by Xiaoyue, her persistence in learning German and constant exploration of the value of being multilingual enabled her to accumulate multilingual experiences, which deepened her understanding of why it was important to become a multilingual person in a globalised world. As illustrated in the work of Fisher *et al.* (2022), language learning experience constitutes a crucial step in developing learners' self-identification with being multilingual. Thus, to some extent, the ought-to multilingual self lays a foundation for learners who have not fully realised the value of LOTE learning to explore and develop important multilingual experiences. As shown in the findings, Xiaoyue even indicated a link between her LOTE learning and her decision to pursue a postgraduate degree in linguistics. In this sense, the ought-to multilingual self seemed to be more than a counterbalancing force to the ideal aspect of her language self (Dörnyei, 2009) and a very important step in stimulating Xiaoyue, as a learner, to explore and construct her ideal multilingual self. This observation can also be substantiated by comparing Xiaoyue's and Ling's experiences.

Where Ling did not regard building up multilingual competence as important for her competitiveness in future, her overall German learning motivation decreased. There was also little evidence that she had explored the value of being multilingual like Xiaoyue did. This situation, to some extent, led to her ambiguous attitudes towards the value of being multilingual throughout the LOTE learning process. This finding suggests a significant difference between the role of the ought-to multilingual self in LOTE learning and that of the ought-to English self in learning English (e.g. Lamb, 2011; Taguchi *et al.*, 2009). As Ushioda (2017) points out, while the instrumental value of English is evident in a globalised world, individuals' attitudes to being multilingual are much more ambiguous. Therefore, language learners may need more opportunities and relevant experiences to understand why it is important to enhance their multilingual competence. In this case, the ought-to multilingual self, which functioned as an external force to sustain language learners' efforts to accumulate multilingual experiences at the exploration stage, appeared to be crucial.

It is also notable that although learners' ought-to multilingual selves can be related primarily to their fear of losing linguistic advantage, they can be internalised when language learners attach personal meaning to being multilingual. As shown in Xiaoyue's case, her ought-to multilingual self was associated with her desire to pursue a career in relation to linguistics at the end of fieldwork, which was internalised to a greater extent compared to the initial stages of her learning. With reference to Lanvers (2016), it became more like an ought-to/own dimension of language self by this stage. Interestingly, although the two learners might have been influenced by their teachers' views of being multilingual, they were not pushed by their parents' or teachers' expectations to be multilingual, similar to the findings of Siridetkoon and Dewaele's (2018) research. This is because there were almost no expectations from significant others (parents, close friends or teachers) regarding the participants' LOTE learning. This result appears to differ from that of Lanvers' (2017) study in which contradictory expectations of individuals' LOTE learning were found to exist in the UK. This difference might be related to the contextual differences between the two countries – for example, different linguistic landscapes and different emphasis placed on multilingualism in education.

Conclusion

By adopting a longitudinal design, this study discussed how learners' ought-to multilingual selves shaped their LOTE motivation in the long term. It has contributed to expanding our understanding of the role of the ought-to multilingual self in developing learners' persistence with LOTE learning, especially in the early stages when they have not identified the personal meaning of being multilingual. As shown in the findings, by helping to sustain learners' LOTE learning motivation, the ought-to multilingual self can contribute to adding to learners' accumulated learning experiences and assisting them in identifying the value of LOTE learning. This research may thus be seen to inform language teachers of the importance of developing LOTE learners' ought-to multilingual selves, i.e. their sense of obligations to learn the LOTE well. The aim of this is not so much to add to learners' learning pressure but to improve their persistence in LOTE learning. However, as a small-scale qualitative study, the results generated here are somewhat context-specific. A further longitudinal quantitative study in the future may therefore be helpful in investigating the role of the ought-to multilingual self in developing learners' persistence in LOTE learning across different student types and contexts. This may help to understand the concept of multilingualism in different cultures more fully and how it may influence individuals' choices.

References

Blackledge, A. and Creese, A. (2010) *Multilingualism: A Critical Perspective*. Bloomsbury.
Chen, S.-A. (2012) Motivation and possible selves: An interview study of Taiwanese EFL learners. *Language Education in Asia* 3 (1), 50–59.
Dörnyei, Z. (2009) The L2 motivational self system. In Z. Dörnyei and E. Ushioda (eds) *Motivation, Language Identity and the L2 Self* (pp. 9–42). Multilingual Matters.
Feng, L. and Papi, M. (2020) Persistence in language learning: The role of grit and future self-guides. *Learning and Individual Differences* 81, 1–10.
Fisher, L., Evans, M., Forbes, K., Gayton, A., Liu, Y. and Rutgers, D. (2022) Language experiences, evaluations and emotions (3Es): Analysis of structural models of multilingual identity for language learners in schools in England. *International Journal of Multilingualism*. https://doi.org/10.1080/14790718.2022.2060235.
Gao, X. and Zheng, Y. (2019) Multilingualism and higher education in Greater China. *Journal of Multilingual and Multicultural Development* 40 (7), 555–561.
Henry, A. (2016) Enablements and constraints: Inventorying affordances associated with lingua franca English. *International Journal of Bilingual Education and Bilingualism* 19 (5), 488–510.

Henry, A. (2017) L2 motivation and multilingual identities. *The Modern Language Journal* 101 (3), 548–565.

Henry, A. and Thorsen, C. (2018) The ideal multilingual self: Validity, influences on motivation, and role in a multilingual education. *International Journal of Multilingualism* 15 (4), 349–364.

Herdina, P. and Jessner, U. (2002) *A Dynamic Model of Multilingualism: Perspectives of Change in Psycholinguistics*. Multilingual Matters.

Jiang, Y. and Dewaele, J.M. (2015) What lies bubbling beneath the surface? A longitudinal perspective on fluctuations of ideal and ought-to L2 self among Chinese learners of English. *International Review of Applied Linguistics in Language Teaching* 53 (3), 331–354.

Kim, U. (1997) Asian collectivism: An indigenous perspective. In H.S.R. Kao and D. Sinha (eds) *Asian Perspectives on Psychology* (pp. 147–163). Sage.

Lamb, M. (2011) Future selves, motivation and autonomy in long-term EFL learning trajectories. In G. Murray, X. Gao and T. Lamb (eds) *Identity, Motivation and Autonomy in Language Learning* (pp. 177–194). Multilingual Matters.

Lanvers, U. (2016) Lots of selves, some rebellious: Developing the self discrepancy model for language learners. *System* 60, 79–92.

Lanvers, U. (2017) Contradictory others and the habitus of languages: Surveying the L2 motivation landscape in the United Kingdom. *The Modern Language Journal* 101 (3), 517–532.

Liu, M. (2022) The emotional basis of the ideal multilingual self: The case of simultaneous language learners in China. *Journal of Multilingual and Multicultural Development* 43 (7), 647–664.

Liu, Y. and Thompson, A.S. (2018) Language learning motivation in China: An exploration of the L2MSS and psychological reactance. *System* 72, 37–48.

Papi, M. and Teimouri, Y. (2012) Dynamics of selves and motivation: A cross-sectional study in the EFL context of Iran. *International Journal of Applied Linguistics* 22 (3), 287–309.

Pavlenko, A. (2005) *Emotions and Multilingualism*. Cambridge University Press.

Ryan, S. (2009) Self and identity in L2 motivation in Japan: The ideal L2 self and Japanese learners of English. In Z. Dörnyei and E. Ushioda (eds) *Motivation, Language Identity and the L2 Self* (pp. 120–143). Multilingual Matters.

Ryan, S. and Dörnyei, Z. (2013) The long-term evolution of language motivation and the L2 self. *Fremdsprachen in der Perspektive Lebenslangen Lernens* 14 (1), 89–100.

Silverman, D. (ed.) (2020) *Qualitative Research*. Sage.

Siridetkoon, P. and Dewaele, J.M. (2018) Ideal self and ought-to self of simultaneous learners of multiple foreign languages. *International Journal of Multilingualism* 15 (4), 313–328.

Taguchi, T., Magid, M. and Papi, M. (2009) The L2 motivational self system among Japanese, Chinese and Iranian learners of English: A comparative study. In Z. Dörnyei and E. Ushioda (eds) *Motivation, Language Identity and the L2 Self* (pp. 66–97). Multilingual Matters.

Thompson, A.S. (2020) My many selves are still me: Motivation and multilingualism. *Studies in Second Language Learning and Teaching* 10 (1), 159–176.

Ushioda, E. (2017) The impact of global English on motivation to learn other languages: Toward an ideal multilingual self. *The Modern Language Journal* 101 (3), 469–482.

Ushioda, E. and Dörnyei, Z. (2017) Beyond global English: Motivation to learn languages in a multicultural world. Introduction to the special issue. *The Modern Language Journal* 101 (3), 451–454.

Wang, T. (2020) An exploratory motivational intervention on the construction of Chinese undergraduates' ideal LOTE and multilingual selves: The role of near peer role modeling. *Language Teaching Research* 27 (2), 441–465. https://doi.org/10.1177/1362168820940097.

Wang, Z. and Zheng, Y. (2021) Chinese university students' multilingual learning motivation under contextual influences: A multi-case study of Japanese majors. *International Journal of Multilingualism* 18 (3), 384–401.

Wang, T. and Fisher, L. (2023) Using a dynamic motivational self system to investigate Chinese undergraduate learners' motivation towards the learning of a LOTE: The role of the multilingual self. *International Journal of Multilingualism* 20 (2), 130–152.

Zheng, Y., Lu, X. and Ren, W. (2020) Tracking the evolution of Chinese learners' multilingual motivation through a longitudinal Q methodology. *The Modern Language Journal* 104 (4), 781–803.

5 Japanese Learners' LOTE Motivation and Persistence in Learning: Focusing on the Influence of English

Chika Takahashi

What motivates learners to learn a language when opportunities for direct contact with target language (TL) speakers are limited? How do learners manage to learn several languages when a strong social, political and economic emphasis is placed on one of the languages? What does language learning mean to learners when they have few pragmatic reasons to study a language?

Japan is a context where both English and languages other than English (LOTEs) can still be described as foreign languages but with a clear emphasis on English compared to LOTE education. On the one hand, there is a strong emphasis on English education for political and economic reasons in the era of globalization (Sugita-McEown *et al.*, 2017). Education is geared toward nurturing citizens' four skills (reading, writing, speaking and listening) in English, with a primary focus on speaking so they can actively participate in the global market. On the other hand, there is little emphasis on LOTE education (JACET, 2002). While both English and LOTEs are foreign languages without daily opportunities to interact in the TLs, there are strong interests in and an acute awareness of just one of these languages – English – and there seems to be little interest in the others.

This chapter reports on a multiple-case study of three LOTE learners who underwent a year-long compulsory period in Japan. Given the unique contextual factors described above, as well as the dearth of research on the topic of LOTE motivation in Japan, investigating Japanese LOTE learners is a worthy task. Since contextual factors can affect LOTE learners' motivations in various ways, examining their motivations in this under-researched, non-multilingual context may add insights to further the theorizing of LOTE learners' motivation.

Research on LOTE Motivation Outside Japan

The growing body of research on LOTE motivation outside Japan has revealed some characteristics that may be unique to LOTE motivation. First, some studies demonstrate that learners may be motivated to learn a LOTE for a wider range of reasons than for English (e.g. Nakamura, 2019): as Dörnyei and Al-Hoorie (2017: 462) suggest: '[a] high level of LOTE proficiency is normally associated with highly specific and personalized reasons on the part of the learner'. These include integrativeness (Gardner, 2001), which may be more applicable in the case of LOTE learning because LOTE learners may have a more definable TL community than in the case of English learning (e.g. Oakes & Howard, 2022). LOTE learners may also have strong intrinsic motivation (Ryan & Deci, 2017), purely enjoying their LOTE studies (e.g. de Burgh-Hirabe, 2019). There may be other aspects of LOTE motivation that are distinct from English motivation.

Second, studies report that many learners hold an instrumentalist view of language learning, involving factors such as 'necessity, utility, advantage, social capital, power, advancement, mobility, migration, and cosmopolitanism' (Ushioda, 2017: 471). This makes learners pursue English rather than LOTE studies. LOTE learning is often seen as having less utility than English, whereas competence in English as a global language pushes learners into believing that they can get by with English alone, which they are already learning and competent in (Henry, 2015; Wang & Liu, 2020). In other words, many learners seem to be content with being competent in only one second/foreign language, i.e. English.

On the basis of these research findings, Henry (2017, 2020, 2023) has proposed two types of higher-order language selves that may exert different motivational powers on the ideal self of each language that learners study. First is the contentedly bilingual self, which is a self-guide or a desired end-state in self-discrepancy theory (Higgins, 1987), 'founded on the person's indifference to multilingual competence' (Henry, 2017: 553). For example, as Henry (2017: 553) illustrates, Swedish learners may be 'comfortable and confident in speaking their native language (e.g. Swedish) and the currently dominant global language (English) … [but may not perceive] any additional need or [have] any particular interest in speaking another language'. In other words, these learners consider that bilingualism is enough. In this case, a higher-order self-guide of the contentedly bilingual self may develop, and indeed has been reported in previous studies (e.g. Busse, 2017; Henry, 2015; Wang & Liu, 2020). A different scenario, however, is also possible. Some learners may develop clear but distinct ideal L2 selves for different languages they learn, and they may have 'a mutually complementary relation' with each other (Henry, 2017: 554). This may lead to the development of an ideal multilingual self, which is a self-guide that reflects a learner's aspirations to become multilingual.

It remains an empirical question as to what types of selves Japanese LOTE learners develop. There may be more cases of developing a contentedly bilingual self. It may even be possible that they do not develop either a contentedly bilingual self or an ideal multilingual self if their competence, even in English, remains low. Low competence level has been linked to both a lack of direct contact with TL speakers and to the country's English and LOTE education systems, as described below.

English and LOTE Education Systems in Japan

In the era of globalization, the Japanese government has implemented a series of English education reforms to boost its citizens' English competence, applying various action/strategic plans (e.g. MEXT, 2003, 2013). Urged by a sense of crisis that the citizens' competence in English is insufficient, the government adopted measures such as starting formal English education as early as 5th grade, increasing the number of non-Japanese assistant English teachers, having teachers conduct English classes in English, setting the achievement targets of standardized proficiency tests and reforming the university entrance examination systems. However, despite such reforms, Japanese learners' competence in English has improved little: 'there is a marked discrepancy in Japan between the significant efforts and resources invested and the rate of success in English language learning' (Boo *et al.*, 2015).

LOTE education in the country sharply contrasts with English education, at both secondary and tertiary levels. Available figures show that less than 2% of high-school students in Japan took LOTE courses in 2018 (MEXT, 2018, 2019). Even at the tertiary level, LOTE courses are optional at many universities/junior colleges (JACET, 2002), and there is presently no specific regulation about which courses should be compulsory at the tertiary level. This is due to the relaxation of guidelines for establishing universities in 1991 (Ministry of Education Higher Education Bureau, 1991). This contrasts with (a) English education in the country, which is compulsory even at most universities/junior colleges, and (b) more intensive LOTE education involving more hours of studies before World War II or the system before 1991 (for more details on the history of LOTE education in Japan, see Takahashi, 2023).

English and LOTE education contexts make learners perceive English and LOTEs differently. Most Japanese learners start studying English as their first second language (L2), now as early as 5th grade (10–11 years old). However, institutional LOTE learning for most starts only at the tertiary level, and is optional in many cases. Even when LOTE courses are compulsory, many learners discontinue their studies once they have earned enough credits. Typical LOTEs offered at the tertiary level include, for example, Chinese, French, German etc., but the specific LOTEs offered depend on each institution. The status of English and LOTEs within such education systems and the strong emphasis on English as a global language are also felt through various media reports. Both English and LOTEs are FLs in the country, but their implied meanings and familiarity differ.

The lack of either English or LOTEs as part of daily life, and the educational systems, contrast with the contexts of much of past LOTE motivation research. For example, Henry and Cliffordson (2017: 719) described English as 'a near-ubiquitous presence' in Sweden. Pirhonen (2022: 3), commenting on the situation in Finland, explained that 'a university student is almost always multilingual'. As previously indicated, Japanese learners do not frequently encounter occasions where they may use English or a LOTE, and most university students are not multilingual.

Furthermore, LOTE education in Japan contrasts with Europe, where learning at least two languages in addition to a first language (L1) is regarded as desirable. LOTE education in Japan has faced 'constant de-emphasis' (Takahashi, 2023: 59), and this de-emphasis differs even from other countries in Asia, e.g. China, where new programs at the tertiary level are promoting multilingualism (e.g. Zheng *et al.*, 2022).

Research Questions

Given past research findings on LOTE motivation in other contexts as well as the characteristics of the Japanese context, this study explores Japanese learners' motivations to study a LOTE both during and after compulsory education, whether and how English as a global language impacts their motivations to study LOTEs, and whether they persist in LOTE studies after the compulsory period. Specifically, the following research questions were posed:

RQ1: How do LOTE motivations of Japanese university students who go through compulsory courses develop during and after the compulsory period?

RQ2: Does English have any impact on students' LOTE motivations?

RQ3: Do students persist in LOTE studies after the compulsory period ends?

Method

The interviewees

As part of a larger study, this chapter reports on three focal cases that were among the 12 interviewees who participated in the study,

Table 5.1 The interviewees

	Ami	Yuko	Miya
Gender	Female	Female	Male
LOTE studied	Korean	German	German
Major	International Law	International Relations	History

selected due to their contrasting LOTE learning experiences. (For a larger survey study of the first two sets of interviews in July/August 2021 and February 2022 that includes other interviewees, see Takahashi, 2022). The interviewees were those who had answered in a preceding questionnaire that they were willing to be individually interviewed, and they also provided personal information. All attended a medium-sized national university's faculty of law and letters in rural Japan. During the first year, they took an obligatory course in one LOTE with a choice of Chinese, Filipino, French, German or Korean, as well as obligatory courses in English. After finishing the compulsory year, they no longer had to take obligatory courses in LOTEs, but some opted to continue their LOTE studies through elective courses. Furthermore, as they only had to officially declare their major field of study in their sophomore year, all declared their majors around the time of the third interview session. Table 5.1 shows further details of the interviewees (names are pseudonyms) in this study.

Data collection and analysis

Three sets of individual interviews took place at approximately half-year intervals, when LOTE courses were compulsory for the first year and then optional afterwards (see Table 5.2 for the timeline of data collection). All the interviews were semi-structured and conducted in our L1 (Japanese). In order to answer the research questions posed above, the interviews closely examined details of the interviewees' LOTE and English learning, development of their motivation and its interactions with English, and (non-)persistence in LOTE and English learning after the compulsory period, focusing on the following categories:

(a) interviewees' classroom English/LOTE learning experience
(b) interviewees' out-of-class English/LOTE learning/use experience
(c) development of English/LOTE learning motivation
(d) attitudes towards English
(e) impact of English on LOTE motivation
(f) persistence in LOTE/English studies

All interviews were audio-recorded and transcribed verbatim.

Table 5.2 Timeline of interviews

Interview	Time	Details	Notes
1	July/August 2021	After the first compulsory semester	Some conducted online due to COVID-19 pandemic
2	February 2022	After the second compulsory semester	
3	August 2022	Half a year after the compulsory period had ended	

The data were analyzed by marking up salient comments related to the six categories above, taking notes of their contents. These comments were then coded using summative phrases, e.g. 'clear ideal LOTE self' and 'no impact of English on LOTE motivation'. The generation of these codes was facilitated by the strategy of 'relying on theoretical propositions' (Yin, 2014: 136), i.e. the theoretical frameworks of ideal/ought-to English/LOTE selves, contentedly bilingual self and ideal multilingual self. The analyses were all carried out in Japanese, and the English transcripts in the following section are direct translations from the originals in Japanese. After examining the intra-case developments as well as inter-case comparisons, my translations and interpretations were member-checked by the interviewees.

Results

The following section provides a detailed description and an analysis of each of the cases as it is important in a case study to present 'an extensive description of the case and its context' (Creswell, 2013: 237) to understand and interpret the data. This is then followed by a more general discussion to answer the research questions.

Ami

Ami's case can be described as a learner who managed to develop an ideal multilingual self and eagerly pursue LOTE and English studies even after the compulsory period was over. She initially chose Korean due to her strong interest in Korean culture. She explained that she 'got hooked' on K-pop when still in junior high school. As she continued to watch various videos, she felt that her listening and speaking skills were already developing even before entering university. In the compulsory Korean classes, she hoped to work on reading Korean characters and further improving her listening skills. After the year-long compulsory period, she took the Test of Proficiency in Korean (TOPIK) I in April 2022 and scored a full mark. She was also planning to participate in a three-week online language program at a university in South Korea during the summer of her sophomore year. Such success helped her gain confidence in learning languages in general and helped her English studies as well, so she was even considering learning another LOTE.

The development of Ami's ideal multilingual self can be explained by several factors, as follows: (a) integrativeness, defined here as the weaker form of having 'an openness to, and respect for other cultural groups and ways of life' (Gardner, 2001: 5); (b) international posture (Yashima, 2009); and (c) 'transferable linguistic confidence from one language experience to the other' (Dörnyei & Chan, 2013: 455), made possible by her habits and behavioral routines (Dörnyei, 2020). These factors initially facilitated the interviewee's Korean studies and later the development of her pursuit of becoming multilingual.

From the very beginning of the present study, Ami described the compulsory classes as 'enjoyable just because of the fact that [she] could learn Korean' (interview, freshman year, August 2021). She further explained that she 'like[d] the Korean culture' and 'love[d] the Korean language' (interview, sophomore year, August 2022). This favorable attitude towards the TL culture had begun even before entering university through her interest in K-pop, and it remained the same throughout the study period. Her attitude towards the Korean language and culture indicates a weaker form of integrativeness.

Throughout the study period, she elaborated on her ideal self of working overseas in the future, and described (a) how she 'like[d] knowing what's happening in the world and what the issues are' and (b) how she hoped to study in South Korea, demonstrating a clear ideal Korean self. Furthermore, her surrounding contexts also seemed somewhat atypical for a Japanese student in that both her parents had had long-term experience abroad and she had a cousin living in the US with whom she communicated in English on a regular basis. Her case seemed typical of a learner with strong international posture, showing the following: (a) intergroup approach tendency; (b) interest in international vocation and activities; and (c) interest in foreign affairs (Yashima, 2009: 146). Such strong international posture facilitated not only her Korean studies but also her English studies, as she perceived that English was 'imperative' in the globalized world.

An ideal multilingual self developed as she realized that her success in learning Korean could be extended to other languages, including English. By first developing an ideal Korean self and then an ideal English self, the interviewee succeeded in developing a clear ideal multilingual self. In contrast to what has been reported in past studies (e.g. Busse, 2017; Henry, 2015), Ami initially experienced a negative impact, not of English on her Korean motivation but of Korean on her English motivation. As she spent almost all her free time watching videos in Korean, she considered that she was 'dominated by Korean, both timewise and psychologically' (interview, freshman year, August 2021). Concurrently perceiving a strong ought-to English self ('English is what someone has to [study], a must') and integrativeness towards the Korean culture and community, her integrativeness had a psychologically negative impact on her. She 'kept watching [Korean] videos' when she had free time, but she knew she should be working more on her English. Interestingly, after some time, such intense Korean studies started to help her gain confidence by continuing to study Korean every day; she therefore considered that she could do the same for English and that she could even study another language. She described such positive development in the following way:

> I've been studying Korean, and really, I gained confidence by the fact that I am continuing [to study Korean] every day. ... My studies [of Korean] are going well. And indeed, English is indeed definitely a must when I think about the career I've been pursuing in future. And English, English is not something I am bad at. So, I feel that if I continue [to study English] every day, I should be able to feel my development [of English] like my Korean. (Interview, freshman year, February 2022)

> Now I consider English and Korean as something completely independent. English is English, Korean is Korean, and I think I'll give each my all. ... [Although for Korean there will naturally be time to study because of the online program], I'm thinking of doing it [studying English] during the summer break by consciously creating the time [to study it]. (Interview, sophomore year, August 2022)

> It'll be the best if I become competent in another language [in addition to English and Korean]. (Interview, sophomore year, August 2022)

These excerpts show the gradual development of Ami's ideal multilingual self over time, by which she clearly foresaw a future that had various language elements. Her ideal multilingual self, in turn exerted a motivational power for both her ideal Korean and her ideal English selves. She was also successful in making it a habit to study Korean and English, which is one of the facilitating conditions for persistence in learning as argued by Dörnyei (2020). Helped by such factors, she persisted in learning both Korean and English after the compulsory period.

Yuko

Yuko can be described as a learner who was initially eager to learn her LOTE – German – but developed a contentedly bilingual self after experiencing difficulties understanding the language. Furthermore, her case demonstrates that having English as a global language may demotivate a learner from studying a LOTE when faced with learning difficulty, making some consider that they can rely on English instead of the LOTE they are studying.

Yuko chose German, as she initially hoped to study in Germany. She believed that English could facilitate her German studies because of the similarities between the two languages. She also expressed intrinsic motivation (Ryan & Deci, 2017), stating: 'it's interesting to know that in German, this word changes [from the equivalent English word] like this, or this word [in English] is derived from German' (interview, freshman year, August 2021). In the first interview, she stated that 'it'd be cool if I can speak [German]'. Overall, she seemed to be enjoying her German studies, and her perceptions of the language were positive.

However, Yuko experienced difficulties keeping up with her German classes during the second semester of the compulsory period. She explained, 'there were many things to memorize', and 'it was beyond my capacity' (interview, freshman year, February 2022). Her German learning experience became more negative compared to her experience during the first semester, so she explained that things were 'difficult' at the end of her compulsory German studies. At the third interview, which was held approximately half a year after she had finished her compulsory German classes, she looked back on her German studies and described them as 'really difficult'. As such, she did not persist in her German studies after the compulsory period, explaining that she 'has not really got in touch with German' (interview, sophomore year, August 2022).

Yuko's motivation, partly sustained by her hopes to study in Germany, disappeared after she realized that studying abroad was probably not possible due to the COVID-19 pandemic. Influenced by her learning difficulties, her German motivation gradually disappeared after the end of the compulsory period. German became 'a language that [she] does not touch in daily life' (interview, freshman year, February 2022), and instead, the interviewee started to rely more on English.

Yuko was interested in studying international relations and possibly working in the field dealing with fair trade. As such, she emphasized the importance and usefulness of English throughout the study period. She explained that 'compared to German, what is useful is English' (interview, sophomore year, August 2022). She was also planning to spend the summer of her sophomore year participating in an internship in Thailand, where she would communicate with students in English. In sum, she seemed to hold a strong instrumentalist view of language, repeatedly stating how useful English is.

At times, Yuko experienced a negative impact of English on her German motivation, particularly after she had difficulty catching up with her German classes. At the first interview, when she still hoped to study in Germany, she explained that she 'c[ould] not think of any particular impact' that English had on her German motivation and that 'they were independent'. However, as she increasingly experienced difficulty following German, she stated that 'frankly, it is perfectly okay if one is competent in English, just English, even if one does not have competence in German' (interview, freshman year, February 2022).

As such, her negative German learning experience appeared to negatively influence her German motivation: at the beginning, she had high hopes for German and even hoped to study in Germany; as her studies became more and more challenging, she started to rely more on English and considered that she could get by just with English. Such changes demonstrate that English may work negatively when one goes through negative LOTE learning experiences, making students think that they can get by without a LOTE. Had Yuko's German learning experiences remained more positive, she might not have experienced the negative impact of English on her German motivation.

Interestingly, despite her emphasis on English, Yuko was positive about the compulsory nature of LOTE courses, and she appreciated their value. This view remained unchanged even after German became increasingly difficult for her:

> We don't have to go and take [LOTE courses] ourselves, because they are compulsory; we have no choice but to touch another language. In that sense, I think it's good that we have an opportunity to touch, to touch something new. (Interview, sophomore year, August 2022)

As such, although Yuko concentrated on her English studies alone and did not persist with her German studies after the compulsory learning period, she nonetheless appreciated LOTE courses being compulsory because they let students 'touch a new field', which she considered to be possible only at the tertiary level.

Miya

Miya was perhaps not the most intensive learner among the interviewees but he held a unique perspective and motivation for studying his LOTE, German. He originally chose German because he aimed to become a researcher in German history. The intensity of his German motivation seemed to fluctuate, as he explained (a) at the first interview that he 'had high motivation'; (b) at the second interview that he sometimes did not engage in his German studies; and (c) at the third interview that he no longer took any classes in German but occasionally learned some German, mainly through reading. Although he was unfortunately unable to major in German history due to the lack of availability of a suitable advisor, he nonetheless majored in history and continued with his German studies on his own even after the compulsory period. He continued his German studies as 'a hobby' and seemed to enjoy them.

Miya's motivation to study German can be categorized into three types: (a) an ideal German self of becoming a researcher in German history; (b) motivation to read in German; and (c) intrinsic motivation. These interrelated LOTE motivations helped him persist with his

German studies, not necessarily always intensively, but even after the compulsory study period had elapsed.

As described above, he first chose German because he aimed to be a researcher in German history, stating: 'in the future, I want to conduct research in modern German history, so the language is a must'. He considered that 'in order to understand history, one needs to start with an understanding of its culture, climate, and of course the language'. He further described language as 'part of culture'. At first, his German studies seemed to be facilitated by his clear ideal German self of becoming a researcher.

When he became a sophomore and officially declared his major subject, however, Miya had to discard this ideal German self. Due to the unavailability of a suitable advisor, he majored in history, but not in German history. Interestingly, this did not de-motivate him, and he simply explained: 'when it comes to German history, it can just be within the realm of my hobby' (interview, sophomore year, August 2022). As such, his ideal German self was an initial motivator to study the language but not the only one.

What sustained Miya's German learning even after he discarded his ideal German self was a distinct type of motivation related to this ideal German self: the motivation to read in German. In the first interview, he explained that when conducting research, 'there are parts that can only be understood in the original text', and this perspective remained the same even after he discarded his ideal professional self. In the third interview, when courses in German were no longer mandatory, he stated that although he did not study German intensively, he was able to refer to the original text to understand 'subtle nuances' when there were parts that he did not understand well in translation, e.g. when he read Goethe. It should also be noted that this motivation for reading in German was similar to his English learning motivation, as he explained: 'I want to read academic articles and books in English' (interview, freshman year, February 2022).

Miya's third type of German learning motivation was his strong intrinsic motivation. As he explained:

> Well, out of mere curiosity, I check German [words/phrases] that are now established as Japanese. (Interview, freshman year, July 2021)

> [German] is a language that is different from Japanese or English, right? That is one aspect [that is enjoyable]. Well, like, when I see words related to Germany, German, in daily life, I say, 'this we learned in [German] class'. (Interview, freshman year, February 2022)

Miya, like other interviewees, perceived English as a global language and considered it 'the most major language' in the world. At the same time, he held a different perspective from that reported by many learners in past studies (e.g. Busse, 2017) and denied the strong economic influence of English on jobs and prosperity:

> Even though the world is globalized, frankly speaking, I don't think that things would change much depending on—how can I put it?—whether one is good or bad at English. ... (Interview, freshman year, July 2021)

> Nowadays, translation tools and AI are much developed, so I don't think there's much meaning in forcing one to try to be competent in English. (Interview, freshman year, July 2021)

As such, he considered that not having competence in English 'would not disadvantage people in Japan'.

Miya's account of the non-necessity of forcing one to study English in the era of machine translation and AI may apply not only to English but also to LOTEs. To him, thanks to the developments in such areas, it seemed that there may be no necessity for forcing one to be competent in any language, including English, but it was a matter of whether he still wanted to learn languages, including German. In this sense, he seemed to be ideal-self driven rather than ought-to self driven.

In part, helped by such a perspective, he never mentioned any negative impact of English on his German motivation throughout the study period. Instead, he considered that English had a facilitative role in understanding German because of the similarities between the two languages. He further explained that English has a less negative impact on many Japanese learners' motivations to learn LOTEs than for other learners 'who speak [English] better'. Put another way, he elaborated that, for many Japanese learners, their competence in either English or LOTEs is not so high, which makes them tend to rely less on English. This, he reasoned, avoids English having a negative impact on LOTE motivation. He explained that compulsory German classes 'helped [him] broaden [his] perspectives a little by getting in touch with a different culture' (interview, sophomore year, August 2022).

In sum, Miya persisted in LOTE learning, albeit perhaps not as intensively as in Ami's case. He continued his German studies (mainly reading) 'like a hobby' and maintained his interests in Germany and German history. This demonstrates that an ideal LOTE self can be an initial motivator but does not have to be the only motivating element throughout one's language learning.

Discussion

The above analysis has demonstrated the distinct motivational trajectories of three Japanese LOTE learners during and after the compulsory language learning period. These trajectories show that their development was different, even in the same context of Japan, as each unique individual interviewee perceived learning a LOTE as 'fitting into (or not fitting into) their personal system of values, goals and identities' (Ushioda, 2013: 10). Although Ushioda was referring to learning English, this applies equally to learning LOTEs.

Firstly, the three interviewees offer both similar and different characteristics compared to past LOTE learning motivation research outside Japan. What is similar to past studies (e.g. Busse, 2017) is Yuko's case. Yuko expressed an instrumentalist view of language, repeatedly stating how useful English is, and her LOTE learning motivation trajectory had a downward trend. Her case demonstrates a contentedly bilingual self, who increasingly realized the value of English and was content with her Japanese and English. This made her stop her German studies after the compulsory LOTE learning period was complete.

In contrast, the case of Ami showed that a learner can pursue LOTE learning by eagerly seeking opportunities for contact with the TL through both institutional and individual learning. In contrast to past studies on LOTE motivation that reported on learners who experienced a negative impact of English on their LOTE motivation (e.g. Henry, 2015; Wang & Liu, 2020), the virtuous cycle of Ami's LOTE and English studies demonstrates that the development of an ideal multilingual self is possible in this foreign language context. The compulsory nature of her Korean classes had little influence on her motivation: her motivation kept developing during and after the compulsory LOTE learning period and is likely to continue. It should also be noted that at the beginning of this study, Ami struggled psychologically because she felt that she should be working more on English when her interest and integrativeness were toward the Korean language and culture. In other words, she initially experienced a negative impact of Korean on her English learning motivation.

Miya is different again in that he may not be described as a learner developing an ideal multilingual self, but he nonetheless persisted in his LOTE learning thanks to other motivational factors that have not necessarily been observed in past studies outside Japan. The interviewee did not seem particularly keen on becoming multilingual *per se*, which is different from Ami. In contrast to Ami, who formed a self-concordant goal (Henry, 2023) of not just being competent in the separate TLs of English and Korean but also of 'becoming multilingual', Miya did not seem to 'formulate goals that ... encompass aspirations of becoming multilingual' (Henry, 2023: 189). Nonetheless, he continued to learn (or read) German and English for other factors.

Miya's motivational trajectory shows that his German studies were supported by his pure enjoyment of knowing about the language and reading texts in the original language, not in translation alone. This resembles extremely successful Japanese learners of multiple languages in Takahashi (2023), in that their motivation was also supported by the motivation to read in the original language. This shows the relevance and importance of reading in original languages among Japanese learners at the tertiary level. As such, Miya's motivation can be described as including both intrinsic and extrinsic components. Not only was he interested in German itself (demonstrating intrinsic motivation), but he also hoped to be an academic, envisioning an ideal German self (showing the self-determined form of extrinsic motivation, Ryan & Deci, 2017). All in all, the three interviewees' motivational trajectories clearly demonstrate 'highly specific and personalized reasons on the part of the learner' (Dörnyei & Al-Hoorie, 2017: 467).

Secondly, regarding the impact of English as a global language, the interviewees' results varied. One, like some reported in a European context (e.g. Busse, 2017; Henry, 2015), experienced a negative impact of English on her German motivation. The others, however, did not perceive the negative impact of English and pursued their LOTE studies. One interviewee experienced a virtuous cycle of first having a positive LOTE learning experience, which then motivated her to pursue her English studies, facilitated by her strong integrativeness and international posture. The other interviewee perceived similar competences between his English and LOTE, which helped him avoid experiencing any negative impact of English. These two interviewees perceived a close relationship between language and culture, which helped them appreciate the value of LOTEs.

When comparing these results to what has been reported in past studies outside Japan (e.g. Busse, 2017), English seems to exert a negative influence on LOTE motivation:

(a) if learners hold an instrumentalist view of language and perceive language as a means of gaining a competitive edge and an economic advantage, perhaps particularly in countries where the issue of a high unemployment rate is salient (e.g. Amorati & Quaglieri, 2023; Busse, 2017); and/or
(b) if their competence in English is already high (e.g. Henry, 2015).

Future research can clarify these possibilities.

Thirdly, persistence in learning a LOTE also varied. Yuko stopped studying German after the compulsory study period, mainly due to the difficulties she experienced in learning German and owing to her contentedly bilingual self. The other two interviewees, however, persisted in their LOTE studies even after the end of the compulsory study period. Ami demonstrated that persistence might be facilitated by habits and behavioral routines (Dörnyei, 2020: 141–142) and a self-concordant goal of becoming multilingual (Henry, 2023: 189). Her case demonstrates that multiple language learning can be managed without English playing a

Table 5.3 Summary of the interviewees' LOTE learning and motivation

	Ami	Yuko	Miya
LOTE motivation trajectories	Positive and intense	Changed from positive to negative	Positive but not intense
Ideal LOTE selves	Clear	Does not develop	Clear
Ideal multilingual selves	Very clear	Develops contentedly bilingual self	Somewhat clear
Impact of English on LOTE motivation	No impact	Negative impact	No impact
Persistence in LOTE studies after compulsory period	Yes	No	Yes
Other characteristics	Initially experienced negative impact of Korean on English learning motivation but managed to balance both		Strong motivation to read

major role but with a LOTE having such a role. Still another case is that of Miya, who did not necessarily aspire 'to be multilingual' but simply enjoyed reading in German and persisted in learning German, albeit not intensively. Such distinct patterns of persistence are only natural given their distinct motivational trajectories.

Table 5.3 summarizes the results of the interviews. The interviewees' LOTE learning motivational trajectories followed different paths even though they were studying in the same faculty. They all perceived English as a global language and seemed to perceive this situation as positive. Each also made sense of the importance of their LOTE studies in their own ways but followed different paths, particularly after the end of the compulsory language learning period – two persisted in LOTE learning but the third did not. At the same time, it should be noted that, regardless of their LOTE learning motivation, all three appreciated the nature of LOTE courses being compulsory.

Conclusion

This chapter has examined three contrasting cases of Japanese LOTE learners who completed compulsory LOTE studies. Their experiences demonstrate that one can manage multiple language learning even when a strong social, political or economic emphasis on one language, i.e. English, is dominant and visible in the media and contexts other than education. Learning a LOTE can be facilitated by having a clear ideal multilingual self or the motivation to read in the original language even without direct contact with TL speakers. Future research outside Japan may examine whether this applies to other learners. Overall, each learner makes sense of the meaning of language learning, and the particular role socially allocated to one of the languages they learn may not de-motivate them from learning other languages.

Pedagogically speaking, the study calls for more balance between English and LOTE education in the country. As all three interviewees appreciated the nature of LOTE courses being compulsory, more Japanese students should be given the opportunity to study a LOTE. Although many may end up not continuing with their LOTE studies after the compulsory period, the compulsory nature provides learners with the initial opportunity 'to touch a new field', as Yuko puts it, and some may then develop their interests in this new field. If this is the case, such opportunities should be given equally to all learners. In addition, instructors should do their best to avoid students having negative LOTE learning experiences. Had Yuko been through a different German learning experience, she might have persisted in German studies even now.

Despite the value of these findings, this study has focused on just three learners in the foreign language context of Japan. More studies on learners who study a greater variety of languages either voluntarily or through compulsory programs both inside and outside Japan are necessary to further understand the complexities of learners' LOTE motivations and persistence in learning.

Acknowledgements

This study was supported by JSPS KAKENHI Grant Number 19K13293. The author would like to thank the interviewees as well as the instructors who cooperated with the study.

References

Amorati, R. and Quaglieri, A. (2023) Commonplace or exotic? A comparative mixed-method study on the instrumental work-related motivations of EFL and LOTE students. *The Language Learning Journal*, 1–18.
Boo, Z., Dörnyei, Z. and Ryan, S. (2015) L2 motivation research 2005–2014: Understanding publication surge and a changing landscape. *System* 55, 145–157.
Busse, V. (2017) Plurilingualism in Europe: Exploring attitudes toward English and other European languages among adolescents in Bulgaria, Germany, the Netherlands, and Spain. *The Modern Language Journal* 101 (3), 566–582.
Creswell, J.W. (2013) *Qualitative Inquiry and Research Design: Choosing Among Five Approaches* (3rd edn). Sage.
de Burgh-Hirabe, R. (2019) Motivation to learn Japanese as a foreign language in an English speaking country: An exploratory case study in New Zealand. *System* 80, 95–106.
Dörnyei, Z. (2020) *Innovations and Challenges in Language Learning Motivation*. Routledge.
Dörnyei, Z. and Chan, L. (2013) Motivation and vision: An analysis of future L2 self images, sensory styles, and imagery capacity across two target languages. *Language Learning* 63 (3), 437–462.
Dörnyei, Z. and Al-Hoorie, A.H. (2017) The motivational foundation of learning languages other than global English: Theoretical issues and research directions. *The Modern Language Journal* 101 (3), 456–468.
Gardner, R.C. (2001) Integrative motivation and second language acquisition. In Z. Dörnyei and R. Schmidt (eds) *Motivation and Second Language Acquisition* (pp. 1–19). University of Hawai'i, Second Language Teaching and Curriculum Center.

Henry, A. (2015) The dynamics of L3 motivation: A longitudinal interview/observation-based study. In Z. Dörnyei, P.D. MacIntyre and A. Henry (eds) *Motivational Dynamics in Language Learning* (pp. 315–342). Multilingual Matters.

Henry, A. (2017) L2 motivation and multilingual identities. *The Modern Language Journal* 101 (3), 548–565.

Henry, A. (2020) Learner-environment adaptations in multiple language learning: Casing the ideal multilingual self as a system functioning in context. *International Journal of Multilingualism* 20 (2), 97–114.

Henry, A. (2023) Multilingualism and persistence in multiple language learning. *The Modern Language Journal* 107 (1), 183–201.

Henry, A. and Cliffordson, C. (2017) The impact of out-of-school factors on motivation to learn English: Self-discrepancies, beliefs, and experiences of self-authenticity. *Applied Linguistics* 38 (5), 713–736.

Higgins, E.T. (1987) Self-discrepancy: A theory relating self and affect. *Psychological Review* 94 (3), 319–340.

JACET (2002) *Waga Kuni no Gaikokugo/Eigo Kyoiku ni kansuru Jittai no Sogoteki Kenkyu: Daigaku no Gakubu/Gakka Hen* [*A Comprehensive Investigation on the Situations Regarding Foreign Language and English Education in Japan: Regarding University Faculties and Departments*]. [In Japanese.] The Japan Association of College English Teachers (JACET).

MEXT (Ministry of Education, Culture, Sports, Science and Technology) (2003) *The National Action Plan to Cultivate 'Japanese with English Abilities'*. [In Japanese.] See https://www.mext.go.jp/b_menu/shingi/chukyo/chukyo3/004/siryo/04031601/005.pdf (accessed 11 October 2022).

MEXT (Ministry of Education, Culture, Sports, Science and Technology) (2013) *English Education Reform Plan Corresponding to Globalization*. See https://www.mext.go.jp/en/news/topics/detail/__icsFiles/afieldfile/2014/01/23/1343591_1.pdf (accessed 11 October 2022).

MEXT (Ministry of Education, Culture, Sports, Science and Technology) (2018) *Heisei 29 Nendo Koto Gakko To ni okeru Kokusai Koryu To no Genjo ni tsuite* [Academic Year 2017 Current Situations Regarding International Exchanges at High School]. [In Japanese.] See https://www.mext.go.jp/a_menu/koutou/ryugaku/koukousei/__icsFiles/afieldfile/2019/09/19/1323946_001_1.pdf (accessed 28 October 2022).

MEXT (Ministry of Education, Culture, Sports, Science and Technology) (2019) *Heisei 30 Nendo Gakko Kihon Chosa (Kakuteichi) no Kohyo ni* tsuite [Academic Year 2018 Regarding Disclosure of Basic Survey on Schools (Definitive Values)]. [In Japanese.] See https://www.mext.go.jp/component/b_menu/other/__icsFiles/afieldfile/2018/12/25/1407449_1.pdf (accessed 28 October 2022).

Ministry of Education Higher Education Bureau (1991) *Daigaku Shiryo* Dai117go [The 117th Information Material on University]. [In Japanese.] Ministry of Education Higher Education Bureau.

Nakamura, T. (2019) Understanding motivation for learning languages other than English: Life domains of L2 self. *System* 82, 111–121.

Oakes, L. and Howard, M. (2022) Learning French as a foreign language in a globalised world: An empirical critique of the L2 motivational self system. *International Journal of Bilingual Education and Bilingualism* 25, 166–182.

Pirhonen, H. (2022) 'I don't feel like I'm studying languages anymore'. Exploring change in higher education students' learner beliefs during multilingual language studies. *Journal of Multilingual and Multicultural Development*, 1–16.

Ryan, R.M. and Deci, E.L. (2017) *Self-Determination Theory: Basic Psychological Needs in Motivation, Development, and Wellness*. Guilford Press.

Sugita-McEown, M., Sawaki, Y. and Harada, T. (2017) Foreign language learning motivation in the Japanese context: Social and political influences on self. *The Modern Language Journal* 101 (3), 533–547.

Takahashi, C. (2022) Fukusuu gengo wo gakushu suru doukizuke no yobiteki bunseki: Eigo no hirogari ni taisuru taido ni chakumoku shite [A preliminary analysis on motivations to study multiple languages: Focusing on attitudes toward the global spread of English]. [In Japanese.] *The Bulletin of the Faculty of Law and Letters: Humanities* 53, 113–141.

Takahashi, C. (2023) *Motivation to Learn Multiple Languages in Japan: A Longitudinal Perspective*. Multilingual Matters.

Ushioda, E. (2013) Foreign language motivation research in Japan: An 'insider' perspective from outside Japan. In M.T. Apple, D. Da Silva and T. Fellner (eds) *Language Learning Motivation in Japan* (pp. 1–14). Multilingual Matters.

Ushioda, E. (2017) The impact of global English on motivation to learn other languages: Toward an ideal multilingual self. *The Modern Language Journal* 101 (3), 469–482.

Wang, T. and Liu, Y. (2020) Dynamic L3 selves: A longitudinal study of five university L3 learners' motivational trajectories in China. *The Language Learning Journal* 48 (2), 201–212.

Yashima, T. (2009) International posture and the ideal L2 self in the Japanese EFL context. In Z. Dörnyei and E. Ushioda (eds) *Motivation, Language Identity and the L2 Self* (pp. 144–163). Multilingual Matters.

Yin, R.K. (2014) *Case Study Research: Design and Methods* (5th edn). Sage.

Zheng, Y., Shen, Q., Zhao, K. and Li, C. (2022) The Shanghai alliance of multilingual researchers: Fudan University, Tongji University, Shanghai University of Finance and Economics, and Shanghai International Studies University, China. *Language Teaching* 55 (4), 583–587.

6 Exploring International Students' Experiences of Learning Japanese in Japan through Multimodal Language Learning Histories

Tae Umino

Introduction

This chapter attempts to understand the long-term learning experiences of international students studying at a university in Japan. In recent years, there has been an increase in the number of learners of Japanese worldwide (Japan Foundation, 2020), along with a wider range of backgrounds and learning needs possessed by such learners. In regions where Japanese has been introduced as an optional second foreign language in primary or secondary education sectors, such as Oceania and Southeast Asia, students may choose to learn it as a school subject. However, in many other contexts, receiving formal instruction in Japanese can be difficult, and an increasing number of learners are attempting to learn through self-instruction – by making use of internet resources, for instance – without relying on formal education resources (Takahashi, 2014). Thus, when international students begin their studies at Japanese universities, teachers often face a heterogeneous group, not only in terms of linguistic and cultural background but also in terms of the types of resources and learning strategies used so far in their language learning.

To better understand the learning experiences of these international students prior to their study in Japan, I collected multimodal language learning histories (MLLHs) from the students at a Japanese university. In essence, MLLHs are language learning histories created by combining the multimodal resources of pictures, videos and sound clips, along with linguistic texts. Block (2014) suggests that there has been an over-reliance on linguistic texts in applied linguistics research and has called for greater attention to multimodal means of expression.

More recently, the use of multimodal data has gained ground (Chik & Melo-Pfeifer, 2020; Kalaja & Pitkänen-Huhta, 2018). Kalantzis *et al.* (2016) have argued that a multimodal approach is better suited to younger-generation learners – who are more used to using multimedia – than an approach that uses a linguistic-only means of self-expression. To better understand the characteristics of the MLLHs of international students, I also collected the MLLHs of Japanese university students learning English, as a basis for comparison. Through the analysis of these students' visuals and written narratives, I hope to increase our understanding of international students' Japanese learning experiences, including their long-term motivation for learning Japanese.

Literature Review

Understanding learning experiences expressed in MLLHs

Language learning histories (LLHs; Oxford, 1996) are a powerful means of understanding learners' subjective perspectives of second language (L2) learning (Benson & Nunan, 2004; Kalaja *et al.*, 2008; Pavlenko, 2007). By incorporating multiple text types, MLLHs can reveal different aspects of L2 learning experiences that may not be easy to express linguistically (Menezes, 2008). By means of 'visual storytelling' (Coffey, 2015: 504), MLLHs provide deeper insights into the person (e.g. a student), the object (e.g. language, learning experiences) and the context (e.g. learning circumstances; Melo-Pfeifer & Chik, 2020: 13).

Some previous studies have employed MLLHs as a method of measuring learners' perspectives. In a pioneering study, Menezes (2008) investigated prospective teachers' perceptions of learning English in Brazil by analyzing 37 text-based MLLHs that contained photographs and media hyperlinks. Chik and Breidbach (2011), meanwhile, used MLLHs as a reflective tool to support the professional development of preservice teachers in Hong Kong and Germany. Paiva and Gomes Jr (2019) analyzed visual metaphors to represent English learning in 70 MLLHs of undergraduate students in Brazil. Melo-Pfeifer and Chik (2020) analyzed 33 visual linguistic biographies using the drawings of prospective foreign language teachers in Germany to examine the construction of the multilingual self. These studies suggest that MLLHs are a powerful tool for shedding light on various aspects of learning experiences through emic views that are not easily captured verbally.

Although these studies described the themes and metaphors that appeared in the visual images, no classification of visuals was developed to allow for the comparison of different groups. In addition, as previous studies have typically analyzed a single image created by each learner, little attention has been paid to how a single learner can make use of multiple visuals to construct a MLLH. Furthermore, the focus has mostly been on learning English; little is known about languages other than English (LOTEs), including Japanese. In a previous study (Umino, 2023), I addressed some of these issues through an analysis of the MLLHs of 21 Japanese and international university students in Japan. In classifying the visuals, I identified four patterns of learner use of particular visual images: 'person-oriented', 'resource-oriented', 'place-oriented' and 'analysis-oriented'. These reflected certain aspects of the students' L2 learning beliefs within their own descriptions. However, the study did not adequately address the differences between international and Japanese students due to the small sample size. In the present study, I attempt to improve upon this and identify the characteristics of the learning experiences of international students learning Japanese in comparison with those of Japanese students learning English.

Motivation for learning LOTEs

L2 motivation has attracted much attention in second language acquisition (SLA) studies as one of the main determinants of second or foreign language learning success. Since the early pioneering work of Gardner and Lambert (1959) in Canada, a large body of literature has been published in this area. In early studies, the focus was on the traditional constructs of instrumental orientation relating to the practical reasons for learning the language (e.g. to enroll in a university) and integrative orientation relating to learners' interests in and/or integration into the target language (TL) culture (Gardner, 1985). More recently, the L2 Motivational Self System (L2MSS) model (Dörnyei, 2005, 2009) has been used to explain motivation in relation to two self-guides: the ideal L2 self, an individual's desire to fill the gap between their current self-conception as an L2 speaker and their desired conception, and the ought-to L2 self, reflecting an individual's need to prevent negative outcomes. Some researchers have proposed a revision of the ought-to L2 self by dividing it into two constructs: self and other (Papi *et al.*, 2018; Teimouri, 2017).

While the idea of self-guides has been widely accepted in studies on motivation to learn L2 English, other theories are also relevant for LOTE learners (Howard & Oaks, 2021) and are complementary rather than mutually exclusive (e.g. Sugita-McEown *et al.*, 2014). The intrinsic and extrinsic motivations described in Deci and Ryan's (1985) Self-Determination Theory may be combined with other motivational constructs to present a more comprehensive understanding of the complexity of these motivations (Noels, 2001).

Intrinsic motivation in L2 learning refers to reasons for L2 learning that are derived from the inherent interest and enjoyment in the activity rather than external incentives or pressure (Ryan & Deci, 2020). In their classic work, Deci and Ryan (1985: 34) argue that the emotion of interest plays an important role in intrinsically motivated activities, since the 'enjoyment and excitement accompanying the experiences of competence and autonomy represent the rewards for intrinsically motivated behavior'. By contrast, extrinsic motivation concerns behaviors arising from motivations other than one's inherent satisfaction. Ryan and Deci (2017) have specified four major subtypes of extrinsic motivation, with varying degrees of integration with the learner's self-concept. *External regulation* (learners' behavior is regulated by an external source) is the least self-determined type, while *integrated regulation* (learners' regulations are fully governed by the self but the activity is viewed as an aspect of self-concept rather than one of enjoyment) is the most self-determined type. *Introjected regulation* (the learner self-imposes pressure or rewards to gain respect from others or avoid embarrassment) and *identified regulation* (the learner engages in an activity because its value is recognized as important and useful for achieving a goal) fall into areas between each end of the continuum.

Another prominent motivational factor for understanding the learning of LOTEs is pop culture (Cheung, 2001; Humphreys & Spratt, 2008). Learning through pop culture is associated with intrinsic motivation, as it is undertaken for its inherent interest and enjoyment (Kao & Oxford, 2014). Although a connection between interest in anime and Japanese language learning has been suggested (Chan & Wong, 2017; Fukunaga, 2006), there have not been sufficient studies on how it motivates learners to pursue learning Japanese long-term. The aim of this study is thus to shed a clearer light on the types of motivation inherent in these cultural activities and their role in long-term Japanese learning.

Regarding methodology, early studies of L2 motivation have traditionally relied on a psychometric approach, typically using quantitative methods to measure motivation as individual traits and/or the differences between groups of learners who share certain characteristics. Such psychometric studies offer little information about each individual student's learning experiences (Ushioda, 2009). Ushioda (2009) proposed a 'person-in-context relational view' of motivation, which focuses more on learners as people located in particular cultural and historical contexts with goals, motives and intentions. Benson (2017) argued that in order to make individual learners visible as people and understand their perspectives, methodologies like individual case studies must be used, and we now see more studies incorporating qualitative approaches (e.g. Henry, 2011).

Furthermore, Nomura and Yuan (2019) point out that little research exists directly addressing L2 long-term motivation across a learner's lifespan. L2 learning often spans extended periods of time, and the motivation at the start of learning may have to change at later stages to sustain learning (Williams & Burden, 1997). Shoaib and Dörnyei (2005) made use of the biographical narratives of 25 young English learners in the United Kingdom and revealed learners' motivational trajectories, including their transformation episodes. While these studies provide insights into the temporal progression of students' motivation, their perspectives on motivation are still under-explored. To further explore ways that learners can autonomously control their motivation (Ushioda, 2011), further studies are needed to understand how learners perceive their own motivation and motivational changes over time. In this study, I aim to understand learners' perspectives regarding their life-long motivation for learning a LOTE (Japanese) by analyzing their MLLHs.

Methodology

Research questions

The main purpose of this study is to understand international students' long-term experiences of learning Japanese through their MLLHs. The data used for this study were collected as part of a larger project to understand the foreign language learning experiences of university students in Japan. The initial research question set for this study was:

(1) What are the characteristics of international students' MLLHs with regard to their long-term Japanese learning experiences?

Data from Japanese students were also analyzed for the purposes of comparison. The analysis of the visuals included the learners' MLLHs identified differences between international and Japanese students. To understand the cause of these differences, I further analyzed the written narratives by focusing on their motivation. Thus, the second research question was formulated as follows:

(2) How do international students perceive their long-term Japanese learning motivation, as represented in their MLLHs?

Data collection and analysis

The data were collected from 47 university students (20 Japanese and 27 international students) whom I met through word of mouth between 2020 and 2022. The international students (ISs) had experienced learning Japanese in foreign language learning settings prior to studying in Japan and consisted of 15 Koreans, 6 Chinese, 2 Americans, 2 Indonesians, 1 Singaporean and 1 Slovak. All the Japanese national students (JSs) had learned English in Japan. All the students were between 18 and 25 years of age.

The participants were asked to provide written LLHs of their respective TLs (ISs of Japanese and JSs of English) of between 1500 and 3000 characters in Japanese (two pages of A4), focusing on the most relevant issues and events they had experienced. They then presented their LLHs orally using PowerPoint. Thus, the data consisted of written narratives, PowerPoint files and oral presentations.

The analysis procedure was as follows. The visual images appearing in the PowerPoint files were analyzed using visual content analysis (Rose, 2012). All the visuals were placed into the five categories identified in Umino (2023): 'language', 'place', 'person', 'learning resource' and 'analysis of learning process'. To observe how learners recount their MLLHs by using visuals, the proportion of the use of visual categories in each MLLH was also examined. It was assumed that focusing on a certain type of visual while telling the story gave significance to that content. Having calculated the percentage of the five categories appearing in each MLLH, a dominant category – accounting for more than one-third of the total number of elements – emerged, thus yielding the following four patterns of MLLHs: person-oriented, resource-oriented, place-oriented and analysis-oriented MLLHs. A comparison was then made between the ISs and JSs.

To understand the differences between the two groups, an analysis of motivation was carried out using their written narratives. The learners' LLHs were divided by their years at preschool, primary school, middle school, high school, preparatory school and university. All sentences mentioning motivation at each of these stages were identified and then grouped according to a set of categories developed based on Ryan and Deci's (2017) intrinsic and extrinsic motivation. The data were quantified according to each of these stages to show the chronological development of the students' motivation.

Results

Use of visual images in the MLLHs of university students

A total of 817 visual images was found in 533 slides (310 slides for ISs and 223 slides for JSs). Classification of the MLLH images revealed that 'language', 'place', 'person', 'learning resource' and 'analysis of learning process' were represented visually (Table 6.1).

The most popular image used to represent 'language' was that of letters. Figure 6.1 shows how Soyeon (Korean) used Hiragana letters to represent the Japanese language and the content she was learning. Learners frequently used photographs to represent places that had significant meaning in their MLLHs. In Figure 6.2, Ubin (Korean) used a

Table 6.1 Types of visual images appearing in the MLLHs of international students (ISs) and Japanese national students (JSs)

Type of visual image	ISs (N = 27)	JSs (N = 20)
Language	16 (4%)	5 (2%)
Place	58 (12%)	30 (11%)
Person (self)	139 (26%)	130 (46%)
Person (others)	81 (15%)	51 (18%)
Learning resource	194 (35%)	55 (20%)
Analysis of learning process	42 (7%)	8 (3%)
Others	7 (1%)	1 (0%)
Total	537	280

Figure 6.1 Soyeon's (Korean) slide showing Hiragana to represent the Japanese language

Figure 6.2 Ubin's (Korean) slide showing the place (Fukuoka) where he decided to study Japanese

picture of Fukuoka to indicate that a visit to this place made him decide to learn Japanese. Images of people were often used to express learners' actions and emotions. In Figure 6.3, Xuyang (Chinese) describes how he was anxious and nervous about speaking Japanese by using images of a nervous person. Regarding learning resources, learners used images of the resources they used for learning Japanese, including classroom-based

Figure 6.3 Xuyang's (Chinese) slide showing his anxiety and the pressure on him to speak Japanese

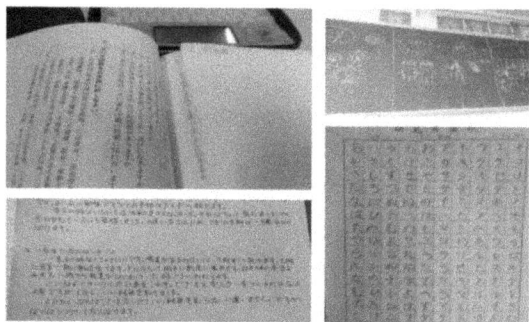

Figure 6.4 Jianguo's (Chinese) slide showing the resources he used to learn Japanese

resources (e.g. textbooks) and out-of-class resources (e.g. YouTube). In Figure 6.4, Jianguo (Chinese) shows images of the textbook, notebook and electronic dictionary he used to learn Japanese. Learners also used graphs and diagrams to illustrate the self-analysis of their 'learning processes'. In Figure 6.5, Qingqing (Chinese) uses a graph to illustrate the ups and downs of her Japanese learning experiences from when she first started her studies.

Although these elements in combination were used to construct a MLLH, students were found to use some elements more frequently than others. Their MLLHs were grouped into four patterns based on the

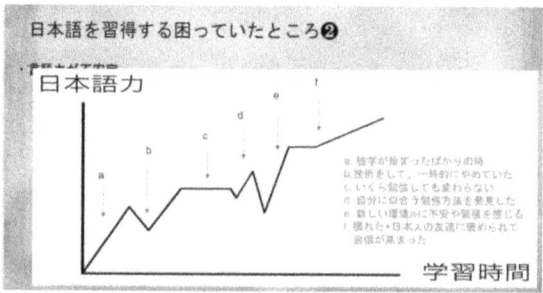

Figure 6.5 Qingqing's (Chinese) slide showing the changes in her Japanese skills

Table 6.2 Percentage of students falling into the four main types of MLLHs

Type of MLLH	ISs	JSs
Person-oriented	7 (26%)	10 (50%)
Resource-oriented	12 (44%)	4 (20%)
Place-oriented	1 (4%)	1 (5%)
Analysis-oriented	1 (4%)	0 (0%)
n.a.	6 (22 %)	5 (25%)
Total	27	20

Note: Percentages have been rounded up.

dominant categories described in the earlier section 'Data collection and analysis' (Table 6.2). ISs tended to produce 'resource-oriented' types of MLLHs more frequently (44%), compared to JSs who tended to produce more 'person-oriented' types more frequently (50%). This suggests that ISs tended to focus on the resources they used to learn Japanese, whereas JSs tended to focus on the actions and emotions they experienced during the learning process when constructing their MLLHs.

Individual case studies

As a first step towards understanding the differences observed above, how each individual learner conveyed their messages through their MLLHs requires closer attention.

An international student: Sora

Sora is an 18-year-old Korean girl who started learning Japanese in Korea when she was six years old. She loved watching Japanese anime (animation) as a child. She watched anime and listened to songs for at least 30 minutes every day (Figure 6.6). After doing this for 10 years, she found

Figure 6.6 Sora's (Korean) slide showing how her motivation for learning Japanese developed

98 Multilingual Selves and Motivations for Learning Languages other than English

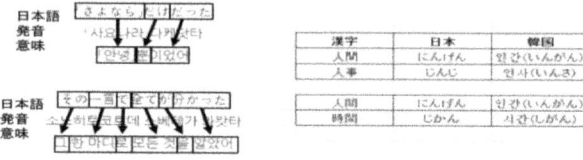

Figure 6.7 Sora's (Korean) slide showing how she used the lyrics of anime songs to learn Japanese

she could understand without having to read the Korean subtitles by age 16. She also learned Hiragana letters using song lyrics. Her method of learning was to obtain a significant amount of Japanese input by listening to various Japanese pop culture artifacts and guessing the meanings of words and grammar from her knowledge of Korean, which has the same word order and Kanji origins. On this basis, she was able to infer the meanings of the Japanese words and sentences by making comparisons (Figure 6.7). After she had the chance to visit Japan on an exchange program in high school, she decided to study abroad at a university in Japan and began to prepare for the entrance exam to a Japanese university. Although her motivation became more extrinsic in nature at that point, she maintained her interest in Japanese culture by communicating with her Japanese friends. She concluded her MLLH by saying: 'I always had a good impression of Japan with nice people, clean cities and tasty food. I will always love Japanese culture, from anime to fashion.'

Sora's MLLH is typical of the pattern followed by most ISs, typically beginning with a description of interests in Japanese anime as children. Their interest then expands to other related cultural artifacts/objects, such as pop songs, dramas and films. Students were intrinsically motivated to learn Japanese because they wanted to enjoy the content of these cultural interests, so they learned largely inductively through massive amounts of listening. At high school, they usually began to think more seriously about their future and decided to study abroad in Japan, and so began a more serious study of the language to pass university entrance exams. Once they began their studies abroad, their motivation became integrative, and they wanted to make friends with Japanese students and to be able to communicate with them.

Like Sora, ISs were inclined to recount their MLLHs by showing visual images from their favorite pop culture artifacts as examples of the resources they used (actual images of anime and idols cannot be shown for copyright reasons). In other words, ISs tended to base their MLLHs on the resources they had used, hence their MLLHs were mainly resource oriented.

A Japanese student: Maki

Maki, an 18-year-old Japanese girl who had been learning English since she was six, provided a contrasting example. She went to a private English-conversation school during her first year of primary school. Her goal was to pass the EIKEN Test (of Practical English Proficiency) because her mother had told her that she could be employed by a prestigious company if she passed this. She managed to pass Grade 4 of the EIKEN test in her third year of primary school.

Maki attended a combined middle and high school. The school required the students to pass the EIKEN Grade Pre-2 to go on to high school and Grade 2 to enroll at an affiliated university. She worked hard to meet the required standard and passed the EIKEN Grade 2 in her second year (see Figure 6.8). Her motivation was extrinsic until a high school teacher introduced her to some cultural aspects of English through Western films and books rather than textbooks alone. This teacher, who was Japanese, talked openly about his own learning experiences, which furthered her interest and motivation to study the English language, culture and people (see Figure 6.9). Having become a university student, Maki felt that learning to speak English enhanced her abilities to speak logically in Japanese. Her future goal was to communicate in English with various English speakers worldwide.

Maki's MLLH resembles that of many other JSs who start learning English in kindergarten or primary school at an English language school. Even though they may find the lessons interesting, they tend to have a utilitarian outlook, perceiving English as necessary for their future careers. At middle school, they begin the serious study of English as a school subject and are motivated to get good school grades or pass the EIKEN exam. At high school, their aim is to pass the university entrance exams. However, if they have the opportunity to develop an

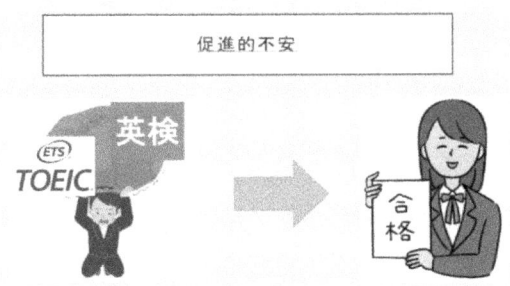

Figure 6.8 Maki's (Japanese) slide showing the notification of passing the EIKEN test

Figure 6.9 Maki's (Japanese) slide showing changes in her image of English

interest in other areas, such as culture or exchange study possibilities, their motivation may become more intrinsic. At university, they develop a more utilitarian sense of what communication in English offers, by engaging with international students through English.

Like many other JSs, Maki's MLLH is person-oriented. She frequently used images of people to express her emotions – like the changes in her motivation. In Figure 6.8, Maki expresses the pressure on her to pass the EIKEN exam by a person carrying a heavy rock on the shoulders (left), as well as her joy at passing by showing a person holding a certificate (right). Figure 6.9 shows the changes in her image of English from 'study with textbooks' and 'pressures of exams' (right) to 'interesting', 'fun' and 'new encounters' (left). Thus, Maki focused more on her emotions and emotional changes in her MLLH.

Analysis of the written LLHs

The differences in the MLLHs of ISs and JSs relate to the differences in motivation concerning their respective TLs. To see whether these motivational differences were reflected in their written narratives, I carried out a content analysis of written LLHs, focusing on what learners perceived their motivation to be for learning their respective TLs (see earlier section 'Data analysis and collection' for the method of analysis).

I identified 11 categories of reasons for learning TLs, which can be understood in terms of intrinsic/extrinsic motivation:

Intrinsic motivation: 'culture', 'language', 'exchange', and 'new experience'

Extrinsic motivation (with more integrated regulations): 'influence of others', 'communication', and 'study abroad'

Extrinsic motivation (with more external regulations): 'cram school', 'test/grades', 'further education' and 'future career'

Table 6.3 Students' reasons for learning their FLs

Reasons for learning an FL	ISs	JSs
Culture	86 (45%)	21 (16%)
Language per se	6 (3%)	6 (5%)
Exchange	17 (9%)	4 (3%)
New experience	6 (3%)	0 (0%)
Influence of others	20 (10%)	8 (6%)
To communicate with others	9 (5%)	22 (17 %)
Study abroad	18 (9%)	4 (3%)
Cram-school requirement	4 (2%)	12 (9%)
Test/grade marks	15 (8%)	32 (25%)
Further education	6 (3%)	19 (15%)
Future career	6 (3%)	0 (%)
Total	193	128

Furthermore, as the students' narratives were produced chronologically, the frequency of these categories was counted (Table 6.3) and plotted according to their years of schooling (Figures 6.10 and 6.11).

ISs' frequently-mentioned reason for learning Japanese was their interest in Japanese culture (45%), particularly pop culture, anime being the most frequent. Other common reasons were the influence of others, such as family members ('My father had studied abroad in Japan'),

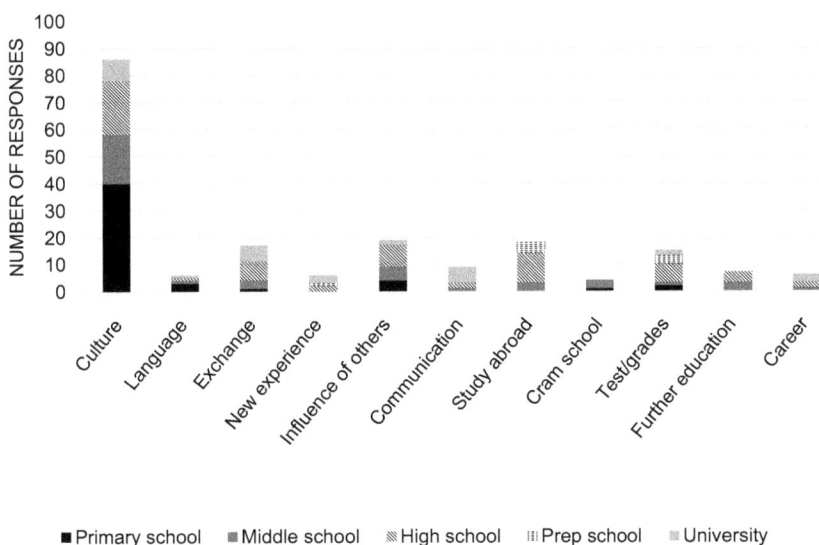

Figure 6.10 International students' reasons for learning Japanese, at different school ages

102 Multilingual Selves and Motivations for Learning Languages other than English

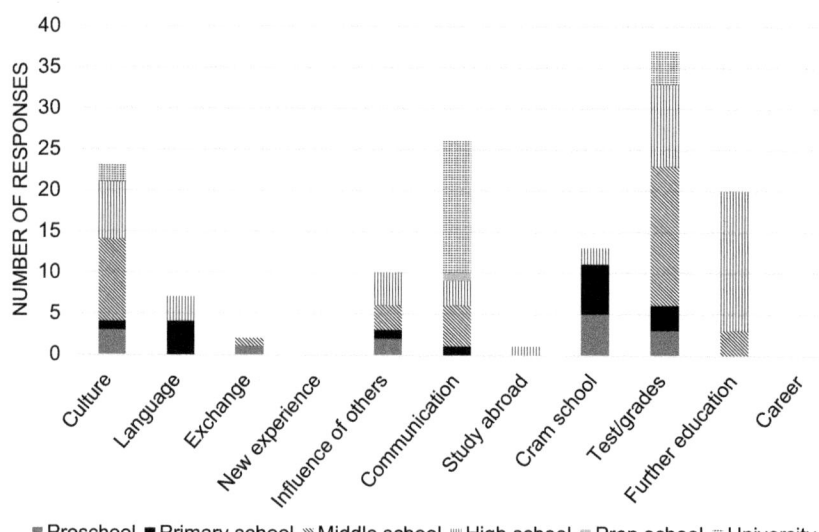

Figure 6.11 Japanese national students' reasons for learning English, at different school ages

and desire for exchange ('I wanted to make Japanese friends'). Some students also mentioned their interest in the language ('I was interested in the Japanese language as it is similar to Korean') and a desire for new experiences ('I wanted to enter a new world by learning a new language'). Overall, their reasons were largely intrinsically motivated.

By contrast, the reasons frequently given by JSs for learning English concerned passing various tests, getting good grades ('I wanted to pass the EIKEN test') and preparing for further education ('I was preparing for university entrance exams', 'I had to take English classes at a cram school'). This was followed by practical reasons, such as a desire to communicate ('I wanted to be able to communicate in English').

Next, I reviewed how these reasons were distributed across different school ages (Figures 6.10 and 6.11). 'Culture' was predominant during the primary school years of ISs, as most initially became interested in Japanese through the influence of anime. 'Culture' was still consistently mentioned during the middle school, high school, and university years, indicating that their interest in Japanese culture sustained their interest in learning Japanese. These results contrast with those of JSs (Figure 6.11). JSs started learning English much earlier, from preschool age, when they attended private English schools. Their motivation changed once intensive English language education had begun at school, and 'tests and grades' were most frequently mentioned from middle school to university. During their middle school and high-school education, preparation for 'further education' was cited as the main reason for learning English. Once at university, more practical reasons, such as 'to communicate with others' were given. Thus, motivation for learning English tends to be extrinsic from middle school onwards, and the awareness of the practical nature of English increases as selecting a career path becomes more of a reality.

The analysis of visual and written narratives indicates that ISs tended to perceive pop culture as the driving force behind learning Japanese for a long period starting in childhood. As Japanese was not a compulsory subject at school, they did not have to study it, making their motivation intrinsic. Following their interests, they then decided to pursue further education or careers in Japanese. This trend contrasts with JSs, who largely described their motivation for learning English in extrinsic terms, such as the need to take tests, get good grades, pass entrance exams, and/or for utilitarian reasons like communicating through English as a lingua franca.

Discussion and Conclusion

The findings of this study have several significant implications. Firstly, the study confirms that the motivation of L2 learners in foreign language learning (FLL) settings depends on whether their TL is English or LOTE, supporting the view that the reasons for the study of a LOTE require further research to understand L2 learner motivation more comprehensively (Howard & Oaks, 2021).

Secondly, the analysis indicates that pop culture is also an important resource for learning Japanese and supports the view that the consumption of pop culture is significant for LOTEs, though its significance for English language learning is more often emphasized (Werner & Tegge, 2021). As Japanese is not a compulsory school subject, learners have more freedom to learn as they wish, without having to worry about passing exams or earning high grades. This gives them more time to pursue their interests in pop culture, making it possible to remain intrinsically motivated for a prolonged period. Conversely, if learners are not interested in Japanese pop culture, they may not have chosen to learn Japanese in the first place. Considering the influence of anime in recent years, the relationship between pop culture and learning Japanese needs further investigation. These results also highlight the significance of out-of-class contexts for L2 learning (Benson & Reinders, 2011).

Thirdly, a long-term view of MLLHs can reveal how learners' motivations are sustained over time. The ISs were able to maintain their intrinsic motivation by broadening their interest to other cultural aspects as they grew older. Although the JSs had extrinsic motivation, they were able to incorporate other interests, such as culture and student exchange programs, and become more intrinsically motivated. This study has confirmed that motivation is not static or fixed throughout the entire period of L2 learning but can change at different ages. As Ushioda (2011) has claimed, learners can exercise their autonomy to change or sustain their motivation based on the goals they set at each stage of education.

By way of implications for pedagogy, given that most of the ISs pursued their Japanese language learning largely on account of their interest in Japanese culture (especially pop culture), incorporating such content in Japanese language programs might help sustain their intrinsic motivation. At the same time, since these learners were already accustomed to studying by processing a massive amount of input (e.g. watching anime, listening to pop music) and did not have sufficient experience of output and communication prior to study abroad, teachers should focus on giving them opportunities for output and communication with other international and Japanese students, so as to enhance their willingness to communicate (MacIntyre et al., 1998) while studying in Japan.

The methodology used highlights the potential offered by multimodal data to record second or foreign language learning experiences. The combined analysis of visual and linguistic narratives allows L2 learning experiences to be expressed from multiple perspectives. Using visuals gives learners the tools to express implicit perceptions that can only be conveyed using non-linguistic means. The combined analysis of multimodal data is a more effective way of appreciating learners' perspectives, which they may not be able to fully verbalize in a two-dimensional linguistic narrative.

This study is still at an exploratory stage and there are issues that need further consideration. I focused mostly on the prominent types of MLLHs: resource-oriented for ISs and person-oriented for JSs. However, I did not investigate whether there were any qualitative differences between the visuals used by the two groups. For example, the actions and emotions expressed in the person-oriented MLLHs may be different in the two groups. Future studies could consider qualitative differences as a means of understanding language learners' perspectives more comprehensively.

Furthermore, the current study could only consider learners' perceptions of those motivating factors that were spontaneously mentioned in their MLLHs, which may only be partial. Further research should focus on how learner motivation develops with the increasing consumption of pop culture and what role learner autonomy plays in this process.

Acknowledgements

I am grateful for the Research Grant awarded by the Institute of Japan Studies, TUFS, and to Grant-in-Aid for Scientific Research (19K00703) for their continued support. I am also thankful to all the learners who participated in this study.

References

Benson, P. (2017) Ways of seeing: The individual and the social in applied linguistics research methodologies. *Language Teaching* 52 (1), 60–70.
Benson, P. and Nunan, D. (eds) (2004) *Learners' Stories: Difference and Diversity in Language Learning.* Cambridge University Press.
Benson, P. and Reinders, H. (eds) (2011) *Beyond the Language Classroom.* Palgrave Macmillan.
Block, D. (2014) Moving beyond 'lingualism': Multilingual embodiment and multimodality in SLA. In S. May (ed.) *The Multilingual Turn: Implications for SLA, TESOL and Bilingual Education* (pp. 54–77). Routledge.
Chan, Y-H. and Wong, N-L. (2017) Learning Japanese through anime. *Journal of Language Teaching and Research* 8 (3), 485–495.
Cheung, C-K. (2001) The use of popular culture as a stimulus to motivate secondary students' English learning in Hong Kong. *ELT Journal* 55 (1), 55–61.
Chik, A. and Breidbach, S. (2011) Online language learning histories exchange: Hong Kong and German perspectives. *TESOL Quarterly* 45 (3), 553–564.
Chik, A. and Melo–Pfeifer, S. (2020) What does language awareness look like? Visual methodologies in language learning and teaching research (2000–2018). *Language Awareness* 29 (3–4), 336–352.
Coffey, S. (2015) Reframing teachers' language knowledge through metaphor analysis of language portraits. *Modern Language Journal* 99 (3), 500–514.
Deci, E.L. and Ryan, R.M. (1985) *Intrinsic Motivation and Self-Determination in Human Behavior.* Springer.
Dörnyei, Z. (2005) *The Psychology of the Language Learner: Individual Differences in Second Language Acquisition.* Lawrence Erlbaum.
Dörnyei, Z. (2009) The L2 motivational self. In Z. Dörnyei and E. Ushioda (eds) *Motivation, Language Identity and the L2 Self* (pp. 9–42). Multilingual Matters.
Fukunaga, N. (2006) 'Those anime students': Foreign language literacy development through Japanese popular culture. *Journal of Adolescent & Adult Literacy* 50 (3), 206–222.
Gardner, R.C. (1985) *Social Psychology and Second Language Learning: The Role of Attitudes and Motivation.* Edward Arnold.
Gardner, R.C. and Lambert, W.E. (1959) Motivational variables in second language acquisition. *Canadian Journal of Psychology* 13 (4), 266–272.
Henry, A. (2011) Examining the impact of L2 English on L3 selves: A case study. *International Journal of Multilingualism* 8 (3), 235–255.
Howard, M. and Oakes, L. (2021) Motivation for LOTE learning: A cross country comparison of university learners of French. *Journal of Multilingual and Multicultural Development.* https://doi.org/10.1080/01434632.2021.1897129.
Humphreys, G. and Spratt, M. (2008) Many languages, many motivations: A study of Hong Kong students' motivation to learn different target languages. *System* 36 (2), 313–335.
Japan Foundation (2020) Survey report on Japanese language education abroad 2018, 11 May 2019. https://www.jpf.go.jp/e/project/japanese/survey/result/survey18.html.
Kalaja, P. and Pitkänen-Huhta, A. (2018) ALR special issue: Visual methods in applied language studies. *Applied Linguistics Review* 9 (2–3), 157–176.
Kalaja, P. and Melo-Pfeifer, S. (eds) (2019) *Visualising Multilingual Lives: More Than Words.* Multilingual Matters.
Kalaja, P., Menezes, V. and Barcelos, A.M.F. (eds) (2008) *Narratives of Learning and Teaching EFL.* Palgrave Macmillan.
Kalantzis, M., Cope, B., Chan, E. and Dalley-Trim, L. (2016) *Literacies* (2nd edn). Cambridge University Press.

Kao, T.A. and Oxford, R.L. (2014) Learning language through music: A strategy for building inspiration and motivation. *System* 43 (1), 114–120.

MacIntyre, P.D., Clement, R., Dörnyei, Z. and Noels, K. (1998) Conceptualizing willingness to communicate in a L2: A situational model of L2 confidence and affiliation. *Modern Language Journal* 82 (4), 545–562.

Melo-Pfeifer, S. and Chik, A. (2020) Multimodal linguistic biographies of prospective foreign language teachers in Germany: Reconstructing beliefs about languages and multilingual language learning in initial teacher education. *International Journal of Multilingualism* 19 (4), 499–522.

Menezes, V. (2008) Multimedia language learning histories. In P. Kalaja, V. Menezes and A.M.F. Barcelos (eds) *Narratives of Learning and Teaching EFL* (pp. 199–213). Palgrave MacMillan.

Noels, K.A. (2001) New orientations in language learning motivation: Towards a model of intrinsic, extrinsic and integrative orientations and motivation. In Z. Dörnyei and R. Schmidt (eds) *Motivation and Second Language Acquisition* (pp. 43–68). University of Hawai'i.

Nomura, K. and Yuan, R. (2019) Long-term motivations for L2 learning: A biographical study from a situated learning perspective. *Journal of Multilingual and Multicultural Development* 40 (2), 164–178.

Oxford, R.L. (1996) When emotion meets (meta)cognition in language learning histories. *International Journal of Educational Research* 23 (7), 581–594.

Paiva, V.L.M.O. and Gomes Jr, R.C. (2019) Multimodal language learning histories: Images telling stories. In P. Kalaja and S. Melo-Pfeifer (eds) *Visualising Multilingual Lives: More Than Words* (pp. 151–172). Multilingual Matters.

Papi, M., Bondarenko, A.V., Mansouri, S., Feng, L. and Jiang, C. (2018) Rethinking L2 motivation research: The 2 × 2 model of L2 self-guides. *Studies in Second Language Acquisition* 41 (2), 337–361. https://doi.org/10.1017/S0272263118000153.

Pavlenko, A. (2007) Autobiographic narratives as data in applied linguistics. *Applied Linguistics* 28 (2), 163–188.

Rose, G. (2012) *Visual Methodologies: An Introduction to Researching with Visual Materials* (3rd edn). Sage.

Ryan, R.M. and Deci, E.L. (2017) *Self-Determination Theory: Basic Psychological Needs in Motivation, Development, and Wellness.* Guilford Press. https://doi.org/10.1521/978.14625/28806.

Ryan, R.M. and Deci, E.L. (2020) Intrinsic and extrinsic motivation from a self-determination theory perspective: Definitions, theory, practices, and future directions. *Contemporary Educational Psychology,* 61, article ID: 101860.

Shoaib, A. and Dörnyei, Z. (2005) Affect in life-long learning: Exploring L2 motivation as a dynamic process. In P. Benson and D. Nunan (eds) *Learners' Stories: Difference and Diversity in Language Learning* (pp. 22–41). Cambridge University Press.

Sugita-McEown, M., Noels, K.A. and Chafee, K.E. (2014) At the interface of the socio-educational model, self-determination theory and the L2 motivational self system. In K. Csizér and M. Magid (eds) *The Impact of Self-Concept on Language Learning* (pp. 19–50). Multilingual Matters.

Takahashi, A. (2014) Gurôbarunettowâku jidai ni okeru "atarashii nihongo gakushûsha" to onrain comyunitî e no juyô ['New Japanese learners' and their need for online communities in the era of global networks]. *Obirin Gengo Kyoiku Ronsou* 10, 139–156.

Teimouri, Y. (2017) L2 selves, emotions, and motivated behaviors. *Studies in Second Language Acquisition* 39 (4), 691–709.

Umino, T. (2023) Using multimodal language learning histories to understand learning experiences and beliefs of second language learners in Japan. *The Modern Language Journal* 107 (1), 308–327. https://doi.org/10.1111/modl.12828.

Ushioda, E. (2009) A person-in-context view of emergent motivation, self and identity. In Z. Dörnyei and E. Ushioda (eds) *Motivation, Language Identity and the L2 Self* (pp. 215–228). Multilingual Matters.

Ushioda, E. (2011) Why autonomy? Insights from motivation theory and research. *Innovation in Language Learning and Teaching* 5 (2), 221–232.

Werner, V. and Tegge, F. (2021) Learning language through pop culture/learning about pop culture through language education. In V. Werner and F. Tegge (eds) *Pop Culture in Language Education: Theory, Research, Practice* (pp. 3–30). Routledge.

Williams, M. and Burden, R.L. (1997) *Psychology for Language Teachers*. Cambridge University Press.

7 Identity, Investment and Language Learning Strategies: Voices of Undergraduate Students Learning Korean in Kazakhstan

Anas Hajar and Syed Abdul Manan

Introduction

English has become a global lingua franca. It dominates language learning motivation research, and is associated with factors such as 'necessity, utility, advantage, social capital, power, advancement, mobility, migration, and cosmopolitanism' (Ushioda, 2017: 471). Boo *et al.* (2015) note that research on L2 motivation in Asian settings has disproportionately focused on English, leaving little knowledge about individuals' motivation for learning a language other than English (LOTE). The imbalance between English and other languages in L2 motivation research has recently encouraged some language researchers to explore individuals' motivations to learn LOTEs across different contexts, including those that are imagined as monolingual and/or consumed by the desire to learn English only (Takahashi, 2023). For example, Liao *et al.*'s (2020) study on Chinese learners' motivation for Arabic as a third language found that by showing empathy for vulnerable families living in some Middle East countries and an imagination of a world characterised by cultural diversity and tolerance, the participants were able to construct an imagined cosmopolitan identity. In this sense, learning LOTEs can contribute to enhancing an individual's intercultural citizenship, implying 'the extension of citizenship beyond national borders, through recognition of the global scale of social relations, the need to respect and value diversity, and participation in and responsibility to communities at multiple levels from the local to the global' (Baker & Fang, 2021: 3).

The learning of a LOTE often occurs concurrently with English learning, especially in non-Anglophone contexts. As Dörnyei and Al-Hoorie (2017: 457) state: 'the most important unique characteristic of the motivation to learn LOTEs is the fact that the process typically takes place in the shadow of Global English'. That is, the motivation to learn LOTEs is an extension of research that seeks to balance global English with other languages in a multicultural world. In this respect, Henry (2017) proposed the idea of the *ideal multilingual self*, which refers to an individual's aspiration to become proficient in multiple languages in the future. He argues that this aspiration can create a powerful motivational force, in addition to the desire to learn specific languages that the learner is currently studying. Elsewhere, Henry (2011) observed the intricate relationship between English and other languages. One learner, Anton, exemplified a multilingual self-image as a Swedish peacekeeping officer using English, French and Russian while working overseas. Anton adopted a self-view that portrayed himself as 'being indomitable, focused and persevering', and this self-image protected his L4-Russian identity from being influenced by his English-speaking/using self (Henry, 2011: 247).

Given that motivation to learn LOTEs is a 'largely uncharted area of language learning motivation' (Ushioda & Dörnyei, 2017: 451), this research study focuses on exploring the experiences of a group of multilingual Kazakhstani students learning Korean as L4 or L5, with a specific focus on their language learning strategy (LLS) use and their ideal multilingual selves across different settings in post-soviet Kazakhstan, the largest Central Asian country. In Kazakhstan, the Kazakh and Russian languages are officially used, and English is the first foreign language. The present study draws on the sociological construct of *investment* to explain the connection between a language learner's desire and commitment to learning the target language(s), and their complex and changing identity (Norton, 2013). Related to this, Oxford (2017: 192) suggests that 'if the language learner makes the decision to invest, it should be followed by a host of cognitive, affective and other strategies to make the investment successful'. In this sense, a language learner needs to exercise their agency by adopting effective LLSs to achieve their desired self-images, otherwise their ultimate vision will turn into having the character of fantasy. From a sociocultural perspective, strategic language learning is defined as 'a language learner's socially mediated plan or action to meet a goal' (Oxford & Schramm, 2007: 48).

It is noteworthy that motivation for learning Korean, the focus of the present study, has unique components that are specific to the language, including 'the popularity of Korean cultural products such as television dramas, movies, video games, popular music (K-pop) and dance (B-boys)' (Jang & Paik, 2012: 198). In what follows, sociolinguistic changes in Kazakhstan are explained, along with prior research on LOTEs in Asia and the theoretical framework of this study. After this, the objectives of this study will be presented, followed by an analysis of the qualitative data in rich detail. This chapter will close by drawing out the pedagogical implications and limitations of the study.

The Case of Ethnic Koreans and the Sociolinguistic Profile of Kazakhstan

Kazakhstan is a former Soviet republic that extends geographically from the Caspian Sea in the west to the Altai Mountains at its eastern border with China and Russia. It is a multilingual and multicultural country with more than 130 ethnic groups, including Russians (23%), Uzbeks (3%), Ukrainians (2%), Uyghur (1.4%), Tartars (1.3%), Germans (1%) and Koreans (1%) (Ahn, 2021). Most Koreans in Kazakhstan are descendants of those forcibly relocated by Stalin from the Russian Far East to Central Asia in the 1930s (Yem & Epstein, 2015). According to the Regulation of the Council of People's Commissars in 1937, this displacement was officially justified due to fear of Japanese espionage (Yem & Epstein, 2015). Under the Soviet Union's language policy, Korean children in Kazakhstan were able to learn their native language in Korean schools (Kokaisl, 2018). The teaching of Korean then ended entirely in the 1970s, after which only Russian was taught (Kokaisl, 2018).

Following the collapse of the USSR in 1991, the Central Asian states – Kazakhstan, Uzbekistan, Kyrgyzstan, Tajikistan, and Turkmenistan – underwent significant education and language policy changes. The shared goal of these newly independent republics was to establish their own national identities and build independent systems and institutions, separate from the Soviet centralised structures. One of the first major moves in this direction was to elevate the role of national languages. Related to this, the attitudes of people in Central Asia towards ethnic Koreans changed due to rising nationalism. The Koreans faced discrimination in government hiring practices because of their use of the Russian language instead of the titular languages of the Central Asian republics. Hwang (2012) pointed out that, as ethnic Koreans felt unwelcome in Central Asia, thousands of them in the 1990s departed with the help of South Korean NGOs. However, the diplomatic and economic relationship between South Korea and Central Asia has markedly improved following South Korean President Lee Myung-bak's visit to Kazakhstan in 2011 in particular (Kokaisl, 2018). The former president of Kazakhstan, Nursultan Nazarbayev, considered South Korea a potential model for Kazakhstan's industrial development (Kokaisl, 2018). Furthermore, South Korea has been involved in setting up a number of enterprises in Kazakhstan, including two construction deals each worth

$4 billion (Hwang, 2012). Taking all of the above into consideration, the present qualitative study seeks to explore the experiences of a group of Kazakhstani university students learning Korean as an additional language, with a specific focus on their strategic language learning efforts and future vision.

Investment, Language Learning Strategies, and Languages Other than English (LOTEs)

Bonny Norton conceptualised the sociological construct of *investment* in the mid-1990s as being a complement to the psychological construct of *motivation* and as a means to explore the socially and historically constructed relationship of the language learner to the target language(s) and their multiple desires and identities, especially in contexts where unequal power structures exist (see Darvin & Norton, 2023; Norton, 2013). Norton's work has in some measure heralded the sociocultural turn in language education (Block, 2003), and the construct of investment provides 'an important critical counterpoint to mainstream research on L2 motivation' (Ushioda, 2020: 28). Norton (2013) questions simplistic L2 motivation theories that conceptualise motivation as a dichotomous, static and unitary construct (e.g. introverted or extroverted, inhibited or uninhibited, motivated or unmotivated) without explaining how highly motivated language learners, on certain occasions, can choose to withdraw from opportunities to participate in learning contexts where they are positioned in unequal ways.

The construct of investment, as Darvin and Norton (2023) note, signals the commitment to the goals, practices and identities that constitute the learning process and that are continually negotiated in different social relationships and structures of power. Norton (2013: 50) indicates that language learners 'expect or hope to have a good return on their investment – a return that will give them access to hitherto unattainable resources'. That is, when individuals invest in the target language, they generally do so with the understanding that the target language will enable them to acquire a wider range of symbolic resources (e.g. education credentials, prestige, social networks) and material resources (e.g. wealth, real estate), which will consequently enhance the value of their cultural capital and lend them more social power. Wang (2023) suggests that LOTE learning has linguistic and pragmatic benefits but that language learners need context-specific examples to recognise the value of learning a LOTE. Wang (2023) further argues that the *near peer role model* (NPRM) can be used as a potentially effective affordance to nurture the development of learners' multilingual selves. The concept of NPRMs was first introduced by Murphey (1998: 201) to describe individuals 'who are close to our social, professional, and/or age level whom we may respect and admire'.

Hajar (2017) points out that although Norton's focus was not on language learning strategies (LLSs), language learners – when capturing the importance of a certain activity – often exercise agency by embracing a particular set of LLSs in attempts to become whoever they want to be. Hajar's (2017) argument is based on Dörnyei and Kubanyiova's (2014) suggestion that one's desired future vision should be associated with the use of appropriate and effective LLSs, which function as a roadmap towards the stated goal. To exemplify this, Hajar (2018) documented the strategic language learning efforts of a female postgraduate learner of English (Noura) from a rural region of Iraq. Noura acted agentively to achieve her overarching goals of being the first female student in her village to pursue her postgraduate studies in England, by employing some effective LLSs, including regularly watching various English programmes and seeking help from her Canadian university colleague to give her additional practice in the Test of English as a Foreign Language (TOEFL) in exchange for teaching him some Arabic, since she could not afford private English tutoring.

While much of the existing L2 motivation research has drawn on the sociological construct of investment to explore individuals' experiences of learning English as a target language (e.g. Manan & Hajar, 2022; Rabbidge & Zaheeb, 2022; Sharif & Channa, 2022), only a few empirical studies have employed it to examine the learning of LOTEs (e.g. Liao *et al.*, 2020; Lu *et al.*, 2022). For instance, Lu *et al.* (2022), drawing on the theoretical model of investment, explored what motivated 15 international undergraduate students studying in mainland China to invest in their Chinese learning. The study found that the participants' investment in learning Chinese was collaboratively driven by both utilitarian incentives (e.g. scholarships, Chinese-related employment opportunities, and educational qualifications) and non-utilitarian incentives (e.g. the enrichment of one's experiences, expressing oneself, and making friends with people from other cultures).

As regards the demand for Korean language learning, there has been growing interest in learning it mainly due to the Korean wave, which refers to 'the phenomenal success of Korean cultures in overseas markets' (Choi, 2015: 33). This has been evident in the few empirical studies that have examined individuals' motivations for learning Korean as an additional language (e.g. Chan & Chi, 2010; Han, 2023; Nourzadeh *et al.*, 2023). Nourzadeh *et al.* (2023), for instance, investigated 174 Iranian learners' experiences and motivations for learning Korean in four private language institutes in Tehran. The study reported that most participants were highly positive regarding their experience in the Korean classroom, describing it as lively, fun and vibrant. Also, they indicated that they were attracted to learning Korean to understand Korean pop music and dramas. Some participants articulated internalised instrumental motives for learning Korean for entertainment and online communication, especially as few Koreans lived in Iran.

Chan and Chi (2010), in turn, analysed quantitatively the factors that motivated 80 undergraduate university students in Singapore to learn Korean. K-pop culture (entertainment news, TV dramas and movies, pop music and fashion) emerged as the most important factor, followed by the participants' perceived value of the Korean language for their future career and South Korea as an Asian economic power. Some participants in Chan and Chi's (2010) study referred to their wish to spend time on academic exchange in South Korea. In spite of Kazakhstan's rich ethnic and linguistic diversity, almost all empirical studies have focused on Kazakhstani individuals' experiences with learning English as an additional language and none of these studies has focused on learning Korean.

Study Details

No previous research has explored Kazakhstani individuals' beliefs, strategic language efforts and future selves while learning Korean as an additional language in Kazakhstan. Drawing on the sociological construct of investment, this qualitative study thus sought to address this research gap by examining six undergraduate Kazakh students' beliefs about Korean language learning as L4 or L5 and the LLSs they used to achieve their ultimate goals while interacting with different contextual factors. The following research questions underpin this study:

(1) What are the participants' changing beliefs about the Korean language and people?
(2) What motivates the participants to invest in learning Korean?
(3) What strategies do they use to achieve their ultimate vision of learning Korean?

The study centred on six female participants, aged between 20 and 22 years old. They were studying at an English-medium instruction university in Kazakhstan. Candidates at the university were chosen according to their overall undergraduate grade point average and International English Language Testing System (IELTS) score. Hence, all participants had already attained an advanced level in English. Also, all of them were attendees of Korean courses run by the university, and their level of Korean was intermediate. The aim of the elective Korean language courses attended by the participants was to build students' proficiency in Korean up to advanced levels by helping them gain an in-depth understanding of Korean society and culture and providing practical support for those who seek educational opportunities in South Korea.

The researchers gained access to the participants through the director of a foreign language centre at the university. The participants were either in their second or third year of their studies at the time of data collection. None of them was an ethnic Korean, nor were they known to the researchers before the data collection stage. Their linguistic repertoires included Kazakh and Russian as their first and second languages, and English as their first foreign language. Pseudonyms were used to protect the participants' privacy. A vignette of each participant's biography from their written accounts of their language learning experiences is presented in the next section.

The data for this qualitative study were collected between September and December 2022 after gaining informed consent. Two research methods were used: narrative writing and individual semi-structured interviews. The participants were first asked to write a short account of themselves and some of their past language learning experiences, together with the reasons that motivated them to learn Korean. The participants sent their responses to the researchers via email. This method enabled the researchers both to enter the life-worlds of the participants based on their own expositions and to construct subsequent interview questions. Two individual semi-structured interviews with each participant were conducted at a time and place convenient to the participants. The first round of interviews took place from September to October, followed by the second round in November and December of 2022. The average length of each interview was approximately one hour. With the permission of the participants, the interviews were audio-recorded.

The data were analysed using Braun and Clarke's (2013) guidelines for conducting thematic analysis, with the aim of identifying and interpreting themes in rich detail. The researchers familiarised themselves with the data by reading and re-reading the interview transcripts and participants' descriptions of their drawings 'actively, analytically and critically' (Braun & Clarke, 2013: 205) to enable them to generate the initial codes in light of the research question and theoretical framework adopted in this study. Following this, codes with common features were collated to create themes derived from the coded data and the entire data set. Once all the themes had been identified, the researchers provided excerpts under each theme to explain the participants' in-depth accounts of their experiences.

Biographical Vignettes of the Participants

Vignettes of each participant, based on their written accounts of their family background, language learning experiences, and future visions are now presented.

Zarina

Zarina was born in 2002 in Aktau, southwestern Kazakhstan. She grew up with one younger brother. Her father was a petroleum engineer and her mother was a physics teacher. She moved with her family to London in the United Kingdom when she was three years old. The family unit returned to Kazakhstan (to Astana) when Zarina was six years old. She studied at a mainstream school that had adopted Russian and Kazakh as the media of instruction. Zarina considered Kazakh and Russian as her native languages, and she was at an advanced level in English. Korean was her L4, and she was at the intermediate level. She was in the second year of her undergraduate studies in applied linguistics. Concerning her motives for learning Korean, Zarina was influenced by the music K-pop band Exo, along with her interest in Korean culture. Zarina planned to take the Test of Proficiency in Korean (TOPIK) and pursue her postgraduate studies in Korea. In addition to attending Korean language courses at her university, she used certain LLSs to improve her Korean, including joining a WhatsApp group to learn Korean, participating in events related to K-pop, and watching Korean dramas and YouTube videos about Korea.

Assel

Assel was born in 2001 in Shchuchinsk, located in northern-central Kazakhstan. She grew up with one younger sister. Her father was an architect and her mother was a housewife. Assel indicated that Kazakh and Russian were her native languages. She was fluent in English, and was at an intermediate level in Spanish and Korean. After completing her school education, she succeeded in gaining a place at a highly selective university in Kazakhstan, where English was the medium of instruction. She was in the third year of her undergraduate studies in political science and international relations. She became interested in learning Korean after she accompanied her parents to South Korea in the Summer of 2018 for their medical treatment. Assel indicated that she was inspired by Korean culture and Korea's role in international politics and economics. This encouraged her to watch Korean dramas and listen to K-pop music.

Nurly

Nurly was born in 2001 in Almaty, Kazakhstan's largest city and former capital. She grew up with one older sister. Her father was an auditor and her mother was a school teacher. Nurly was in the third year of her undergraduate studies in economics. She could speak four languages: Kazakh, Russian, English and Korean. Nurly started learning Korean (for almost a year and a half) by attending Korean language courses at her university. She was at the intermediate level. Nurly indicated that her mother encouraged her to learn Korean to pursue her postgraduate studies and work in South Korea. She was also impressed by the Korean economy, stating: 'South Korea is one of the four *Asian Tigers*; its economy is growing rapidly. [...] the Korean language will be in demand while getting a job in highly paid competitive companies'. Nurly mainly employed the strategies regulated by her instructor, including the written repetition of new words and reading the grammatical rules several times before working on the textbook exercises. She also liked to construct a monologue aloud in Korean in order to improve her pronunciation.

Malika

Malika was born in 2002 in Oskemen, eastern Kazakhstan. She had one older brother and a younger sister. Her mother had an administrative position at a public university in Kazakhstan, and her father was a businessman. Malika mentioned that Kazakh and Russian were her native languages. She was fluent in English and at an intermediate level in German and Korean. She was in the second year of her undergraduate studies in world languages, literature and culture. She had been learning Korean for almost one year by attending Korean language courses at her university. Malika's interest in Korean culture and her desire to pass the TOPIK and then pursue her postgraduate studies in Korea were the main reasons that encouraged her to learn Korean. She employed a number of LLSs, such as borrowing books about Korean grammar from the university library and watching YouTube videos to learn the Korean language.

Talshyn

Talshyn was born in 2003 in Astana, the capital of Kazakhstan. She had one older sister and a younger brother. Her father was a police officer, and her mother was an accountant in an export company. Talshyn indicated that she could speak five languages: Kazakh and Russian (native languages), English (at advanced level), Chinese (at beginner level) and Korean (at intermediate level). She was in the second year of her undergraduate studies in economics. Although she started to learn Korean formally for one year, Talshyn indicated that she used to watch her favourite Korean show, *The Running Man*, when she was in Grade 10. This in turn encouraged her to start learning Hangul, the Korean alphabet, by herself. She believed that learning and mastering Korean could open up job opportunities for her in the future, along with her desire to widen her knowledge of Korean culture and complete her postgraduate studies in South Korea. Participating in volunteering events organised by Astana Zhastary Youth Centre in Kazakhstan helped her meet some Korean delegates and practice her Korean with them.

Diana

Diana was born in 2002 in Ekibastuz, northeastern Kazakhstan. She had one younger sister. Her father was an engineer in a local telecommunications company and her mother was a housewife. She was in the second year of her undergraduate studies in political science and international relations. Diana indicated that Kazakh and Russian were her native languages. She was fluent in English, and at an intermediate level in Korean. One of Diana's classmates in Grade 10 encouraged her to learn Korean by introducing her to K-pop music. Therefore, Diana became interested in understanding the meaning of song lyrics. At university, she wanted to develop her Korean to pass the TOPIK and pursue her postgraduate studies in South Korea. To achieve her goals, she borrowed some textbooks from her university library, such as *Korean Grammar for International Learners* (Ihm *et al.*, 2004). She also regularly watched K-dramas in Korean with subtitles in English and listened to K-pop songs.

Interpreting the Participants' Experiential Accounts of Learning Korean

Participants' changing beliefs about the Korean language and people

The interview data revealed that almost all participants were initially wary of their ability to learn Korean. Their fear stemmed from the assumption that, as both China and Korea shared a Confucian heritage, Korean and Chinese languages may have derived from the same root, and hence that Korean – similar to Chinese – has unique characters rather than letters and each character is a complicated square graph. However, they gradually discovered through watching Korean dramas and K-pop music videos on YouTube that Korean Hangul is a transparent orthographic system with direct letter/sound correspondences. After joining the Korean language courses at their university, they became aware of the association between Korean and Kazakh languages, especially regarding grammar.

The data analysis also showed that all participants had a positive attitude towards Korean people, describing them as hardworking, polite, fashionable and patriotic. The participants further indicated that the instructors of the Korean courses enabled them to increase their awareness of Korean culture in relation to family harmony, the extensive use of kinship terms (e.g. *hyong* 'older brother' and *enni* 'older sister') among close friends, proper filial piety and showing respect to older people by using honorific forms when talking to them. For example, Koreans use the suffix 님 (nim) in words 선생님 *(seon-saeng*-nim — teacher) or a 목사님 *(mok-sa*-nim — pastor).

> I thought it was difficult to learn Korean and that its spelling is like Chinese. I had to learn hieroglyphs. After I started to watch K-drama and listen to K-pop when I was a secondary school student, I discovered there's a correspondence between the sounds and letters in the Korean alphabet, Hangul. [...] The image I had of Koreans was influenced by the media, which showed their interest in skin care and plastic surgery, along with presenting good-looking K-pop stars. After I enrolled on the Korean course, I learnt from the instructor and the internet about Korean traditions and culture. They are hardworking and patriotic. Also, they – like Kazakh people – show great respect for elders. (Malika, first interview)

> I thought Korean would be completely different from Kazakh and similar to Chinese. After I attended the Korean courses, I found that Kazakh shares some grammatical features with Korean. Both languages are left-branching, and agglutinative and the canonical word order is SOV. In terms of the Korean people, they are famous for being polite. After I watched different bloggers living in Korea and read some books during the Korean courses, I expanded my knowledge about Koreans. They are hardworking and firmly abide by rules. They also built a technocratic country. (Diana, first interview)

Regarding Assel, she was the only one who had visited South Korea and her positive image of the Korean people is crystallised in the following excerpt:

> I went with my parents to South Korea in the Summer of 2018 for their medical treatment. At that time, I used to watch K-dramas but wasn't really interested in learning Korean. When we wanted to go from the airport to the hotel, we took the wrong bus and got lost. We stopped a man and asked him for directions in English. Although he didn't know English, he helped us using Google Translate. We also went to the city of Incheon. I found that all people there were polite, friendly and willing to help foreigners. This visit left a positive impression on me about Korea and its people. (Assel, first interview)

Participants' incentives for Korean learning investment and their future vision

The participants articulated three main incentives that motivated them to learn Korean, related to cultural, economic/academic and personal gains. More specifically, all participants (apart from Nurly) indicated that they were influenced by the Korean Wave, and their interest in K-pop and K-drama represented their primary incentive to start learning Korean. Appearance (i.e. good-looking people, plastic surgery) and attributes (e.g. politeness) were also reported by most participants. Along with Korean cultural products, the participants gradually developed the academic and economic benefits of learning Korean, namely well-paid occupations and opportunities for studying abroad in Korea. The following excerpts elucidate this aspect.

> The more I learn Korean, the more I want to go to Korea to pursue my Master's degree there. I met a Korean professor from Hankuk University at one of the events in Kazakhstan. He encouraged me to apply for a Master's degree in Korea and he will write a recommendation letter for me. I am also a K-pop fan. [...] Learning new languages enabled me to become more open-minded. I now think of myself not as a citizen of one country, but as a citizen of the world. (Talshyn, first interview)

> There are two main things that encouraged me to learn Korean. The most important one is that as I'm majoring in Political Science and International Relations, it's essential to learn other languages, including Korean because Korea is expected to play an important role in the international arena. My future vision is to work in Kazakhstan's embassy in South Korea. In addition to employability, I have a passion for learning more about Korean culture because I am a K-pop and drama lover. Learning languages helps us be more tolerant and show respect to other cultures. (Assel, first interview)

Regarding Nurly, she pointed out that she was not greatly attracted by the Korean culture but her mother played a pivotal role in encouraging her to choose the Korean language module as an elective at university, mainly because of the utilitarian benefits associated with being able to speak Korean, such as a respectable job and further educational opportunities:

> My mother is a history teacher. She advised me to learn Korean because Korea has a strong economy and has more than 150 contracts with Kazakhstan. I didn't have a passion for learning Korean before selecting it as an elective course at university. Initially, I didn't like watching K-pop videos and K-dramas because Koreans wear lots of makeup. They seemed spoiled to me. Then, I gradually realised that the K-pop industry is a business and attracts tourists. It has even entered the United States. ... My plan is to complete my Master's studies or find a job in South Korea. (Nurly, second interview)

The data analysis also showed the significance of NPRMs for learning a LOTE. Zarina explained how a K-pop band – Exo – and one particular member of this band inspired her not only to learn Korean but also to become a K-pop singer, organising some events on the university campus. This was because that member was more similar to her because his parents were ethnic Koreans who lived in Kazakhstan and he was a university student with a sense of humour and a lot of fans. NPRMs have similar features (e.g. gender, ethnicity, interests, age level or social background) to the language learners and can foster the learners' willingness and confidence to perform similarly to their nearest role model's ways to success (Murphey, 1998):

> I am a K-pop singer. I am a big fan of songs performed by one K-pop group called Exo. I have a dream of attending an Exo members' fan meeting and communicating with them in Korean. I access their blog for their latest news, especially one member. He is my idol because we are similar to each other. He mentioned in one of the interviews that his parents used to live in Kazakhstan. Both of us are university students and have a sense of humour, I believe. I envision having a lot of fans like him [...] I recently have another goal to enrol in a Master's degree programme in South Korea. (Zarina, first interview)

Learners' exercise of their agency

As described in the previous section, the participants articulated their linguistic, academic, intercultural and professional goals in learning Korean. The data analysis revealed that the participants, to varying degrees, displayed their agency to achieve their goals. Learner agency can be perceived as 'the human ability to act through mediation, with awareness of one's actions, and to understand their significance and relevance' (Lantolf, 2013: 19). That is, an individual needs to employ certain effective strategies and to invest more time in learning and practising the target language across different settings. Four participants (Assel, Diana, Talshyn and Zarina) described how they had used several LLSs that were not confined to those mediated by their language instructors. Examples of these strategies were listening to K-pop music and watching Korean movies with subtitles (i.e. cognitive strategies), learning new vocabulary in some meaningful context, planning for a language task and participating in events to widen knowledge about the Korean language and culture (i.e. metacognitive strategies), and cooperating with others and self-talk to maintain motivation and confidence (i.e. social and affective strategies). The following excerpts vividly exemplify this interpretation:

> I participated in some competitions organised by the Korean embassy in Kazakhstan. I wrote an essay about the Korean Wave. I also made a video about Exo, a K-pop group ... I sang two K-pop songs at an event on the university campus on International Women's Day. ... I keep searching for internships in South Korea. I joined a WhatsApp group called The Korean Club. This group helped me have useful information

about TOPIK and widen my knowledge about grammatical rules, learn new vocabulary and be informed about any events related to the Korean language and culture in Kazakhstan. (Zarina, second interview)

I watch several Korean TV shows such as *Running Man*, *Knowing Bros* and *Sixth Sense*. This helps me expand my vocabulary inventory and understand everyday language. ... I enrolled in a volunteering club. There were many international events. In one of these events, I was in charge of helping Korean delegates. I met them at the airport, escorted them to their hotel, and accompanied them to different events. They were friendly to me, helping me improve my Korean by practising it with them and encouraging them to correct my mistakes. (Talshyn, second interview)

Unlike the other participants, the experiential accounts of Nurly and Malika in the current research revealed that there was something of a mismatch between the long-term goals of learning Korean they articulated and their actions to achieve these goals. More specifically, the two participants' LLSs were largely exam-oriented and were less likely to lead to mastering Korean necessary for academic and professional gains in particular. This point is elucidated in the following excerpts:

I only work on the activities covered in the Korean course. The activities involve a lot of repetition and writing short sentences using the new vocabulary we learnt in the course. I don't want to confuse myself by studying extramural activities. However, I use certain strategies for my homework and quizzes. For example, when I write a short essay in Korean for my homework, I often think aloud and record the sentences I utter. Then, I listen to the audio and jot everything down. After that, I polish the sentences and make them grammatically correct. (Nurly, second interview)

I don't employ many strategies to learn Korean. I just studied the material provided by the course instructor. For example, when I wrote my last assignment, I went through the PowerPoint presentation slides and handouts shared by the instructor. I also checked the notes I took during the sessions and asked some classmates about vocabulary and grammatical rules I was not sure about. [...] Some friends advised me to watch Korean dramas and listen to K-pop songs but I am busy preparing for other courses at university. (Malika, second interview)

Discussion and Implications

The findings of the present study show that Zarina's investment in learning Korean was somewhat stronger than the other participants, possibly due to the modelling effect of the NPRMs. Dörnyei and Kubanyiova (2014) suggest that NPRMs can help raise individuals' hopes for the future and motivate them to pursue similar excellence in learning and mastering the target language. This is because language learners may attempt to interact and/or emulate their nearest role model's ways to success and can generate a possible future image for themselves. As Bandura (1997) points out, language learners can enhance their language learning beliefs when they observe people who respect and admire their achievement of success. In line with this argument, Wang (2023) conducted a mixed-methods study to explore the role that NPRMs played in constructing 17 English major students' motivation for learning French as a LOTE in China. The study found that the NPRMs inspired most participants to invest their time and efforts in learning French and that their ideal French selves became more emotionally constructed. The NPRMs' success also promoted the participants' awareness that it was unnecessary to evaluate their French learning achievements based on how they appraised their English learning. Wang (2023: 462) concluded her study by emphasising that the NPRMs can support the development of learners' ideal LOTE selves, as 'they reduce participants' uncertainty about the sufficiency of LOTE-using opportunities and their ability to seize those chances'.

In this regard, Dörnyei and Kubanyiova (2014) suggest that language teachers need to adopt specific strategies inside the classroom to foster their students' awareness of the motivational power of NPRMs. For example, language teachers can invite successful speakers of LOTEs from the same school, region or city into the classroom to share their experiences and success stories, and may use the experiences of these successful learners as teaching material (Dörnyei & Kubanyiova, 2014). Language teachers themselves may also share their own language learning experiences of success. Moreover, they can create a platform for sharing students' successful strategies for learning LOTEs, e.g. classroom displays, classroom online blogs and newsletters (i.e. a selection of inspiring extracts from the students' language learning histories). Therefore, more research is needed to explore this relatively under-researched domain – namely, how the NPRMs may impact the development of learners' ideal LOTE and multilingual selves.

While most participants in the present study indicated how they exercised their agency, reporting on the LLSs they adopted to reach their desired goals for learning Korean, the LLSs used by two participants (Nurly and Malika) were largely confined to those mediated by their language instructors and these strategies were not sufficient to transform their vague imaginations of achieving academic and professional gains of learning Korean into concrete ambitions. This finding aligns with Norton's (2013) argument that resistance to investing in language learning tends to be a logical choice if one's access to material and symbolic resources is limited or one's professional achievement is denied. In this regard, Oxford (2017: 189) underlines that making the decision to invest to achieve the state of the ideal self 'logically requires the intelligent selection and implementation of learning strategies'. That is, learners' ideal LOTE and multilingual selves need to be 'accompanied by relevant and effective procedural strategies that act as a roadmap towards the goal', similar to an elite athlete's training plan (Dörnyei & Kubanyiova, 2014: 11); otherwise, one's future vision turns into having 'the character more of fantasy rather than concrete ambition' (Lamb, 2013: 24).

The present study also demonstrates that learning LOTEs helped some participants to develop their intercultural/global citizenship identity by, for example, respecting different opinions (e.g. attitudes towards individuals who have undergone plastic surgery and wear lots of makeup and luxury clothes), understanding some similarities between cultures (e.g. proper filial piety and showing respect to older people), developing tolerance of cultural differences and feeling changed as a person. Further research needs to be conducted to explore language learners' development of intercultural citizenship while learning LOTEs, especially because almost all previous studies on how language learners became more global-minded and interculturally competent have focused on English as the target language and were conducted in study abroad contexts.

Conclusion

This chapter has provided new insights from the experiences of a group of Kazakhstani university students learning Korean as L4 or L5 in Kazakhstan. Special focus was placed on their changing beliefs towards the Korean language and people, and on their investment or disinvestment in learning Korean. Schwieter *et al.* (2021: 135) point out that care must be taken when interpreting participants' experiential accounts because 'first-person accounts may not be complete or fully accurate due to the limitations of memory and other factors (e.g. desire to please the researcher)'. Therefore, the researchers in this study used member checks, that is, they gave the participants transcripts of their interviews to review and asked them if they accurately represented their perceptions and experiences of learning LOTEs. Future studies might use a mixed-methods approach and consider the perceptions and actions of other individuals (e.g. language instructors, family members) who can influence the participants' strategy choices and their endeavours to strengthen their ideal multilingual selves to offer a stronger way of validating the findings obtained from each individual source.

Acknowledgements

This work was supported by the Nazarbayev University Graduate School of Education (grant number 20122022FD4117).

References

Ahn, S.H. (2021) The political and historical implications of Koreans in the former Soviet Union: Their social historic dynamics with Turkic people. *Journal of Asian and African Studies* 56 (8), 1935–1952.

Baker, W. and Fang, F. (2021) 'So maybe I'm a global citizen': Developing intercultural citizenship in English medium education. *Language, Culture and Curriculum* 34 (1), 1–17.

Bandura, A. (1997) *Self-efficacy: The Exercise of Control*. Freeman.

Block, D. (2003) *The Social Turn in Second Language Acquisition*. Edinburgh University Press.

Boo, Z., Dörnyei, Z. and Ryan, S. (2015) L2 motivation research 2005–2014: Understanding a publication surge and a changing landscape. *System* 55, 145–157.

Braun, V. and Clarke, V. (2013) *Successful Qualitative Research: A Practical Guide for Beginners*. Sage.

Chan, W.M. and Chi, S.W. (2010) A study of the learning goals of university students of Korean as a foreign language. *Electronic Journal of Foreign Language Teaching* 7 (1), 125–140.

Choi, J.B. (2015) Hallyu versus Hallyu-hwa. In S. Lee and A.M. Nornes (eds) *Hallyu 2.0: The Korean Wave in the Age of Social Media* (pp. 31–52). University of Michigan Press.

Darvin, R. and Norton, B. (2023) Investment and motivation in language learning: What's the difference? *Language Teaching* 56 (1), 29–40.

Dörnyei, Z. and Kubanyiova, M. (2014) *Motivating Learners, Motivating Teachers: Building Vision in the Language Classroom*. Cambridge University Press.

Dörnyei, Z. and Al-Hoorie, A.H. (2017) The motivational foundation of learning languages other than global English: Theoretical issues and research directions. *The Modern Language Journal* 101 (3), 455–468.

Hajar, A. (2017) Identity, investment and language learning strategies of two Syrian students in Syria and Britain. *Language, Culture and Curriculum* 30 (3), 250–264.

Hajar, A. (2018) Motivated by visions: A tale of a rural learner of English. *The Language Learning Journal* 46 (4), 415–429.

Han, Y. (2023) Motivations for learning Korean in Vietnam: L2 selves and regulatory focus perspectives. *Journal of Language, Identity & Education* 22 (6), 559–573.

Henry, A. (2011) Examining the impact of L2 English on L3 selves: A case study. *International Journal of Multilingualism* 8 (3), 235–255.

Henry, A. (2017) L2 motivation and multilingual identities. *The Modern Language Journal* 101 (3), 548–565.

Hwang, B. (2012) A new horizon in South Korea–Central Asia relations: The ROK joins the 'Great Game'. *Korea Compass*, 1–8.

Ihm, H.B., Hong, K.P. and Chang, S.I. (2004) *Korean Grammar for International Learners*. Yonsei University Press.

Jang, G. and Paik, W.K. (2012) Korean Wave as tool for Korea's new cultural diplomacy. *Advances in Applied Sociology* 2 (3), 196–202.

Kokaisl, P. (2018) Koreans in Central Asia – A different Korean nation. *Asian Ethnicity* 19 (4), 428–452.

Lamb, M. (2013) Your mum and dad can't teach you! Constraints on agency among rural learners of English in Indonesia. *Journal of Multilingual and Multicultural Development* 34 (1), 14–29.

Lantolf, J.P. (2013) Sociocultural theory and L2 learner autonomy/agency. In P. Benson and L. Cooker (eds) *The Applied Linguistic Individual: Sociocultural Approaches to Identity, Agency and Autonomy* (pp. 17–31). Equinox Publishing.

Liao, J., An, N. and Zheng, Y. (2020) What motivates L3 learners' investment and/or divestment in Arabic? Understanding learning motivation in terms of 'identity'. *Círculo de Lingüística Aplicada a la Comunicación* 84, 27–39.

Lu, J., Wang, Y., Shen, Q. and Gao, X. (2022) Investment in learning Chinese by international students studying Chinese as a second language (CSL). *Sustainability* 14 (23), 15664.

Manan, S.A. and Hajar, A. (2022) 'Disinvestment' in learners' multilingual identities: English learning, imagined identities, and neoliberal subjecthood in Pakistan. *Journal of Language, Identity & Education*, 1–16.

Murphey, T. (1998) Motivating with near peer role models. In B. Visgatis (ed.) *The Proceedings of the JALT 23rd Annual International Conference on Language Teaching and Learning* (pp. 205–209). Japan Association for Language Teaching.

Norton, B. (2013) *Identity and Language Learning: Extending the Conversation* (2nd edn). Multilingual Matters.

Nourzadeh, S., Fathi, J. and Davari, H. (2023) An examination of Iranian learners' motivation for and experience in learning Korean as an additional language. *International Journal of Multilingualism* 20 (2), 115–129.

Oxford, R. (2017) *Teaching and Researching Language Learning Strategies: Self-Regulation in Context* (2nd edn). Routledge

Oxford, R.L. and Schramm, K. (2007) Bridging the gap between psychological and sociocultural perspectives on L2 learner strategies. In A.D. Cohen and E. Macaro (eds) *Language Learner Strategies: Thirty Years of Research and Practice* (pp. 47–68). Oxford University Press.

Rabbidge, M. and Zaheeb, A.S. (2022) The cost of change: How ideological shifts impact Afghans' investment in learning English. *TESOL Quarterly* 57 (4), 1041–1065.

Schwieter, J.W., Jackson, J. and Ferreira, A. (2021) When 'domestic' and 'international' students study abroad: Reflections on language learning, contact, and culture. *International Journal of Bilingual Education and Bilingualism* 24 (1), 124–137.

Sharif, S. and Channa, L.A. (2022) Lived narratives: Female investment and identity negotiation in learning English in rural Pakistan. *Linguistics and Education* 72, 101119.

Takahashi, C. (2023) *Motivation to Learn Multiple Languages in Japan: A Longitudinal Perspective*. Multilingual Matters.

Ushioda, E. (2017) The impact of global English on motivation to learn other languages: Toward an ideal multilingual self. *The Modern Language Journal* 101 (3), 469–482.

Ushioda, E. (2020) *Language Learning Motivation*. Oxford University Press.

Ushioda, E. and Dörnyei, Z. (2017) Beyond global English: Motivation to learn languages in a multicultural world: Introduction to the special issue. *The Modern Language Journal* 101 (3), 451–454.

Wang, T. (2023) An exploratory motivational intervention on the construction of Chinese undergraduates' ideal LOTE and multilingual selves: The role of near peer role modeling. *Language Teaching Research* 27 (2), 441–465.

Yem, N. and Epstein, S.J. (2015) Social change and marriage patterns among Koryo Saram in Kazakhstan, 1937–1965. *Seoul Journal of Korean Studies* 28 (2), 133–152.

8 Indonesian Students' Mental Images of Portugal and their L2 Motivation

Raan Hann Tan and Larisa Nikitina

Introduction

The Portuguese language and its local varieties are spoken by 258 million people, which makes it the ninth most widely spoken language in the world (Eberhard *et al.*, 2022). Portuguese has deep historical and cultural links with Asia that go back to the 16th century. Portuguese once served as the lingua franca of maritime Asia. Consequently, Portuguese-based creoles developed in the region, including in Malacca, Batavia (present-day Jakarta, Indonesia), Sri Lanka, India and Macau. Even though most Portuguese creoles are perilously endangered nowadays, there remain traces of Portuguese language influence in the lexicons of the Malay and Indonesian languages. For example, the Malay language has 300–400 Portuguese loan words. Many more can be found in the Indonesian language or Bahasa Indonesia, since the Portuguese presence was not limited to the islands – the Moluccas, Ambon, Makassar, Solor, Banda – but it was also strong in Batavia where speakers of creoles Portuguese from Melaka and Ceylon migrated after the Dutch conquest (Baxter, 1995). Another example of cross-cultural pollination is the popular Indonesian music style known as *keroncong*, which has elements derived from the Portuguese music of the 16th and 17th centuries (Yampolsky, 2010: 7).

In more recent times, Portugal established a Representative Office in Indonesia in 1950. However, diplomatic relations between the two countries were severed in 1975 due to the conflict in East Timor. East Timor became the 27th province of Indonesia in 1976 and Bahasa Indonesia became the official language. In December 1999, diplomatic relations between Indonesia and Portugal were restored and, in 2002, the Timor-Leste government proclaimed Portuguese to be an official language, alongside Bahasa Tetun, the dominant local vernacular. Following these developments in politics, bilingual dictionaries and reference books were published, among which is the *Kamus Melayu-Indonesia Portugis* (Malay Indonesian Portuguese Dictionary), aimed at assisting young East Timorese to learn Portuguese (Hull, 2012). Several other published volumes target speakers and learners of Portuguese in Indonesia, Malaysia, Singapore and Brunei and also learners of Malay and Indonesian in Portuguese-speaking countries. Prominent examples are *Bahasa Portugis Sehari-hari* (Everyday Portuguese) (Araujo, 2014) and *Kamus Portugis Indonesia* (Portuguese Indonesian Dictionary) (Manhitu, 2015).

Despite the deep cultural and historical roots outlined above, the Portuguese language is not widely taught in Indonesia. A Portuguese course was offered at the private Catholic University of Atma Jaya in 2000 but has since been discontinued. Currently, the Universitas Indonesia (UI) is the only university in the country to offer Portuguese as a foreign language and does so in the Faculty of Human Sciences. The course was launched in 2004.

Generally, as far as the research literature is concerned, explorations of aspects pertaining to the teaching and learning of Portuguese are scarce compared to studies concerning other European languages such as German, French and Spanish. The current exploratory study addressed this gap. The study is part of a larger research project on the teaching and learning of Portuguese in Indonesia and Malaysia. To the best of our knowledge, it is the first scholarly investigation of Indonesian learners of the Portuguese language.

This empirical study on Indonesian learners of Portuguese aimed to explore the language learners' mental images of Portugal and to assess their motivation to learn Portuguese (L2 motivation). The next section provides a brief review of earlier scholarly studies of Portuguese language learners' images of countries and cultures where Portuguese is spoken and their motivations for learning this language. In addition, it states the research questions that guided this study.

Literature Review

Learners' mental images of Portuguese in Portuguese-speaking countries

Available studies that focus on learners of the Portuguese language are comparatively scarce. Nevertheless, those that do exist have addressed a variety of pertinent issues, including learner motivation (Bateman & Oliveira, 2014; Kelm 2002, 2018). Only a handful of earlier studies have explored Portuguese learners' mental images or stereotypes of countries where the target language is spoken (Nikitina,

2016; Nikitina *et al.*, 2014, 2022). Nikitina (2016) investigated the mental images of Portugal held by Malaysian learners of European Portuguese in a public university. The images formed 11 categories: 'football', 'culture', 'language', 'people', 'food', 'Portuguese dance and music', 'former colonial power', 'beautiful country', 'obscure country', 'European country' and 'weather' (Nikitina, 2016: 867). Football star, Cristiano Ronaldo, was the most frequently mentioned image and, overall, the students held positive attitudes to Portugal.

In another study, Nikitina *et al.* (2014) examined mental images held by Malaysian learners of the Brazilian variety of Portuguese. The images shared by the students formed 14 categories|: 'football and sporting events', 'beach and ocean', 'culture and arts', 'cities and sites', 'travel destination', 'national flag', 'food', 'nature and scenery', 'people', 'festivals and dance', 'country size and geographical location', 'crime', 'economy' and 'language' (Nikitina *et al.*, 2014: 79). The ratings the students gave their images indicated predominantly positive attitudes towards the target language country, Brazil.

A more recent study by Nikitina *et al.* (2022) collected data from 91 Malaysian learners at two public universities. The 128 images of Portugal provided by the students were divided into 10 categories: 'people', 'food', 'football and sports', 'cities, places, sites, scenery', 'culture', 'history', 'cultural impact', 'language', 'country descriptions' and 'tourism' (Nikitina *et al.*, 2022: 151). Among the images mentioned by more than one student were 'Cristiano Ronaldo', 'football', 'egg tart', 'Lisbon', 'colonization', 'architecture', 'food', 'culture', 'Alfonso de Albuquerque' and 'language spoken in other parts of the world'. The findings also revealed that the language learners held overall positive attitudes towards Portugal, as indicated by a relatively high composite mean valence of the images of Portugal (CMV = 0.989).

Studies of Portuguese language learners' goals and L2 motivation

Research into the motivational drivers of learners of Portuguese is scarce compared to learners of languages other than English (LOTE). For the most part, these studies have been conducted in American universities. Kelm (2002, 2018) explored language learners' reasons for choosing Portuguese and discovered that the students wanted to acquire Portuguese for various reasons, including for academic purposes, for future work or doing business in Portuguese-speaking countries. Many of the respondents were keen to learn Portuguese because they had significant others who were native speakers of the language. Some students stated they were attracted by the target language cultures. Notably, very few respondents mentioned the university's foreign language requirement as a reason for following their Portuguese language course.

While the studies by Kelm (2002, 2018) were not anchored in any particular theoretical framework, Bateman and Oliveira (2014) adopted a broad framework of L2 motivation from Csizér and Dörnyei's (2005) study. Bateman and Oliveira conducted a survey of American undergraduates' motivation and preferences when learning foreign languages, including Portuguese. They discovered that, for the most part, the students were motivated by various pragmatic considerations, including their future career plans, and also by family members (e.g. spouses and parents) and friends who were native speakers of Portuguese. Some respondents decided to learn Portuguese because of its similarities with Spanish. Several students mentioned affective or emotional factors: they considered Portuguese a beautiful and interesting language and wished to communicate with people in Portuguese-speaking countries. Similar to the findings reported by Kelm, very few respondents in Bateman and Oliveira's study chose Portuguese in order to fulfil university requirements. At the same time, a very small percentage of Portuguese learners mentioned their interest in the target language culture. The researchers pointed out that this did not necessarily indicate a lack of interest in culture; rather, it reflected the educational priorities of this particular cohort of students.

Interesting and useful insights into Portuguese language learners' motivation come from Sommer-Farias *et al.*'s 2020 study. The respondents mentioned their wish to be able to communicate fluently in Portuguese when travelling in Portuguese-speaking countries and read and write everyday texts, such as emails and social media, as well as read scholarly literature. The students also wished to learn more about the culture and history of Portuguese-speaking countries to better appreciate various cultural products, such as popular songs.

As this review of the literature indicates, for the most part, exploration of the L2 motivation of learners of Portuguese has been qualitative and without any underlying formal theory of motivation. Taking a different approach, Nikitina (2019) adopted Gardner's socio-educational theory. In her study of learners of European and Brazilian Portuguese, she operationalized L2 motivation as consisting of instrumental orientation (i.e. a range of pragmatic reasons) and integrative orientation (i.e. cultural interest and the desire to communicate with native speakers of the target language). Nikitina's findings indicated a statistically significant positive relationship between the students' mental images of the target language countries (i.e. Portugal and Brazil) and their L2 motivation. The strongest links were found to exist between these images and integrative orientation. Against such a background, this study raised the following research questions:

(1) What mental images do Indonesian students have of Portugal? What categories do these images form?

(2) What are the main features of these categories?
(3) What is the nature of the students' motivation to learn Portuguese? Is there a relationship between the attitudes embedded in the mental images of Portugal and the students' L2 motivation?
(4) Why did the students decide to learn Portuguese?

The following section explains the methodology adopted in this study.

Methodology

Study context and participants

This study was conducted with undergraduate students who learned Portuguese at the Universitas Indonesia, the only university in Indonesia to offer Portuguese language courses. The university signed an agreement of cooperation with the Camões Institute, Portugal, so the language instructor is a native speaker of Portuguese from Portugal. One course focuses on Portuguese culture, while the other is geared towards Portuguese history. Both are elective courses, intended primarily for students majoring in linguistics and literature, but they are open to students from other faculties. The classes are three hours in duration per week, using the bilingual (Bahasa Indonesia and Portuguese) method. The teaching manual was developed by a teacher of Portuguese. Students are assessed on their video essays and classroom presentations.

Forty-eight ($N = 48$) students between 19 and 23 years of age (Mean, $M = 20.85$; Standard Deviation, $SD = 0.91$) took part in this study, the majority being female ($n = 41$ or 85.4%). The participants were majoring in various social sciences and humanities disciplines, such as communication studies, Russian literature, English literature, French literature and Chinese literature. All the students were multilingual. Besides the national language, Bahasa Indonesia, they could speak one or more local languages (e.g. Javanese, Minangkabau) and had previously learned at least one foreign language (e.g. Arabic, English, French, German or Russian). Participation in the study was on a voluntary basis. The questionnaire contained a statement that answering and submitting the questionnaire online implied the students' consent to participate in the survey.

Research instrument

A parallel mixed-methods research design (QUAL+QUAN) was used to gather and analyse the data. To be more specific, the qualitative data on the students' mental images were gathered simultaneously with the quantitative data on the rankings of these images. Furthermore, the QUAL and QUAN analytical procedures were intertwined and enmeshed throughout the study. The questionnaire used in this study was adapted from Nikitina (2020) and translated into Indonesian. The instrument had two open-ended and 24 closed-ended items measuring L2 motivation. One open-ended question asked: 'What images or mental pictures come to mind when you hear the words "Portugal" and "Portuguese"?'. The respondents were asked to give a rating from –2 to +2 for each image they wrote. Thus, qualitative data (i.e. the students' mental images) and quantitative data (the ratings given to the images) were collected simultaneously. These ratings allowed the attitudes embedded in the students' images of Portugal to be measured. The other open-ended question was: 'Why are you learning Portuguese?'.

The questionnaire contained three key measures from the Gardnerian model of L2 motivation (Gardner, 1985a, 1985b; Gardner & Lambert, 1972). The model is premised on the fact that motivation is goal-directed behavior, and that effort is required to achieve one's goals (Gardner *et al.*, 1978). It also recognizes the role of numerous external and internal factors that might influence motivated behaviour. Based on these main tenets, the questionnaire in this study had three measures of L2 motivation, namely:

(1) General motivation (9 statements) assessed key aspects inherent in motivated behaviour, such as effort and perseverance. Higher scores indicated a higher degree of determination and greater effort that the students were willing to expend to learn Portuguese.
(2) Instrumental orientation (7 items) related to pragmatic goals for learning Portuguese. Higher scores suggested a greater desire to learn Portuguese for practical benefits, such as fulfilling university requirements or financial reasons.
(3) Integrative orientation (8 items) evaluated the importance of learning Portuguese in order to enable social interactions with the speakers of Portuguese and to enhance one's cultural knowledge and aptitude. Higher scores indicated a stronger aim to learn Portuguese to communicate with native speakers of Portuguese in various parts of the world, including their own country, to have a better knowledge of the target cultures and ways of life in Portugal and Portuguese-speaking countries.

The language learners' motivation to learn Portuguese was assessed from their responses to the 24 questionnaire statements (see Table 8.2) on a 5-point Likert-type scale that ranged from 'strongly disagree' to 'strongly agree' as a choice for answers. The statements were adapted from a number of questionnaires on L2 motivation (Gardner, 1985b; Nikitina, 2019; Nikitina *et al.*, 2022). One section of the questionnaire gathered information on the demographic and linguistic backgrounds of the participants.

Data collection and management

The data were collected in November 2021 via the Google Forms platform. To observe research ethics, a statement on implicit consent to participate in this study was included in the research instrument (i.e. 'Answering this questionnaire means that you agree to take part in this survey'). A link to the questionnaire was sent to the students. The total number of students in this class was 66. Of these, 48 students responded to the questionnaire. The purpose of the study was explained in the introductory section of the questionnaire.

The Excel files with raw data generated by Google Forms were downloaded to the researcher's personal computer and cleaned using OpenRefine. During this stage, the answers were translated from Indonesian into English by the researchers, who both know Indonesian.

Data analysis

This mixed-methods study used qualitative and quantitative approaches to analyse the data. Qualitative content analysis (Krippendorff, 2013) was used to analyze the data from the open-ended items in the questionnaire in order to answer research questions (RQs) #1 and #4. Specifically, the students' responses to each open-ended question (i.e. their images of Portugal and reasons for learning Portuguese) were compared for similarity and then placed in categories on a data-driven basis; no categories were established *a priori*.

The difference between 'item' and 'image' terms of reference needs to be stated clearly: 'item' refers to the images used by the students; 'image' refers to the different images identified during the qualitative data analysis. For instance, 'Lisbon', 'the city of Lisbon' and 'Lisbon, the capital' were identified as different descriptive phrases (items) all referring to the same, single image 'Lisbon'. Hence, the number of 'images' was smaller than the number of 'items'.

Next, to answer RQ #2 and identify the main features of the categories for images of Portugal, we calculated the salience and favourability (i.e. mean valence) of the categories of mental images of Portugal formed during the context analysis. Salience refers to the importance or prominence of a category of images. This concept was assessed using ANTHROPAC 4.0 software (Borgatti, 1996). The software computes the Modified Free-List Salience (MFLS) Index (Smith *et al.*, 1995), which considers both the frequency and the position of the images in the lists. This means that categories with higher salience indices (the highest value is 1) contained images mentioned more often by the respondents, images that came more readily to their collective mind and so were placed higher in their lists. The positive/negative/neutral attitudes embedded in these images were assessed using the ratings from –2 to +2 that the students assigned to each image. Their attitude responses were computed to give the mean value (MV) of the ratings awarded to all the images in one category. We also calculated the composite mean valence (CMV) or the level of favourability of all the images of Portugal given by the students.

The reliability of the qualitative content analysis was checked using 'intracoder reliability' (Van den Hoonaard, 2008: 445). Two weeks after the initial analysis, the same researcher re-analysed a portion of the data and calculated the agreement rate between the two analyses. The reliability rate was 95%, exceeding the recommended 80–90% level (Loewen & Plonsky, 2015).

The quantitative part of the study used descriptive and inferential statistics to answer RQ #3. The descriptive statistics explored the nature of the students' L2 motivation while the inferential statistics assessed whether the attitudes embedded in the students' mental images of Portugal were associated in a statistically significantly way with the students' L2 reasons for learning Portuguese. Due to the small sample size ($N = 48$), which undermined the normality of the data and the presence of outliers, we opted for a robust statistical procedure. This study performed a one-tailed bootstrapped Pearson's correlation test with 1000 bootstrap samples. The analysis was conducted using SPSS software version 27.

Findings

Students' mental images of Portugal

In total, the students listed 179 descriptive phrases and words as their images of Portugal. The shortest list had only one image, while the longest had 13 images. On average there were 4.38 items per student list and the mode was 4. Figure 8.1 presents a word cloud of the images of Portugal that the students shared with us. The word cloud was generated by LIWC-22 software (Pennebaker et al., 2022).

The most frequently mentioned distinct images (indicated as f_i) were 'Lisbon' ($f_i = 16$), 'football' ($f_i = 13$), 'Cristiano Ronaldo' ($f_i = 10$), 'colonialism' ($f_i = 5$), 'Luis de Camoes' ($f_i = 5$), 'Vasco da Gama' ($f_i = 5$), 'pasteis de nata' ($f_i = 5$), 'food' ($f_i = 4$) and 'obrigada' ($f_i = 4$). Next, 10 distinct categories of images of Portugal were identified (see Table 8.1), excluding the category 'Miscellaneous' which had 6 items that could not be placed in any other category. However, this category was included to assess the composite mean valence (CMV) of the images of Portugal.

As shown in Table 8.1, the category with the highest mean valence (MV) value was 'Culture and Arts' (MV = 1.73). Besides being one of the biggest image clusters ($f_i = 22$) it had the highest salience index (SI = 0.236). This category contained references to 'Portuguese music',

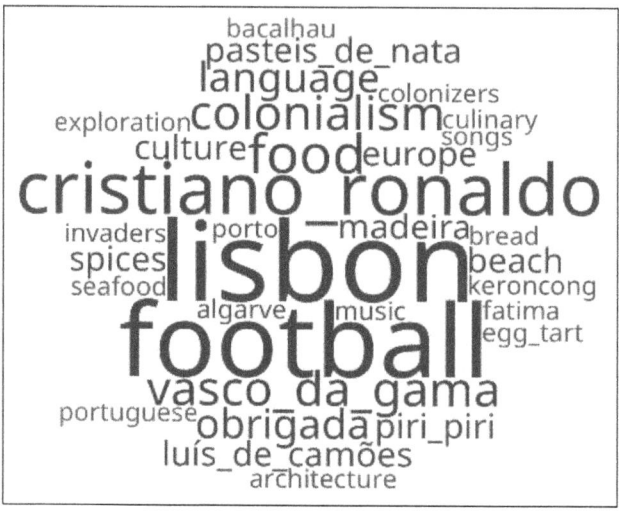

Figure 8.1 Students' images of Portugal

Table 8.1 Categories of images, their favourability (MV) and salience (SI)

Category	f_i	MV	SI
Culture and arts	22	1.73	0.236
Religion	3	1.67	0.024
Geography and sites	16	1.63	0.373
People	26	1.46	0.184
Football	9	1.44	0.257
Food	44	1.41	0.355
European country	5	1.40	0.067
Festivals and events	5	1.20	0.032
Language	23	1.17	0.147
Colonial past and history	20	0.15	0.181

Note: f_i = number of items in the category; MV = mean valence; SI = salience index.

'Portuguese songs', 'Portuguese viola' (a string instrument similar to a guitar), '*fado*' (a form of song with a traditional structure), '*keroncong* music' (a form of Indonesian music influenced by a Portuguese musical style), 'architecture', 'old buildings' and 'musical instruments'. Two students mentioned 'Azulejo tiles' (painted and tin-glazed ceramic tilework) and 'Portuguese traditional clothing'. For the most part, these images received the highest rating: +2. They also tended to be placed high in the students' lists, as indicated by the category's high cognitive salience index rating of 0.236.

The second highly favorable category was 'Religion' (MV = 1.67). However, it was also the smallest group of images (f_i = 3) and with the least salience (SI = 0.024). The category contained the images 'Catholic' and 'Our Lady of Fatima', which received positive ratings of +2 and +1.

The third category, according to the favorability of its images, was 'Geography and sites' (MV = 1.63). It also had the highest salience index (SI = 0.373), which means that its 16 images tended to be placed at the top or very near the top of the students' lists. The image 'Lisbon' was most frequently mentioned (f_i = 5), followed by references to 'beaches', 'the Algarve region' (a southernmost region in Portugal famous for its beaches), 'Madeira', 'beautiful places', 'Minho' (a region in Portugal) and 'ocean'. Only one student gave a neutral, 0, rating to the image 'Lisbon'. All other images were rated positively +2 and +1.

The category 'People' (MV = 1.46) was formed with references to famous football players Cristiano Ronaldo, Luís Figo, Nuno Gomes, and by reference to great cultural and historical figures like Luís de Camões (the greatest Portuguese poet of the 16th century), Vasco da Gama and Afonso de Albuquerque. The category also had more general images, such as 'sea explorers', 'conquistadors', 'football players', 'Caucasians' and 'Portuguese people'. The images in the 'People' category were not only positive for the most part (with a few neutral ratings): they were also quickly recalled and placed higher in the students' lists, which is indicated by this category's salience index (SI = 0.184).

The next category, Football, (MV = 1.44) was dominated by the image 'football', mentioned six times. Other images were 'FC Porto' (mentioned by two respondents) and 'Portugal national football team'. These images were mostly rated +2 and +1.

'Food' (MV = 1.41) was the biggest category (f_i = 44) and the second most salient (SI = 0.355) group of images. Some images were mentioned by several students; for example, *'bacalhau'* ('cod' in Portuguese, which can also refer to 'dried and salted cod'), *'pasteis de nata'* (the English equivalent of 'egg tart'), *'piri-piri* chicken', 'chestnuts' and 'spices'. General references to 'food', 'seafood', 'bread' and 'cuisine' were less frequent. The images mentioned only once were 'coffee', 'cheese', 'mackerel', 'sardine', 'lamprey fish', 'street food', 'tea' and *'bolo rei'* ('King Cake' in English). Most of the images in this category were given positive ratings +2 and +1; only three students gave negative ratings to their 'spices' and 'lamprey fish' images.

The next category, 'European country' (MV = 1.40), contained references to Portugal's location in Europe. The students mentioned 'Europe' and 'a developed European country'. Although the perceptions of the target language country were favorable, this category was small (f_i = 5) and it had low salience (SI = 0.067).

Similarly, the next category 'Festivals and events' (MV = 1.20) had only five images (f_i = 5), some being rather general in nature (e.g. 'Portuguese festivals') and others more concrete (e.g. 'Portugal National Horse Fair' and 'Portuguese Grand Prix'). Although these images were positively evaluated by the respondents, the students tended to write them as afterthoughts, as reflected by the lowest salience index (SI = 0.032) of this category.

The category 'Language' (MV = 1.17) contained various Portuguese words and phrases. There were the greetings such as *'Bom dia'* ('Good morning'), *'Boa tarde'* ('Good afternoon'), *'Boa noite'* ('Good evening' or 'Good night') and also *'obrigada/o'* ('Thank you'), as well an odd assortment of words (e.g. *'segurada'* meaning 'insured' and *'listras'* meaning 'stripes').

Finally, the least favorable category, 'Colonial past and history' (MV = 0.15)' contained the images 'colonialism', 'colonized Indonesia' and 'invaders', all with negative ratings of −2 and −1. However, some images in this cluster were rated positively, like 'exploration', 'big exploration', 'history' and 'rose revolution'. The latter is erroneous – probably the 'carnation revolution' in Portugal in 1974 was the intended reference.

Overall, the students had positive attitudes to the target language country, as indicated by the composite mean valence value (CMV = 1.326) of all the images of Portugal. The next step of the analysis assessed whether these positive attitudes had statistically significant associations with the language learners' L2 motivation.

Students' L2 motivation

Findings from the descriptive statistics

Table 8.2 presents the descriptive statistics of the students' responses to the closed-ended questionnaire items to assess the nature of the language learners' L2 motivation. As Table 8.2 shows, not all items received equally strong endorsement. The strongest agreement was with the statements 'Knowledge of the Portuguese language will give me some advantages in future' (M = 4.10; SD = 0.51), 'Knowledge of the Portuguese language will help me when I travel abroad' (M = 3.98; SD = 0.56), 'I learn the Portuguese language because this will enable me to know the way of life in various countries where Portuguese is spoken' (M = 3.96; SD = 0.54) and 'I learn the Portuguese language because I am interested in Portuguese culture' (M = 3.94; SD = 0.66). The mean values of these statements exceeded or closely approached 4.0, while the standard deviation values indicated fairly minor discrepancies in the students' opinions.

The statements that had less support and mean values less than 3.0 were 'I always volunteer to answer questions my Portuguese language instructor asks in class' (M = 2.98; SD = 0.69), 'If my Portuguese language instructor wanted someone to do an optional assignment for the class, I would certainly volunteer' (M = 2.92; SD = 0.70), 'Knowledge of the Portuguese language is important because Portuguese is spoken by some people in my country' (M = 2.75; SD = 0.90) and 'If the Portuguese

Table 8.2 Findings concerning language learners' L2 motivation

L2 Dimension	Questionnaire items**	Mean	SD***
General motivation ($\alpha = 0.674$)*	I am working hard at learning the Portuguese language.	3.69	0.62
	If my Portuguese language instructor wanted someone to do an optional assignment for the class, I would certainly volunteer.	2.92	0.70
	I would rather spend my time on subjects other than Portuguese.	3.06	0.56
	After I complete the current level of the Portuguese language program I wish to continue learning Portuguese to a more advanced level.	3.23	0.77
	I always volunteer to answer questions my Portuguese language instructor asks in class.	2.98	0.69
	If the Portuguese language was not offered in my university I would try to find Portuguese language classes somewhere else.	2.67	0.66
	I like learning Portuguese very much.	3.75	0.52
	I seldom do more than the minimum in my Portuguese classes.	3.36	0.80
	I would like to spend lots of time learning Portuguese	3.15	0.68
Instrumental orientation ($\alpha = .678$)	I am taking the Portuguese language course only to fulfil university requirements.	3.08	1.11
	Knowledge of the Portuguese language will help me to find a job.	3.27	0.76
	Knowledge of the Portuguese language will bring me financial benefits (e.g. translation work, being a tour guide etc.).	3.42	0.93
	Knowledge of the Portuguese language can be useful for my further studies, such as at Master's or PhD level.	3.5	0.84
	Knowledge of the Portuguese language will give me some advantages in future.	4.10	0.51
	Knowledge of the Portuguese language will help me when I travel abroad.	3.98	0.56
	Knowledge of the Portuguese language will be useful for my future career.	3.63	0.75
Integrative orientation ($\alpha = .691$)	I learn the Portuguese language because I am interested in Portuguese culture.	3.94	0.66
	I learn the Portuguese language because it will enable me to better understand the way of life in Portugal.	3.73	0.73
	I learn the Portuguese language because this will enable me to find out about the way of life in various countries where Portuguese is spoken.	3.96	0.54
	I learn the Portuguese language so that I can get to know its speakers and their cultures better.	3.85	0.50
	Knowledge of the Portuguese language is important to me because I am very interested in the values and cultures of people who speak Portuguese.	3.81	0.67
	Knowledge of the Portuguese language is important to me because I would like to make friends with foreigners.	3.67	0.72
	Knowledge of the Portuguese language is important because it will enable me to get to know new people from different parts of the world.	3.79	0.58
	Knowledge of the Portuguese language is important because Portuguese is spoken by some people in my country.	2.75	0.90

Note: *α stands for Cronbach's alpha; ** the items were presented in random order in the actual questionnaire; *** SD refers to standard deviation.

language was not offered in my university I would try to find Portuguese language classes somewhere else' (M = 2.67; SD = 0.66). As the standard deviation values indicate, there was a greater dispersion in the student opinions about these statements.

The next step examined the relationship between the attitudes embedded in the students' images of Portugal and their L2 motivation.

Relationships between the students' attitudes toward Portugal and their L2 motivation

We also wanted to know whether the attitudes embedded in the language learners' images of Portugal had any statistical associations with their L2 motivation to learn Portuguese. As explained in the section 'Research instrument', L2 motivation in this study was measured by three variables – namely, general motivation, instrumental orientation and integrative orientation.

The findings from the one-tailed bootstrapped Pearson's correlation test with 1000 bootstrap samples indicated that the students' attitudes toward Portugal had a statistically significant positive linear association only with integrative orientation (95% CI: .019, .604, $r = .370$). In other words, when the students had more positive attitudes to Portugal they also had a greater motivation to learn Portuguese in order to know the target culture, to communicate with speakers of Portuguese and to better understand their ways of life. The other two variables – general motivation (95% CI: −.079, .489, $r = .231$) and instrumental orientation (95% CI: −.045, .504, $r = .230$) – had positive but not statistically significant relationships with attitudes to Portugal.

To understand the language learners' underlying motives better, their responses to the open-ended questions that sought to find out, in the students' own words, why they had decided to learn Portuguese, were analyzed. The findings are reported in the next section.

Reasons for learning Portuguese

As the next step, we analysed the students' answers to the open-ended question 'Why are you learning Portuguese?'. Their responses were analysed by content analysis. The findings are presented in Table 8.3. As several students gave more than one reason, the total number of responses (f_m) was greater than the number of students.

The most frequently cited reason was 'Interest' ($f_m = 23$). While some students simply stated that it was 'interesting' to learn Portuguese, others gave more specific answers. They cited their interest in the culture(s) of the target language country, in varieties of Portuguese language and how Portuguese people live. Desire 'to know more languages' ($f_m = 10$) was the second most often given reason; some students stated they

Table 8.3 Reasons for learning Portuguese

Category	f_m
Interest	23
To know more languages	10
To fulfil university requirements	7
Cultural interest	6
Like learning foreign languages	3
Future career and work	2
Other	4

Note: f_m = number of responses in the category.

wanted to know world languages other than English. A slightly lower frequency (f_m = 7) was the need to fulfil 'university requirements'. It was followed by the category 'Cultural interest' (f_m = 6), where some students cited their love of Portuguese songs, music and their interest in Brazilian TV dramas. Several responses (f_m = 3) came under the heading 'Like learning foreign languages' and two responses revealed that the students considered knowledge of Portuguese useful for their 'Future careers and work' (f_m = 2). The category 'Other' (f_m = 4) contained the answers 'I want to communicate with speakers of Portuguese', 'I learned Spanish before and decided to learn Portuguese because of similarities between the languages', 'Because of Cristiano Ronaldo. I am interested in football' and 'I plan to study in Europe or England'.

Discussion and Pedagogical Implications

The findings revealed that the Indonesian learners of Portuguese had a diverse set of mental images of the target language country. Besides ubiquitous references to Cristiano Ronaldo (Nikitina, 2016; Nikitina *et al.*, 2014, 2022) they mentioned historical and cultural figures, such as Luís de Camões and Vasco da Gama. The students were also aware of the cultural influence of Portugal. Like their Malaysian peers, the participants in this study acknowledged the linguistic impact of Portuguese on the Indonesian language; they were also aware of Portugal's impact on other spheres of culture and art (e.g. *keroncong* music). Overall, there were no great differences in the mental imagery of Portugal of the students in Indonesia and Malaysia. Moreover, the students in these two countries had a positive attitude to Portugal, although the Indonesian language learners in this study viewed Portugal in a slightly more positive light (CMV = 1.326) than their Malaysian peers (CMV = 0.989).

Regarding the reasons and motivations for learning Portuguese, the participants in this study provided a narrower range of answers. The predominant reason for learning Portuguese was personal interest, while the Malaysian students were overwhelmingly driven by a desire to expand their knowledge (Nikitina et al., 2022). However, there were many similarities as well. For example, the language learners in both countries said they liked learning new languages and realized that knowledge of Portuguese could benefit their future careers. Furthermore, the statistical analyses indicated statistically significant positive associations between the Indonesian students' mental images of Portugal and their desire to learn Portuguese to enhance their knowledge of Portugal.

The pedagogical implications are that various classroom activities could incorporate the language learners' images of Portugal – for example, a lighthearted quiz to discover the students' perceptions and knowledge of any target language country, its people and cultures, and also to make them aware of the gaps in their knowledge. The quiz could ask: 'Who is the most famous Portuguese person in the world?' and 'What kind of music has its roots in traditional Portuguese music?'.

Since an important objective of the Portuguese language courses at Universitas Indonesia is to introduce a European culture that has had a deep impact on Indonesian history, the students might benefit from background information about historical figures and events with links to the Indonesian archipelago. Language learners could be introduced in class to poems by the revered Portuguese poet, Luís de Camões, and may be interested in learning about the devoted friendship between Camões and António, a Javanese Christian, also known as Jau. Camões and António probably met in 1565, in the aftermath of a shipwreck in Cambodia while Camões was waiting for a ship to take him to India. According to some accounts, António cared for Camões until he himself died in 1580, a few months before Camões' death. The students could be asked to create imaginary dialogues between António and Camões to practise new vocabulary and grammar (for example, tenses). Another activity might centre on reading *Os Lusíadas*, the epic poem by Camões that mentions some islands in Indonesia, including Ternate and Tidore. The poem also contains references to the 'spicy cloves' found in the archipelago. Such historical facts and cultural insights can be used as stepping stones to the students' own explorations of shared Portuguese and Indonesian history and the cultural cross-pollination that has enriched both cultures.

Conclusion

Exploring mental images of a target language country enables the elucidation of conceptions – and misconceptions – about the country, its cultures and its people, that language learners bring to the language classroom. Stereotypes of other countries and cultures are deeply rooted notions about the world around us, which we absorb unconsciously from early years in life. Language learners' mental images of other countries do not necessarily reflect their actual knowledge. Instead – and importantly – they are saturated with deeply seated attitudes, such as the potent 'likes' and 'dislikes', which have an impact on the students' choice of a foreign language to learn and their learning goals or L2 motivations. This study has provided additional empirical evidence in support of earlier studies that postulate such claims (Nikitina, 2019; Nikitina et al., 2022).

Language educators, besides imparting linguistic skills, have another important mission, which is to deepen the cultural knowledge of their students and enhance their intercultural communication skills. Exploring stereotypes of a target language country in the form of the mental images that language learners spontaneously recall and proceeding to analyze these images systematically, as described in this study, can help language educators to make better informed decisions about the cultural content of a language program and to design appropriate classroom activities. Empirically-rooted pedagogical decisions will help to address the students' educational needs and enhance their L2 motivation. To conclude, although the current study was conducted in the context of learning Portuguese, it is hoped that its methods of discovery and empirical findings may have some implications for language pedagogy and the teaching of foreign languages.

Acknowledgements

This study was supported by the Research University Grant (Code: GUP-2020-070) from the Universiti Kebangsaan Malaysia (UKM). The authors are grateful to Dr Filipe Delfim Santos for his help with collecting the data and for sharing insights regarding the teaching of Portuguese.

References

Araujo, B.D. (2014) *Bahasa Portugis Sehari-hari*. Kesaint Blanc Publishing.
Bateman, B.E. and de Almeida Oliveira, D. (2014) Students' motivations for choosing (or not) to study Portuguese: A survey of beginning-level university classes. *Hispania* 92 (2), 264–280.
Baxter, A.N. (1995) The linguistics reflexes of the historical connection between the Malay and Portuguese language in the Malay world. In G. Fernandis (ed.) *Save Our Portuguese Heritage Conference 95* (pp. 40–64). Published by Gerard Fernandis.
Borgatti, S.P. (1996) ANTHROPAC 4.0. Analytic Technologies.
Csizér, K. and Dörnyei, Z. (2005) The internal structure of language learning motivation and its relationship with language choice and learning effort. *Modern Language Journal* 89 (1), 19–36.
Eberhard, D.M., Simons, G.F. and Fennig, C.D. (eds) (2022) *Ethnologue: Languages of the World* (25th edn). SIL International. Online version: http://www.ethnologue.com.
Gardner, R.C. (1985a) *Social Psychology and Second Language Learning: The Role of Attitudes and Motivation*. Edward Arnold.

Gardner, R.C. (1985b) The Attitude/Motivation Test Battery: Technical report *(1985)*. Accessed 1 March 2020. Available at https://publish.uwo.ca/~gardner/docs/AMTBmanual.pdf.

Gardner, R.C. and Lambert, W.E. (1972) *Attitudes and Motivation in Second-Language Learning*. Newbury House Publishers.

Gardner, R.C., Gliksman, L. and Smythe, P.C. (1978) Attitudes and behaviour in second language acquisition: A social psychological interpretation. *Canadian Psychological Review/Psychologie Canadienne* 19 (3), 173–186.

Hull, G. (2012) *Kamus Melayu–Indonesia Portugis. Dictionário de Malaio de Indonésio–Português*. Lidel.

Kelm, O.R. (2002) Opportunities in teaching Portuguese for special purposes: Business Portuguese. *Hispania* 85 (3), 633–643.

Kelm, O.R. (2018) Student motivation in learning Portuguese. *Hispania* 100 (5), 297–298.

Krippendorff, K. (2013) *Content Analysis: An Introduction to Its Methodology* (3rd edn). Sage.

Loewen, S. and Plonsky, L. (2015) *An A–Z of Applied Linguistics Research Methods*. Palgrave.

Manhitu, Y. (2015) *Kamus Indonesia–Portugis*. Gramedia.

Nikitina, L. (2016) Language learners' representations of Portugal: Implications for culture teaching/Las representaciones de Portugal de los estudiantes de Português: Implicaciones en la enseñanza de aspectos culturales. *Cultura y Educación* 28 (4), 863–879.

Nikitina, L. (2019) Do country stereotypes influence language learning motivation? A study among foreign language learners in Malaysia. *Moderna språk* 113 (1), 58–79.

Nikitina, L. (2020) *Stereotypes and Language Learning Motivation: A Study of L2 Learners of Asian Languages*. Routledge.

Nikitina, L., Don, Z. and Loh, S.C. (2014) Focus on Brazil: Country images held by Malaysian learners of Brazilian Portuguese. *Calidoscópio* 12 (1), 73–82.

Nikitina, L., Tan, R.H., and Mohamad, J. (2022). Malaysian university students' mental images of Portuguese-speaking countries and their motivations to learn Portuguese. *Moderna språk* 116 (2), 140–166.

Pennebaker, J.W., Boyd, R.L., Booth, R.J., Ashokkumar, A. and Francis, M.E. (2022) *Linguistic Inquiry and Word Count, LIWC-22*. [Software]. Pennebaker Conglomerates.

Smith, J.J, Furbee, L., Maynard, K., Quick, S. and Ross, L. (1995) Salience counts: A domain analysis of English color terms. *Journal of Linguistic Anthropology* 5 (2), 203–216.

Sommer-Farias, B., Carvalho, A. and Picoral, A. (2020) Portuguese language program evaluation: Implementation, results and follow-up strategies. *Journal of Less Commonly Taught Languages* 28, 1–50.

Van den Hoonaard, W.C. (2008) Inter- and intracoder reliability. In L.M. Given (ed.) *The SAGE Encyclopedia of Qualitative Research Methods* (pp. 445–446). Sage.

Yampolsky, P.B. (2010) Kroncong revisited: New evidence from old sources. *Archipel* 79 (1), 7–56.

9 Multilingual Language Profiles, Perceptions and Motivations within the Context of Majoring in a Foreign Language in Malaysia

Stefanie Pillai and Roshidah Hassan

Introduction

Malaysia is a multilingual country with a complex linguistic landscape with an estimated 131 languages, 85% of which are indigenous (Eberhard *et al.*, 2023). The official and national language of the country is Malay but there are also social and regional dialects of Malay, as well as languages spoken by Malaysian Chinese and Indian ethnic groups; Mandarin, Hokkien and Cantonese by the former, and Tamil, Malayalam and Punjabi by the latter. The indigenous languages include Iban, Kadazan, Semai and Temiar (Pillai *et al.*, 2021). English is widely spoken and used in Malaysia, particularly in business, education and tourism. In the public education sector, Malay is the main medium of instruction. However, there are also Chinese (Mandarin)- and Tamil-medium primary schools. English, in the meantime, is taught as a compulsory second language (L2) in schools and is a compulsory subject at public universities.

The teaching and learning of a third language (L3) is mentioned in the Malaysia education blueprints for schools and higher education (Ministry of Education Malaysia, 2013, 2015). The need to study L3 also appeared in an earlier document, the *National Higher Education Strategic Plan Beyond 2020* (Ministry of Higher Education, 2007), which sees proficiency in a third language as being essential for Malaysians and Malaysia to be globally competitive. Although there is a mention of Arabic, Mandarin and Tamil at the primary school level, the focus at secondary and higher education leans towards the learning of foreign languages like French, German, Japanese and Korean. For example, it was reported that 129 residential and 117 day-schools in Malaysia teach these languages (Ministry of Education Malaysia, 2018: 2.25–2.26). The teaching and learning of foreign languages in Malaysia was reiterated in the Education Act 1996, and is in fact not a new practice, having already been introduced in residential schools in the 1970s (Hassan & Riget, 2020).

At the tertiary level, foreign languages are also offered as electives. At one public university, languages include Japanese, Korean, Portuguese, Russian, and Southeast Asian languages like Filipino and Thai. In addition, this university also offers five undergraduate degree programmes in language and linguistics: French, German, Italian, Japanese and Spanish. Unlike English, these languages can be classified as 'foreign' languages as they are not used or learnt in the same way that English is used in Malaysia. The question then arises as to what would motivate Malaysians to not only learn a foreign language from scratch but also to major in this language for an undergraduate degree. It has been said that 'learners' motivations are inevitably influenced by how they perceive the individual characteristics and value of particular languages in connection with their own identities and future aspirations' (Wang et al., 2021: 42). In the case of pursuing foreign language degree programmes in Malaysia, the learning of the new language also needs to be situated within the context of the languages that are already in the linguistic repertoires of the students in the programme. This is because most Malaysian students already know and use at least two languages, such as Malay and English, before beginning a foreign language degree programme.

In light of these points about perception, motivation and multilingualism, based on a questionnaire of closed and open-ended questions, this study set out to address two research questions:

(1) How do undergraduates majoring in languages other than English (LOTE) at a public university in Malaysia perceive themselves as multilinguals in relation to the languages they already know and the new one they are learning in their degree programme?
(2) What are their motivations for pursuing a foreign language degree programme?

Literature Review

The Malaysian multilingual context

In countries like Malaysia, where people are likely to know and use two or more languages, the connection between language and identity is multifaceted, with different languages and varieties of a language being used to express one's identity. Regional varieties of Malay such as Kelantan and Sarawak Malay can be used by Malays and non-Malays alike, thus transcending ethnic boundaries, unlike ethnic languages. In the case of Malaysian Chinese speakers, Vollmann and Soon (2018: 53) found that 'the Chinese identity (based on education, tradition, habits, culture, literature) is more important than smaller identities (e.g. being Hakka)', with Mandarin 'seen as a symbol of a wider, ethnic identity'. This phenomenon among the Malaysian Chinese may in part be due to a language shift from their heritage Chinese dialects to Mandarin (Low *et al.*, 2010), and the fact that many Malaysian Chinese attend Chinese-medium primary schools (Rahimy *et al.*, 2020). At the same time, when a language shift has occurred, ethnic identity is not necessarily inextricably linked to a heritage language, as can be seen in the case of the Portuguese–Eurasians (Pillai & Khan, 2011) and Sindhis (Khemlani-David, 1998) in Malaysia, who have mainly shifted to English as their first language (L1).

In the case of the Malay language, its status as a symbol of national identity is enshrined in the Malaysian constitution. Malay is used for inter-ethnic communication (Ng & Cavallaro, 2019) but does not appear to have had the same effect as a national lingua franca as Bahasa Indonesia has had in Indonesia (Dardjowidjojo, 1998). The complexities of dealing with the concept of one language for national identity in multilingual contexts is a point of contention for some. How *et al.* (2015: 133), for instance, contend that in a multilingual nation such as Malaysia, 'national identity cannot be formed based only on the use of the national language, but should involve the embodiment of linguistic diversity to give the concept a more accurate and holistic meaning'. This concept of one language for national identity can result in the suppression of indigenous and minority languages. It can also lead to questions about one's national identity and loyalty (see, for example, Mohamad, 2023).

In other cases, the language legacy of a former colonial power may continue to have considerable influence. In the case of Malaysia, this legacy is English, and debates about its use, role and status continue to this day. As an example, the colloquial variety of Malaysian English is a commonly used spoken variety among Malaysians (Gill, 2002), and can be considered as a marker of Malaysian identity (Pillai & Ong, 2018; Schneider, 2003, 2007). However, there are persisting tensions between the use of this colloquial variety and the standard variety of spoken English, particularly in the context of education (e.g. Mohd Don, 2016; Ng & Diskin-Holdaway, 2023).

In sum, the language context in Malaysia highlights the complexities of trying to link language and identity in a simplistic, one-to-one relationship. There are choices to be made about the use of particular languages or a combination of languages in a speaker's repertoire to construct, perform and negotiate particular identities. There is also the question of how multilinguals perceive themselves in relation to their ability to speak and understand multiple languages (Forbes & Rutgers, 2021; Pavlenko, 2006).

The multilingual self

With reference to Kramsch and Huffmaster (2015), Henry and Thorsen (2018: 3) explain that 'multilinguals who experience a close affinity to their different languages can be understood as possessing a "multilingual self"'. In addition, the conceptualisation of how people see themselves, and perhaps how they want to portray themselves, are linked in part to the languages they speak. This can be influenced by a variety of factors, including language proficiency, cultural background, personal experiences and social context (Thomson, 2020). Thus, multilingualism should be seen as a dynamic entity (Henry, 2023), where individuals' perceptions of their multilingual selves may change as they continue to learn and use languages.

In relation to language learning, Henry and Thorsen (2018: 11) suggest that 'the ideal multilingual self can perhaps best be understood as creating a context of meaning within which the ideal L2 self is nurtured'. The *context of meaning* referred to here can be seen as a mainly practical reason for learning new languages, such as to develop new language skills as part of one's multilingual repertoire. This context is also seen as a protective mechanism – for instance, against negative views about LOTE (Henry & Thorsen, 2018). Drawing on self-discrepancy theory, it is posited that people have self- or other-directed guides: 'ideal/own, ideal/other, ought/own, and ought/other' (Higgins, 1987: 321). Where language learning is concerned, learners may be motivated, for instance, by what they hope to achieve (ideal/own) or what they think they should achieve (ought/own) as a language learner. When faced with two or more languages, the interactions between these languages result in multilingual self-guides, part of which is the ideal multilingual self (Henry, 2017). Henry (2017) posits that the guides reflect one's aspirations to become multilingual, and hence are related to motivation. Thus, an individual's vision of themselves as a successful and proficient multilingual speaker of the various languages they speak or are learning was found to be positively associated with language learning motivation and language proficiency. However, within the context of learning two languages it has been suggested that there is a tendency for learners to be less motivated to learn an L3 than an L2, and that they frequently lose their LOTE selves (Howard & Oakes, 2021; Wang & Liu; 2020; Wang & Zheng; 2019; Zheng *et al.*, 2019).

Henry (2017) highlights the importance of understanding and promoting the development of the ideal multilingual self in multilingual language education as it can have a positive impact on language learning motivation and success. A harmonious relationship between the ideal self-guides for two languages is seen as a facilitating factor as interactions leading 'to the emergence of a self-guide reflecting the person's aspirations to be/become multilingual, an ideal multilingual' acts as a strong motivator to learn a language (Henry, 2017: 554).

More recently, Henry (2023) found that the external context in which multilingual language learning is taking place interacts with identity systems in the emergence of multilingual self-guides. An instance of a facilitative environment would be a school or learning environment that provides opportunities to use the language being learnt outside the classroom. In the context of higher education, this could be through student mobility programmes, where students spend time in the country where the language is spoken as an L1 (e.g. Japan for learners of Japanese). Another example is the deliberate creation of a multilingual environment that encourages the use of the languages being learnt in interactions outside the classroom (Henry, 2023).

Although language learning has become increasingly important in a world without boundaries, many students struggle to find the motivation to learn a third or foreign language. Previous studies by Dörnyei (1994, 1998), Gardner (1985, 2007) and Noels and Clément (1996) have identified various factors that affect motivation for language learning. These include attitudes towards the target language and its culture, perceived usefulness, and relevance of the language, self-efficacy beliefs and social support. The students' emotional state can also have an impact on how motivated they are to study the languages, which is why it has been found that positive feelings help students stay motivated and enthusiastic about their studies (Dewaele & MacIntyre, 2022; MacIntyre et al., 2019). All these factors interact differently depending on the learners' backgrounds, goals and the contexts of the motivational variables. In the case of English, its dominance at the global level is one of the key motivating factors to learning this language, as it can provide access to cross+-border education and job opportunities (The British Council, 2013).

In the context of learning LOTE in Malaysia, Chien et al. (2021), Chua and Azlan (2019), and Zubairi and Sarudin (2009) suggest that learners are motivated to learn the target language for extrinsic reasons, especially for their future careers. Similar findings were reported by Nikitina et al. (2020), whose study of Malaysian learners of Korean also found no significant relationship between learners' attitudes towards speakers of the target language and their motivation to learn Korean language. Instead, they found that the career dimension was the main factor that motivated Malaysian university students in their study to learn Korean. Studies have also shown that mastery of a new language and language exposure increased the confidence level of learners. Azmi

(2013), who focused on Malay students learning Mandarin in Chinese vernacular schools, found that students became more extroverted and confident upon mastering the language. This finding was similar to Wong (2020), who explored the experiences and perceptions of Japanese language learners from Malaysia who were taking part in mobility programmes to Japan. In this study, students had developed a new identity after completing their mobility programme in Japan (Wong, 2020). They were more confident, flexible and culturally sensitive at the end of the programme.

Despite the studies mentioned in the previous paragraph, there is still a lack of understanding regarding the complex ways in which individuals experience and navigate their multilingual identities. In particular, little attention has been paid to LOTE in Malaysia, such as French, Spanish, German or Japanese.

Methodology

The following sections describe the methodology used to explore how undergraduates majoring in LOTE perceive themselves as multilinguals. It also accounts for their motivation in pursuing a degree programme in LOTE.

Respondents

Students from four undergraduate degree programmes at a public university in Malaysia were selected for this study. One programme did not have many students and was excluded. Upon obtaining permission from the dean of the faculty, the coordinators of these degree programmes were contacted to seek their help in sending the questionnaire to the Malaysian students in their programmes. There was no compulsion for the students to respond to the questionnaire and, thus, the numbers across the programmes are not equal. It was indicated that by answering the questionnaire, the respondents were deemed to have consented to participating in the study. They were informed that their personal information would not be shared with other parties, and that their responses would be anonymised. The respondents comprised 83 undergraduate students (68 females and 15 males) majoring in foreign languages at one of the higher education institutions in Malaysia (see Table 9.1). This represented 34% of the total number of students ($n = 245$) enrolled in the four selected programmes. The respondents consisted of undergraduate students majoring in French ($n = 30$), German ($n = 19$), Japanese ($n = 16$) and Spanish ($n = 18$) (see Table 9.1). Their ages ranged from 18 to 28 years, with an average age of 22 years ($SD = 1.8$). The participants were all Malaysians, with a majority of them being Malays ($n = 63$). As shown in Table 9.1, the rest of the

Table 9.1 Respondents' language major and ethnicity

Bachelor's degree	Bajau*	Chinese	Indian	Ethnicity Kadazan*	Malay	Siamese*	Total
French Language and Linguistics		3	1		26		30
German Language and Linguistics		6			13		19
Japanese Language and Linguistics	1	5			9	1	16
Spanish Language and Linguistics		2		1	15		18
Total	1	16	1	1	63	1	83

*Bajau and Kadazan are indigenous groups in the state of Sabah, while Siamese refers to Malaysians of Thai descent.

Malaysian respondents comprised 16 Chinese students and 1 Indian, Bajau, Kadazan and Siamese student, respectively.

Instrument

Data were collected over four weeks in December 2022, through an online questionnaire that comprised four sections (see Appendix A):

- Section A sought to obtain basic demographic information about the respondents, such as their degree programme, age and ethnicity.
- Section B aimed to obtain the multilingual profiles of the respondents, including questions about their first languages and other languages they knew and used.
- Section C consisted of five parts aimed at eliciting the perception of respondents as multilinguals.
- Section D comprised three parts focusing on their motivation to learn a new foreign language.

Together, sections B, C and D were designed to provide a better understanding of the respondents' multilingual profile, their perceptions of themselves as multilinguals and their motivations for pursuing a foreign language degree programme.

There were two types of questions in Section C: open-ended and closed-ended questions. Cronbach's alphas were calculated for the closed-ended questions.

The first set of closed-ended questions on perceptions about learning their language major and about being multilinguals comprised 10 items (statements) that respondents had to rate on a 5-point Likert scale from *strongly agree* to *strongly disagree* ($\alpha = .85$). In the second set, the respondents replied on a scale ranging from *very much* to *not at all* to four statements on perceptions about their language majors and the speakers of these languages ($\alpha = .64$).

There were three open-ended questions. The first sought to elicit their perceptions on their language major prior to beginning their degree programme, while the second asked how the respondents felt they changed the way they communicated when using their language major. The third open-ended question was a follow up to a *yes–no* question of whether the respondents identified themselves differently when they spoke different languages.

In Section D, motivation was measured through three types of questions. In the first type, the respondents were asked to rate how important five elements (culture, cuisine, history, communicating with local people and travel) were in motivating them to learn a language on a scale ranging from *very important* to *not important at all* (α = .67). The second was a *yes–no* question, which was followed by an open-ended one seeking more information about their responses to the *yes–no* question. The third type of question required respondents to rate eight statements on a scale ranging from *very important* to *not important at all* (α = .75).

Prior to the dissemination of the online questionnaires, a pilot study was conducted by asking students from another foreign language major, which was not included in this study due to the small number of students across this particular degree programme. Based on the responses and feedback obtained, there appeared to be no issues in understanding the questions. However, the sections self-rating for L1, L2, and their language major were removed from the questionnaire as they were not relevant to the present study.

Data analysis

The responses to the closed questions in Sections B to D were analysed in terms of frequencies (n) and percentages (%). The mean score for each statement was also calculated:

$$\text{Mean score} = \frac{\Sigma \, (n^i \times \text{Likert Scale Score})}{\text{Number of Respondents}}$$

where

n^i = frequency of each Likert scale score

The scores for the Likert Scale were *strongly disagree*: 1; *disagree*: 2; *neutral*: 3; *agree*: 4; *strongly agree*: 5.

The open-ended questions were categorised in relation to the keywords used in the answers. The keywords could be in the form of single words or phrases. For instance, in answer to the question in Part 1 of Section C (see Appendix A), the words used by the respondents included 'difficult' and 'interesting' (see the findings section on 'Perception'). The categories were organised by the second author and subsequently checked and verified by the first author.

Findings

The presentation of the findings begins with the language profiles of the respondents, as we believe it is important to show the multilingual makeup of the respondents before delving into their perceptions and motivations.

Language profiles

Figure 9.1 shows the L1s of the respondents. The majority of the Malay respondents ($n = 41$) said that their L1 was Malay, while seven of them said it was a Malay regional dialect or dialects, such as the Kelantan, Pahang and Terengganu Malay dialects. Four of the Malay respondents put both Malay and a Malay dialect or two dialects as their L1. The use of the term 'Malay' here needs to be treated with caution, as it could refer to an informal form of Malay rather than a particular regional Malay dialect such as a northern Malay dialect.

The influence of a regional language can be seen in the L1 of the Malay respondent from Sarawak who reported the Sarawak Malay dialect as one of their L1s. The other L1 for this respondent was a majority indigenous language in that state, Iban. On the other hand,

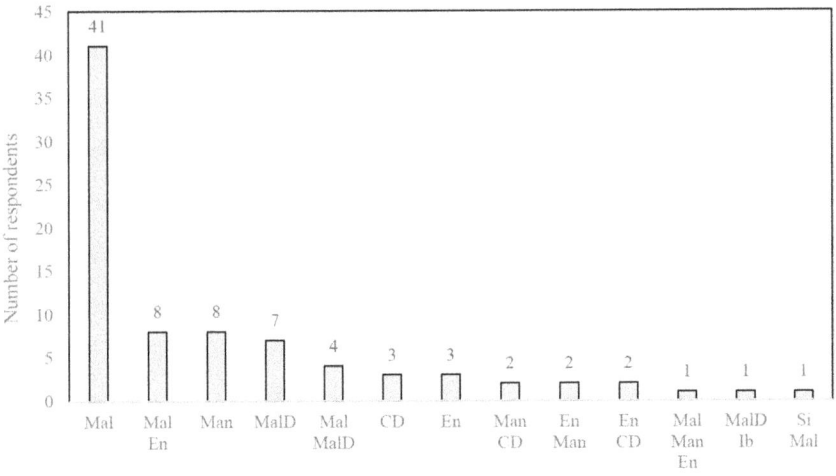

Figure 9.1 First languages of respondents
Mal: *Malay*; En: *English*: Man: *Mandarin*; MalD: *Malay Dialects*; CD: *Chinese Dialects*; Ib: *Iban*; Si: *Siamese* (Thai)

the Bajau speaker from Sabah, indicated that Malay, and not Bajau, was their L1. Similarly, the Kadazan respondent did not report the Kadazan language as their L1, but instead said their L1s were Mandarin and a Chinese dialect, Hakka. The shift from a heritage language or dialect to another language can also be observed among the Chinese respondents, as more than half of them ($n = 10$) said that Mandarin was their L1 or was one of their L1s, with only three of the Chinese respondents declaring a dialect – for example, Cantonese – as their only L1. In fact, 10 of the Chinese respondents reported that their L1 was not the same as their heritage language (e.g. Cantonese, Hakka, Hokkien and Teochew). For the Malay respondents, the heritage languages they no longer speak include Javanese and Minang. Eight of the Malay respondents indicated that both Malay and English were their L1s. The use of English as one of the L1s, together with either Mandarin or a Chinese dialect, was also reported by one Malay and three Chinese respondents.

However, where the national language was concerned, only the Siamese respondent cited Malay as another of their L1s. In contrast, none of the Chinese respondents did so. Nevertheless, the majority of the respondents indicated that they knew and used Malay as an L2. The other most mentioned language by the respondents as an L2 was English (80%, $n = 66$). The majority of the respondents said that they used English in their communication with friends and lecturers at the university and in their assignments. In fact, only six respondents reported not using English with their lecturers. Most respondents did use English and, in most cases, this was along with their language major (e.g. Arabic).

Figure 9.2 shows the number of languages the respondents know and use ($M = 21$, $SD = 6.13$). In total 12 of the respondents reported knowing and speaking only two languages, including their L1, and for eight of them, who were all Malay respondents, it was Malay (and/or a Malay dialect) as an L1 and English as the other language, while for the sole Indian respondent, their L1 was English and their L2 Malay. Two other respondents, one Malay and one Chinese, also declared English as their L1 (see Figure 9.1). A total of 25 respondents reported knowing three languages, and, for 15 of them, their language major was one of these languages. Another 25 of the respondents reported knowing four languages, with 19 of them mentioning their language major as one of the four languages. In fact, more than half the respondents (63%, $n = 52$) indicated their language major as one of their L2s. A total of 21 respondents reported knowing five or more languages. Other foreign languages mentioned, which were not related to their degrees, were Korean and Japanese. Seven of the Malay respondents also indicated Arabic as one of the other languages they knew and used.

In terms of the languages learnt before majoring in the language of their degree programme, half the respondents ($n = 41$) stated that their

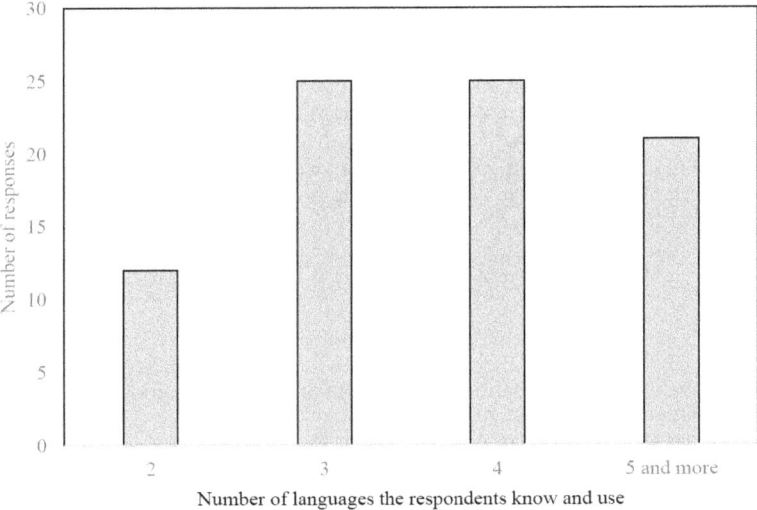

Figure 9.2 Number of languages the respondents know and use

language major was the first non-Malaysian language that they had learnt. The other half said that they had learnt other non-Malaysian languages prior to their degree programme. These languages included Arabic, Japanese, Korean, French, German and Italian.

Perceptions: Learning LOTE and being multilinguals

In the first part of the section C related to the research question on the perceptions of the respondents as multilinguals, the respondents were asked how they perceived the language that they were currently majoring in before they began their degree programmes. Figure 9.3 shows a word cloud that was generated to represent visually the most commonly occurring words used in the responses to this open-ended question. About one-third of the respondents perceived the language to be difficult to learn. This was especially in relation to German. Another 20% of them, the majority of whom were in the French programme, thought that it was an 'interesting' language. About 15% and 12% respectively perceived their language major as being 'useful' and 'beautiful'.

The next part in section C was related to learning their language major and their perceptions of being multilinguals. Table 9.2 presents the total scores and mean values for each of the 10 statements that the respondents rated on a 5-point Likert scale from *strongly agree* to *strongly disagree*. Their responses suggested that now that they were pursuing their degree programmes, the majority of them were positive,

Figure 9.3 Word cloud representing the perceptions of the respondents towards their language majors prior to studying it
Note: The bigger the word, the more frequent the response.

with an overall mean score (MS) of 4.17 about the language they are learning and with only 3 respondents consistently *strongly disagreeing* or *disagreeing* with most of the statements provided. Most respondents agreed that they very much enjoyed learning their language major (MS = 4.16) and that learning this language was really interesting (MS = 4.31). Most of the respondents also agreed that they were really proud of themselves for studying a foreign language (MS = 4.36).

In terms of seeing themselves as multilinguals, 80% ($n = 66$) of the respondents *strongly agreed* and *agreed* that they identified as a multilingual person (MS = 4.10), and 73% ($n = 61$) *strongly agreed* and *agreed* that their language major was part of their multilingual identity (MS = 3.94). As part of their future, 81% ($n = 67$) of them *strongly agreed* and *agreed* that they liked to think of themselves as someone who would be able to speak their language major fluently (MS = 4.10). Three quarters of the respondents (75%, $n = 62$) *strongly agreed* and *agreed* that whenever they thought of their future careers, they imagined themselves as being able to use their language major very well (MS = 4.04).

In the third part of section C, the respondents were asked to respond, on a scale ranging from *very much* to *not at all*, to four statements in the questionnaire on perceptions about their language majors and the speakers of these languages (see Table 9.3). A total of 90% of the respondents liked their language major *very much* (39%, $n = 32$) and *quite a lot* (52%, $n = 43$), with a mean score of 4.22. In addition, slightly more than half the respondents would like *very much* (51%, $n = 42$) to become similar to the people who speak their language major (MS = 4.24). In fact, 78% ($n = 65$) of the respondents responded that they liked the people who speak their language major *very much* (39%, $n = 32$) and *quite a lot* (40%, $n = 33$) with a mean score of 4.06. As to how much

Table 9.2 Language major and perceptions of being multilinguals: Total responses, percentages, scores and mean scores

Statements	1		2		3		4		5		Total score	Mean score
	n (%)	Score	n (%)	Score	n (%)	Score	n (%)	Score	n (%)	Score		
1. People around me tend to think that it is a good thing to know foreign languages.	3 (4)	3	0 (0)	0	9 (11)	27	36 (43)	144	35 (42)	175	349	4.20
2. Learning my language major is really great.	3 (4)	3	0 (0)	0	6 (7)	18	38 (46)	152	36 (43)	180	353	4.25
3. I feel really proud of myself for studying a foreign language.	3 (4)	3	0 (0)	0	7 (8)	21	27 (33)	108	46 (55)	230	362	4.36
4. I really enjoy learning my language major.	3 (4)	3	0 (0)	0	10 (12)	30	38 (46)	152	32 (39)	160	345	4.16
5. I like to think of myself as someone who will be able to speak my language major fluently.	2 (2)	2	4 (5)	8	10 (12)	30	35 (42)	140	32 (39)	160	340	4.10
6. I find learning my language major really interesting.	2 (2)	2	1 (1)	2	6 (7)	18	34 (41)	136	40 (48)	200	358	4.31
7. Whenever I think of my future career, I imagine myself being able to use my language major very well.	4 (5)	4	1 (1)	2	16 (19)	48	29 (35)	116	33 (40)	165	335	4.04
8. I identify as a multilingual person.	3 (4)	3	0 (0)	0	14 (17)	42	35 (42)	140	31 (37)	155	340	4.10
9. My language major is part of my multilingual identity.	3 (4)	3	3 (4)	6	16 (19)	48	35 (42)	140	26 (31)	130	327	3.94
10. Youngsters should be encouraged to speak their local languages/dialects as part of their identity.	2 (2)	2	1 (1)	2	13 (16)	39	23 (28)	92	44 (53)	220	355	4.28
											Overall mean score	4.17

Note: Likert Scale Scores: 1: *Strongly disagree*; 2: *Disagree*; 3: *Neutral*; 4: *Agree*; 5: *Strongly agree*.
n: Frequency of responses.
(%): Percentage in parentheses.

Table 9.3 Perceptions about language major and speakers: Total responses, percentages, scores and mean scores

Statements	Likert item										Total score	Mean score
	1		2		3		4		5			
	n (%)	Score	n (%)	Score	n (%)	Score	n (%)	Score	n (%)	Score		
1. How much do you like your language major?	2 (2)	2	2 (2)	4	4 (5)	12	43 (52)	172	32 (39)	160	350	4.22
2. How much would you like to become similar to the people who speak your language major?	2 (2)	2	3 (4)	6	10 (12)	30	26 (31)	104	42 (51)	210	352	4.24
3. How much do you like the people who speak your language major (e.g. the French/Germans/Spanish/ Italians)?	3 (4)	3	3 (4)	6	12 (14)	36	33 (40)	132	32 (39)	160	337	4.06
4. How much do you think knowing your language major would help your future career?	3 (4)	3	3 (4)	6	12 (14)	36	30 (36)	120	35 (42)	175	340	4.10
									Overall mean score			4.15

Note: Likert scale scores: 1: *Not at all*; 2: *Not really*; 3: *So-so*; 4: *Quite a lot*; 5: *Very much*.
(%): Percentage in parentheses.

they thought knowing their language major would help them in their future careers, a majority of the respondents (78%, $n = 65$) selected *very much* ($n = 35$) and *quite a lot* ($n = 30$) (MS = 4.10).

The next section on perception was an open-ended question that sought to understand how the respondents felt they changed the way they communicate when they used their language major. The most cited reason among almost 30% ($n = 25$) of the respondents was that they changed their accent or pronunciation, to sound more like the native speakers of the language. The other change mentioned by almost 15% ($n = 12$) of the respondents was that they now used this new language with their friends, mostly those from the same language programme.

In relation to identity, only 37% ($n = 31$) of the respondents felt that the different languages that they spoke identified them differently. A total of 21 of these 31 respondents provided reasons for their response. Eight of the responses alluded to the fact that the languages they used identified, for example, their nationality (as Malaysians), their ethnicity, and their geographical origins, as shown in the following excerpts. (All the excerpts have been edited for language.) The first extract, from Respondent 5, reflects the geographical distribution of different Chinese communities in Malaysia, where it was common for particular Chinese language groups to settle in different parts of the country. Hence, assumptions are made about a Malaysian Chinese person's geographical origins based on the Chinese language that they speak (Ong & Ting, 2023), such as Hokkien from Penang, Foo Chow from Sibu in Sarawak, Hakka from Sabah and Cantonese from Kuala Lumpur.

Respondent 5

… when I speak Cantonese and Mandarin, people immediately know my ethnic group and assume that I come from Kuala Lumpur.

The extract from Respondent 15 shows the demarcation between one's ethnic and national identity being marked by the different languages. There is also an age factor when it comes to identity as there was a stronger move for Chinese-medium education and the use of Mandarin among the Malaysian Chinese community in the 1980s (Ong & Ting, 2023).

Respondent 15

For example, I feel that Mandarin, for the most part, identifies me as part of the younger generation of Malaysians of Chinese descent, whereas Malay usually identifies me as a Malaysian by nationality.

The use of the Malaysian variety of English is also another identifier, as expressed by Respondent 23, this time as a form of recognisably national identity even if official discourse only links the national language to national identity:

Respondent 23

Malaysians can be identified when they speak Manglish.

A total of 52 (63%) respondents did not think that a language changed or affected their identity, with 38 of them providing reasons for their response. Most of these respondents felt that they were the same person regardless of the language they used ($n = 18$), or that their national and/or ethnic identity remained the same ($n = 18$), as exemplified in the excerpts from Respondents 33 and 57:

Respondent 33

Regardless of whatever languages I speak, my nationality and identity as a Malaysian are still intact.

Respondent 57

Even though I can speak English and Spanish, I'm still Malay and I identify with Malaysian culture.

Such thinking, in a way, supports the learning of English and LOTE as there is no fear of losing one's ethnic and national identity and culture or of being 'influenced' by the other cultures, especially if they are deemed to be in conflict with one's own (Lee et al., 2020).

Motivation to learn LOTEs

To address the second research question – about the motivations for pursuing a foreign language degree programme – we begin with how important the five elements were in terms of motivating the respondents to learn their language major (see Table 9.4). Travel to the country was selected by 84% of the respondents ($n = 70$) as a *very important* and *important* motivating factor for them in the selection of their language major ($MS = 4.27$). Another important motivating factor was culture ($MS = 4.07$). For about 72% ($n = 60$) of the respondents, communicating with local people using the language major was a *very important* and *important* motivating factor ($MS = 4.04$). The other two elements – the history ($MS = 3.80$) and cuisine ($MS = 3.82$) of the country concerned – were not rated as highly in terms of being important motivating factors. In response to a follow-up open-ended question about what other motivating factors there were, the most cited ones were entertainment and future job opportunities. Next, in response to a *yes–no* question, an overwhelming percentage agreed that they would have privileges as a multilingual speaker (93%). When asked to

Table 9.4 Motivations to learn language major: Total responses, percentages, scores and mean scores

Statements	Likert item										Total score	Mean score
	1		2		3		4		5			
	n (%)	Score	n (%)	Score	n (%)	Score	n (%)	Score	n (%)	Score		
1. Culture	2 (2)	2	2 (2)	4	14 (17)	42	35 (42)	140	30 (36)	150	338	4.07
2. Cuisine	2 (2)	2	4 (5)	8	27 (133)	81	24 (29)	96	26 (31)	130	317	3.82
3. History	1 (1)	13	5 (6)	10	22 (27)	66	37 (45)	148	18 (22)	90	315	3.80
4. Communicating with locals	1 (1)	1	3 (4)	6	19 (23)	57	29 (35)	116	31 (37)	155	335	4.04
5. Travel	1 (1)	1	3 (4)	6	9 (11)	27	30 (36)	120	40 (48)	200	254	4.27
									Overall mean score			4.00

Likert scale scores: 1 = *Not important at all* to 5 = *Very important*.
(%): Percentage in parentheses

elaborate on this in a follow-up open-ended question, the majority of them indicated *future opportunities* as well as *being more knowledgeable* and *being able to communicate* and *network* with people as the privileges of a multilingual speaker.

The final set of questions in this section explored how true the respondents felt each of the eight statements provided was (see Table 9.5). A majority of the respondents indicated that the statement that learning a foreign language had increased their intercultural competence was true ($MS = 4.02$). In addition, almost 80% ($n = 67$) of them stated that it was *absolutely* and *mostly true* that their way of thinking had changed by learning a foreign language ($MS = 4.07$). A total of 61 (73%) of the respondents found that it was *absolutely* and *mostly true* that the feeling of belonging to a multilingual group motivated them to learn a foreign language ($MS = 3.86$). A total of 59 (71%) respondents indicated that they felt empowered as a multilingual person ($MS = 3.83$). A total of 66 (80%) and 59 (71%) of the respondents respectively indicated that it was *absolutely* and *mostly true* that they felt more confident now that they were majoring in a new language ($MS = 4.02$) and that they could express their feelings using the foreign language in ways they could not do in the other languages that they spoke ($MS = 3.82$). When it came to whether it was true that learning their language major had influenced or changed their identities, 66% ($n = 55$) of the respondents felt that it was *absolutely* and *mostly true* ($MS = 3.73$). The percentage of respondents (49%, $n = 41$) who found that it was *absolutely* and *mostly true* decreased in relation to learning a foreign language affecting their cognitive ability ($MS = 3.54$).

Discussion

The language profiles, perceptions as multilinguals and motivation for learning languages as majors highlight several points about the respondents' language use and language education, including their language major itself. For one thing, the findings show that being multilingual is a norm among the respondents, with the majority of them speaking at least three languages. The self-reported L1(s) of several of the respondents show the presence of dialects in their language repertoires. This could be a Malay regional dialect and/or a Chinese dialect. However, for the Malay respondents, it appears that the term 'Malay' is all-encompassing, as the majority of them reported their L1 simply as Malay, when it is likely that they speak a dialectal variety of Malay as well as a standard form of both spoken and written Malay. The latter can be assumed, as all the participants were educated in public schools, where Malay is the main medium of instruction. This does raise the issue of whether this means different varieties of a language, such as Malay, constitute being multilingual, which seems to be the case going by

Multilingual Language Profiles, Perceptions and Motivations 161

Table 9.5 Perceptions about learning/knowing a foreign language: Total responses, percentages, scores and mean scores

Statements	Likert scale score										Total score	Mean score
	1		2		3		4		5			
	n (%)	Score	n (%)	Score	n (%)	Score	n (%)	Score	n (%)	Score		
1. The feeling of belonging to a multilingual group motivates me to learn a foreign language.	3 (4)	3	6 (7)	12	13 (16)	39	39 (47)	156	22 (27)	110	320	3.86
2. Learning a foreign language affects my cognitive ability: e.g. more creative and have better semantic memory.	3 (4)	3	11 (13)	22	28 (34)	84	20 (24)	80	21 (25)	105	294	3.54
3. Unconsciously, learning a foreign language has changed or influenced my identity.	2 (2)	2	8 (10)	16	18 (22)	54	37 (45)	148	18 (22)	90	310	3.73
4. I feel more confident since studying a foreign language.	3 (4)	3	2 (2)	4	12 (14)	36	39 (47)	156	27 (33)	135	334	4.02
5. Learning a foreign language has changed my worldview or way of thinking.	3 (4)	3	1 (1)	2	12 (14)	36	38 (46)	152	29 (35)	145	338	4.07
6. Learning a foreign language has increased my empathy/intercultural competence.	2 (2)	2	3 (4)	6	17 (20)	51	30 (36)	120	31 (37)	155	334	4.02
7. I feel empowered as a multilingual person.	2 (2)	4	9 (11)	18	13 (16)	39	36 (43)	144	23 (28)	115	318	3.83
8. I can express my feelings using the foreign language in ways I cannot do in the other languages I speak.	2 (2)	3	9 (11)	18	13 (16)	39	37 (45)	148	22 (27)	110	317	3.82
									Overall mean score			3.86

Note: Likert scale scores: 1: Absolutely untrue; 2: Mostly untrue; 3: Neutral; 4: Mostly true; 5: Absolutely true
n: Frequency of responses
(%): Percentage in parentheses

the following definition: 'The set of varieties used in a speech community in various speech situations is called its linguistic repertoire or its verbal repertoire' (Finegan, 2015: 362). Chinese speakers, on the other hand, make a distinction between Mandarin and other Chinese dialects, with many of them claiming Mandarin as their L1. The shift from a heritage language to another one – such as in the case of Chinese dialects to Mandarin among the Malaysian Chinese (e.g. Low et al., 2010; Ong & Ting, 2023) and Indian communities – has been previously reported (e.g. Khemlani-David, 1998; Krishnan & Sharmini, 2022).

Despite the occurrence of language shift among non-Malay respondents, there is still a clear link between ethnicity and language among the Chinese and Malay respondents. However, Malay was still the other language that non-Malay respondents knew and used. This is to be expected, given the status of Malay as a national language and the main medium of instruction in public schools. However, the national language – Malay – has not replaced the ethnic languages of the non-Malay respondents, with only the Bajau (an indigenous group in the state of Sabah) respondents claiming Malay as their only L1.

The next point relates to English. Because English is a compulsory subject in this school system, it can also be anticipated that English will be another language in their repertoire. However, the level of proficiency among Malaysians varies and this has caused considerable concern among parents, educators and employers, leading to the implementation of strategies under the English Language Roadmap (see Pillai et al., 2021). At the same time, English also emerged as one of the L1s that cut across ethnic groups. It was one of the first languages of several Malay and Chinese respondents, reflecting a bilingual home language context. The use of English as a main language of communication at university also emerges, reflecting the use of English in higher education in the country, including in public universities.

The respondents' inclusion of the language major as one of the other languages used after their L1(s), regardless of which semester of their degree programme they were in, suggests a sense of ownership of this relatively new language they are learning. However, at the same time, the exclusion of the language major as one of the languages they know by 31 of the respondents suggests otherwise, i.e. they do not consider it as one of the languages in their repertoire. Nevertheless, we hesitate to speculate on this finding, as there may be other reasons why the respondents did not report their language major as one of the languages they know. For the respondents who included their language major, it should be noted that they have already acquired at least two languages before learning their major language, and they now appear to consider this new LOTE part of their already bilingual or multilingual language repertoire. This may be because they are not just learning the language but are using it with their lecturers teaching the foreign language component of their degree programme and, to a certain extent, with their course mates on the same programme. Thus, their language major is a part of their daily communication whilst they are at university, which in turn creates a facilitating external context for language learning and use (Henry, 2023).

The inclusion of the participants' language major as part of their language repertoire can be linked to their perceptions of their language major. The respondents had mostly positive perceptions about learning their language major, even if initially they thought that it would be difficult to learn a foreign language. The latter may be attributed to the lack of exposure to foreign language learning despite the education policy calling for the teaching of another language. Now that they are learning a new language, there is a sense of pride and accomplishment in doing something that may have been deemed a difficult endeavour. There appears to have been a shift in their pre-degree perception as their responses suggest that now that they are in their degree programmes, they like learning their language major and find it interesting and enjoyable. The inclusion of their language major as part of their language repertoire can also be tied to their perception of the language major being a part of their multilingual identity. This is perhaps also why the respondents tended to have a positive perception of themselves as competent users of the language in the future. This vision of themselves aligns with their motivation for learning their language major in relation to future opportunities, similar to the findings of Chien *et al.* (2021), Chua and Azlan (2019), Nikitina *et al.* (2020) and Zubairi and Sarudin (2009). Other motivating factors are the ability to expand their communication network, as well as being more interculturally competent and empowered as a multilingual person. Being multilingual is thus considered an asset. This is consistent with the positive link between people's vision of themselves as successful multilingual speakers and their motivations to learn the language suggested by Henry (2017) and mentioned by, for example, Forbes and Rutgers (2021), Pavlenko (2006) and Wang *et al.* (2021).

The participants' perceptions about their language major could also stem from their generally positive attitude towards the native speakers of their language major, with some of them wanting to become like the people who spoke that particular language. Perhaps this was in terms of the way they communicated, especially in relation to using a native-like accent. This trend of wanting to use such an accent sets the foreign language majors apart from the English used in Malaysia, where there are distinguishing pronunciation features that have developed over the years and which are discernible even among fluent Malaysian speakers of English (Pillai *et al.*, 2010). As students of these foreign languages, they are motivated to sound native when speaking a foreign language because it may be seen as a measure of success. This might also make them feel more confident and accepted by the community that speaks that language. For some learners, sounding native-like may be a personal goal that contributes to their future aspirations because a native-like accent may be important for certain jobs, such as those in international business or diplomacy. Unlike English, which is taught by Malaysian teachers, foreign language degree programmes usually have a mix of L1 and L2 speakers of the language major in the teaching team. The team includes both Malaysian and non-Malaysian lecturers, who are likely to insist on a native speaker's target pronunciation.

In relation to wanting to sound native-like, there is also the question of whether using a foreign language changed their identity. The divided response to this statement suggests that there may be a reluctance to identify with the culture, even if the respondents liked the language and the people. This is despite the fact that there was a general sense of agreement among the respondents that learning the new language had changed their thinking and cognitive ability. This may be because of a fear of being perceived as someone who has taken on values from another culture that may be perceived as being incompatible with one's own, or as someone who has forgotten their own identity. Such perceptions have been reported in the use of English in Malaysia (Mohd-Asraf, 2005). In short, there appears to be an underlying assumption that learning a foreign language or engaging with a new culture may result in losing touch with one's own cultural identity. There was also the assumption of a one-to-one relationship between a language and ethnic and national identity, as can be seen in Mohamad (2023), and this may be an assumption that is entrenched in the minds of the respondents due to the way ethnic and national identity are not only portrayed in official statements and documents (How et al., 2015; Pillai et al., 2021) but also on social media platforms.

Conclusion

This study discussed the multilingual profiles of the respondents who were majoring in four foreign language undergraduate programmes at a public university in Malaysia in relation to how they perceived themselves as multilinguals vis-à-vis the languages that they already know and use, and their motivations for pursuing a LOTE degree programme. There is both a sense of a utilitarian use for their language major (e.g. for travel and work opportunities) and also what could be considered as a more socially driven sense of motivation, such as communicating with locals and networking. Taken together, the multilingual profiles, the perceptions of the respondents about their language majors, and the inclusion of the new language as part of their multilingual repertoire along with a perception of themselves as fluent users of these languages, can be linked to their motivation for learning these languages. In short, interacting links between components like perceptions about a language and its people, perceived usefulness and motivations, emerged from the findings (Dörnyei, 1994, 1998; Gardner, 1985, 2007; Henry, 2017; Noels & Clément, 1996). At this point in their language education and multilingual persona, the respondents generally perceived themselves as multilinguals who continue to maintain their ethnic and/or national language without 'fear' of losing it to a new language such as their language major.

Findings from this study suggest that LOTE teachers need to increase students' passions and interests in and outside classrooms. This is especially as previous findings (e.g. Howard & Oakes, 2021; Wang & Liu, 2020; Wang & Zheng, 2019; Zheng *et al.*, 2019) have shown that the vitality of an L3 motivation tends to be weaker than that of an L2, in addition to them often losing their LOTE selves in the course of their language learning journey. Thus, more opportunities should be given for students to develop their ideal language self (desires of students to use the target language in the future) and ideal multilingual self (desire to add to their linguistic repertoire). Strategies that can be employed to help students stay engaged and motivated in their learning include encouraging students to develop attainable language learning objectives, as these can increase motivation. These objectives can be to obtain a good grade at a particular language proficiency level, to communicate with a native speaker, or to comprehend a certain amount of content in the target language. Besides this, celebrating students' progress and accomplishments can generate positive emotions in them, thus motivating them to continue learning the language. This is because positive emotions can be strong motivators in themselves (Dewaele & MacIntyre, 2022; MacIntyre *et al.*, 2019).

Although this study is limited to only one university in Malaysia and had a relatively small sample of 83 respondents from four undergraduate programmes in foreign languages and linguistics who voluntarily answered the questionnaire, the university is only one of two universities in the country that has such programmes, and the only one that has that five such degree programmes. Given that the education policy in the country highlights the need for the learning of LOTEs at the schools and tertiary level, there is a need for more Malaysian graduates with foreign language degrees to teach languages such as French and German. Thus, the findings from this study contribute to our understanding of multilingual learners' perceptions about their language majors and elements related to them (e.g. people, culture, usefulness) and how these relate to their motivations to learn these languages. Such an understanding can have practical use if translated into promotional materials for related degree programmes.

At the same time, the findings also point to the need to take into account the multilingual makeup of students so that the promotion, teaching and learning of these new foreign languages are carried out in isolation but conceptualised as part of their multilingual self's development.

One other element that emerged from the study was the concept of identity related to the use of different languages in the respondents' repertoire, which was very strongly tied to an ascribed sense of identity (e.g. ethnic or national identity). The use of different languages or language varieties by multilinguals to construct or perform, depending on one's theoretical learning, different identities merits further investigation.

Acknowledgements

We would like to thank the programme coordinators for their assistance in disseminating the online questionnaire and Nurmahfuzah Razak for assisting us with the data collection and collation of the data for analysis. This project was funded by a RMF grant from Universiti Malaya (RMF0273-2021).

Appendix A
Questions in the online questionnaire
Section A: Demographic information
1. Gender: Male   Female
2. Age:
3. Ethnic Group: Malay   Chinese   Indian
   Other Ethnicity: (Indicate)
4. Current Semester: 1   2   3   4   5   6
5. Bachelor Programme:
   Bachelor of French Language and Linguistics
   Bachelor of German Language and Linguistics
   Bachelor of Japanese Language and Linguistics
   Bachelor of Spanish Language and Linguistics

Section B: Multilingual profiles
1a. What do you consider as your first language/s (L1)?
    [Note: This could be a Malay dialect/variety, Chinese dialect/variety, an Indian language, an indigenous language etc., and you can have more than one first language (L1).]
1b. Why do you consider this to be your first language/s?
2a. Is (one of your) first language(s) the same as your heritage language/s?   Yes   No
    [Note: E.g. Your first language is Mandarin, but the language that your parents or grandparents grew up in was Cantonese.]
2b. If you answered No, state what your heritage language/s is/are:
3. State other languages that you know and use:
4a. Is your language major the first non-Malaysian language that you have learnt?   Yes   No
4b. If you answered No, what other non-Malaysian language did you learn before learning your language major?
5. Which languages/s do you use the most to write academic papers?
6. Which languages/s do you use the most to read academic materials?
7. Which languages/s do you use the most to speak to your course mates in the SAME language major during lectures/tutorials?
8. Which language/s do you use the most to speak to your course mates from the SAME language major outside of class?

9. Which languages/s do you use the most to speak to your lecturers teaching you courses in your language major programme?

Section C: Perceptions about learning LOTE and being multilingual

Part 1: Before starting your degree programme, what was your perception towards your language major (as a language)?

Part 2: Select the option that best indicates your level of agreement from *strongly agree* to *strongly disagree*:

1. People around me tend to think that it is a good thing to know foreign languages.
2. Learning my language major is really great.
3. I feel really proud of myself for studying a foreign language.
4. I really enjoy learning my language major.
5. I like to think of myself as someone who will be able to speak my language major fluently.
6. I find learning my language major really interesting.
7. Whenever I think of my future career, I imagine myself being able to use my language major very well.
8. I identify as a multilingual person.
9. My language major is part of my multilingual identity.
10. Youngsters should be encouraged to speak their local languages/dialects as part of their identity.

Part 3: In the following section, answer the following questions by rating the level of frequency: 5 = *very much*, 4 = *quite a lot*, 3 = *so-so*, 2 = *not really*, 1 = *not at all*

1. How much do you like your language major?
2. How much would you like to become similar to the people who speak your language major?
3. How much do you like the people from your language major (e.g. the French/Germans/Spanish/Italians)?
4. How much do you think knowing your language major would help your future career?

Part 4: In what way do you change the way you are communicating when you use your language major?

Part 5:

5a. Do the different languages that you speak identify you differently (e.g. ethnic, geographical, national identity etc.)? Yes/No
5b. Tell us more about your answer.

Section D: Motivation to learn LOTE

Part 1:
1. How important were each of the following motivating you to learn French/German/Spanish/Italian as your language major on a scale of 1 = *not important at all* to 5 = *very important*.
   1. Culture
   2. Cuisine
   3. History
   4. Communicating with locals
   5. Travel
2. Were there other motivating factors?

Part 2:
1a. Do you think you (will) have certain privileges as a multilingual speaker?   Yes   No
1b. Tell us more about your answer.

Part 3: With reference to your language major, select the option which best expresses how true the following statements are about your feelings or situations.
[*absolutely true* to *not true at all*]
1. The feeling of belonging to a multilingual group motivates me to learn a foreign language.
2. Learning a foreign language affects my cognitive ability: e.g. more creative and have better semantic memory.
3. Unconsciously, learning a foreign language has changed or influenced my identity.
4. I feel more confident since studying a foreign language.
5. Learning a foreign language has changed my worldview or way of thinking.
6. Learning a foreign language has increased my empathy/intercultural competence.
7. I feel empowered as a multilingual person.
8. I can express my feelings using the foreign language in ways I cannot do in the other languages I speak.

References

Azmi, M.N.L. (2013) Multilingualism and personality traits among Malay primary school students in vernacular schools. *IOSR Journal of Humanities and Social Science (IOSR-JHSS)* 8 (3), 24–31.

Chien, G.K., Fu, D.L.E., Boon, E.S., Phong, S.Y. and Ying, L.Y. (2021) Motivation in foreign language learning among Malay undergraduates in a Malaysian public university. *International Journal of Academic Research in Business and Social Sciences* 11 (7), 162–168.

Chua, H.W. and Azlan, M.A.K. (2019) Factors influencing foreign language learners' motivation in continuing to learn Mandarin. *EDUCATUM Journal of Social Science* 5 (1), 1–6.

Dardjowidjojo, S. (1998) Strategies for a successful national language policy: The Indonesian case. *International Journal of the Sociology of Language* 130, 35–47.

Dewaele, J. and MacIntyre, P. (2022) 'You can't start a fire without a spark': Enjoyment, anxiety, and the emergence of flow in foreign language classrooms. *Applied Linguistics Review*. https://doi.org/10.1515/applirev-2021-0123.

Dörnyei, Z. (1994) Motivation and motivating in a foreign language classroom. *The Modern Language Journal* 78 (3), 273–284.

Dörnyei, Z. (1998) Motivation in second and foreign language learning. *Language Teaching* 31 (3), 117–135.

Eberhard, D.M., Simons, G.F. and Fennig, C.D. (eds) (2023) *Ethnologue: Languages of the World* (26th edn). SIL International. Retrieved 20 September 2023 from http://www.ethnologue.com.

Finegan, E. (2015) *Language: Its Structure and Use* (7th edn). Cengage Learning.

Forbes, K. and Rutgers, D. (2021) Multilingual identity in education. *The Language Learning Journal* 49 (4), 399–403.

Gardner, R.C. (1985) *Social Psychology and Second Language Learning*. Edward Arnold.

Gardner, R.C. (2007) Motivation and second language acquisition. *Porta Linguarum Revista Interuniversitaria de Didáctica de las Lenguas Extranjeras* 8, 9–20. Retrieved from http://doi.org/10.30827/Digibug.31616.

Gill, S.K. (2002) *International Communication: English Language Challenges for Malaysia*. Universiti Putra Malaysia Press.

Hassan, R. and Riget, P.N. (2020) *Foreign Language: Teaching and Learning in the Malaysian Context*. University of Malaya Press.

Henry, A. (2017) L2 motivation and multilingual identities. *The Modern Language Journal* 101 (3), 548–565.

Henry, A. (2023) Learner–environment adaptations in multiple language learning: Casing the ideal multilingual self as a system functioning in context. *International Journal of Multilingualism* 20 (2), 97–114.

Henry, A. and Thorsen, C. (2018) The ideal multilingual self: Validity, influences on motivation, and role in a multilingual education. *International Journal of Multilingualism* 15 (4), 349–364.

Higgins, E.T. (1987) Self-discrepancy: A theory relating self and affect. *Psychological Review* 94 (3), 319–340.

How, S.Y., Chan, S.H. and Abdullah, A.N. (2015) Language vitality of Malaysian languages and its relation to identity. *Gema Online Journal of Language Studies* 15 (2), 119–139.

Howard, M. and Oakes, L. (2021) Motivation for LOTE learning: A cross-country comparison of university learners of French. *Journal of Multilingual and Multicultural Development*. https://doi.org/10.1080/01434632.2021.1897129.

Khemlani-David, M. (1998) Language shift, cultural maintenance, and ethnic identity; A study of a minority community: The Sindhis of Malaysia. *International Journal of the Sociology of Language* 130, 67–76.

Kramsch, C. and Huffmaster, M. (2015) Multilingual practices in foreign language study. In J. Cenoz and D. Gorter (eds) *Multilingual Education* (pp. 114–136). Cambridge University Press.

Krishnan, M.R. and Sharmini, S. (2022) English language use of the Malaysian Tamil diaspora. *Journal of Multilingual and Multicultural Development*. https://doi.org/10.1080/01434632.2021.2020800.

Lee, Y.L., Jung, M., Nathan, R.J. and Chung, J.-E. (2020) Cross-national study on the perception of the Korean wave and cultural hybridity in Indonesia and Malaysia using discourse on social media. *Sustainability* 12 (15), 1–33.

Low, H.M., Nicholas, H. and Wales, R. (2010) A sociolinguistic profile of 100 mothers from middle to upper-middle socio-economic backgrounds in Penang-Chinese community: What languages do they speak at home with their children? *Journal of Multilingual and Multicultural Development* 31 (6), 569–584.

MacIntyre, P.D., Ross, J. and Clément, R. (2019) Emotions are motivating. In M. Lamb, K. Csizér, A. Henry and S. Ryan (eds) *The Palgrave Handbook of Motivation for Language Learning* (pp. 183–202). Springer International.

Ministry of Education Malaysia (2013) *The Malaysia Education Blueprint 2013–2025 (Preschool to Post-Secondary Education)*. Ministry of Education Malaysia.

Ministry of Education Malaysia (2015) *Malaysia Education Blueprint 2015–2025 (Higher Education)*. Ministry of Education Malaysia.

Ministry of Education Malaysia (2018) *2018 Annual Report Malaysia Education Blueprint 2013–2025*. Ministry of Education Malaysia.

Ministry of Higher Education (MOHE) (2007) *National Higher Education Strategic Plan Beyond 2020*. Ministry of Higher Education Malaysia.

Mohamad, M. [@chedetofficial] (2023) But the Chinese and Indians in Malaysia insist on speaking in Chinese and Indian languages, 9 March. [Tweet]. Twitter. twitter.com/chedetofficial/status/1633740302463934465?s=20.

Mohd-Asraf, R. (2005) English and Islam: A clash of civilizations? *Journal of Language, Identity & Education* 4 (2), 103–118.

Mohd Don, Z. (2016) It's all in the pronunciation. *New Straits Times*, 7 August, p. 5. Retrieved 1 September 2023 from www.nst.com.my/news/2017/03/196764/its-all-pronunciation.

Ng, B.C. and Cavallaro, F. (2019) Multilingualism in Southeast Asia: The post-colonial language stories of Hong Kong, Malaysia and Singapore. In S. Montanari and S. Quay (eds) *Multidisciplinary Perspectives on Multilingualism: The Fundamentals* (pp. 27–50). de Gruyter.

Ng, J.C. and Diskin-Holdaway, C. (2023) Attitudes to English in contemporary Malaysia. *World Englishes* 42 (30), 562–578.

Nikitina, L., Furuoka, F. and Kamaruddin, N. (2020) Language attitudes and L2 motivation of Korean language learners in Malaysia. *Journal of Language and Education* 6 (2), 132–146.

Noels, K.A. and Clément, R. (1996) Communicating across cultures: Social determinants and acculturative consequences. *Canadian Journal of Behavioral Science* 28 (3), 214–228. https://doi.org/10.1037/0008-400X.28.3.214.

Ong, T.W.S. and Ting, S-H. (2023) Children deciding the family language in Chinese families in multiethnic Malaysia. *Notion: Journal of Linguistics, Literature, and Culture* 5 (1), 32–46.

Pavlenko, A. (2006) Bilingual selves. In A. Pavlenko (ed.) *Bilingual Minds: Emotional Experience, Expression and Representation* (pp. 1–33). Multilingual Matters.

Pillai, S. and Khan, M.H. (2011) I am not English but my first language is English: English as a first language among Portuguese Eurasians in Malaysia. In D. Mukherjee and M.K. David (eds) *National Language Planning and Language Shifts in Malaysian Minority Communities: Speaking in Many Tongues* (pp. 87–100). Amsterdam University Press.

Pillai, S. and Ong, L.T. (2018) English(es) in Malaysia. *Asian Englishes* 20 (2), 147–157.

Pillai, S., Don, Z.M., Knowles, G. and Tang, J. (2010) Malaysian English: An instrumental analysis of vowel contrasts. *World Englishes* 29 (2), 159–172.

Pillai, S., Kaur, S. and Chau, M.H. (2021) The ideological stance of multilingualism in education in Malaysia in the press 2000–2020. *Austrian Journal of South-East Asian Studies* 14 (2), 173–193.

Rahimy, R., Tan, T. and Carvalho, M. (2020) More non-Chinese enrol in Chinese schools now compared to a decade ago. *The Star*, 11 November. Retrieved from www.thestar.com.my/news/nation/2020/11/11/more-non-chinese-enrol-in-chinese-schools-now-compared-to-a-decade-ago.

Schneider, E.W. (2003) Evolutionary patterns of New Englishes and the special case of Malaysian English. *Asian Englishes* 6 (2), 44–63.

Schneider, E.W. (2007) *Postcolonial English*. Cambridge University Press.

The British Council (2013) *The English Effect: The Impact of English, What It's Worth to the UK and Why It Matters to the World*. The British Council. Retrieved 1 September 2023 from www.britishcouncil.org/sites/default/files/english-effect-report-v2.pdf.

Thompson, A.S. (2020) My many selves are still me: Motivation and multilingualism. *Studies in Second Language Learning and Teaching* 10 (1), 159–176.

Vollmann, R. and Soon, T.W. (2018) Chinese identities in multilingual Malaysia. *Grazer Linguistische Studien* 89, 35–61.

Wang T. and Liu Y. (2020) Dynamic L3 selves: A longitudinal study of five university L3 learners' motivational trajectories in China. *The Language Learning Journal* 48 (2), 201–212.

Wang Z. and Zheng Y. (2019) Chinese university students' multilingual learning motivation under contextual influences: A multi-case study of Japanese majors. *International Journal of Multilingualism* 18 (3), 384–401.

Wang, Z., McConachy, T. and Ushioda, E. (2021) Negotiating identity tensions in multilingual learning in China: A situated perspective on language learning motivation and multilingual identity. *The Language Learning Journal* 49 (4), 420–432.

Wong, N.L. (2020) Study abroad programme: The case of Japanese language programme learners. In R. Hassan and P.N. Riget (eds) *Foreign Language Teaching and Learning in the Malaysian Context* (pp. 47–62). University of Malaya Press.

Zheng, Y., Lu, X. and Ren, W. (2019) Profiling Chinese university students' motivation to learn multiple languages. *Journal of Multilingual and Multicultural Development* 40 (7), 590–604.

Zubairi, A.M. and Sarudin, I.H. (2009) Motivation to learn a foreign language in Malaysia. *GEMA Online Journal of Language Studies* 9 (2), 73–87.

10 Understanding Pakistani University Students' Motivations for Learning Chinese in Pakistan: A Bourdieusian Perspective

Muhammad Yasir Khan, Liaquat Ali Channa and Muhammad Mohsin Khan

Introduction

Second language acquisition (SLA) studies over the years have attempted to theorize L2 motivation by seeking to identify factors that influence language learning, such as integrative motivation (Gardner, 1985; Gardner & Lambert, 1959), instrumental motivation (Gardner & MacIntyre, 1991), imagined communities and identities (Pavlenko & Norton, 2007), ideal and ought-to L2 selves (Dörnyei, 2009), and international posture (Yashima, 2009). Motivation serves as the driving force and gives impetus to learning new language/languages; it is the learner's disposition towards learning the target language (Crookes & Schmidt, 1991). People's motivations to learn a target language can range from the desire to obtain something material or practical – 'necessity, utility, advantage, social capital, power, advancement, mobility, migration, and cosmopolitanism' (Ushioda, 2017: 471) – to the desire to integrate into a culture or society out of sheer admiration.

The urge to learn a second language for upward mobility, gaining access to resources and availing oneself of opportunities, is known as instrumental motivation (Gardner & McIntyre, 1991). Such motivation renders language learning a 'tool of narrowly conceived economic interests' rather than a 'humanistic, cultural, and intellectual' endeavor (Lo Bianco, 2014: 322), and much of this has to do with the neo-liberalization and marketization of education around the world. Influenced by the same discourses, language education is also underpinned by the pragmatic focus on transferable, employable and competitive communication skills inducing economic benefits at individual and societal levels (Kubota, 2016). Moreover, there are growing concerns regarding the impact of globalization in terms of the way we think and learn, especially its influence on language education (Kramsch, 2014).

Heller and Duchêne (2012: 3) point out that, in a globalized economy, the motivation to learn a target language (TL) is increasingly dependent on its exchange value, namely its symbolic and economic currency: 'During the 1990s and into the 21st century, language and culture have come to be seen primarily in economic terms'. This is evident from the growing status of English as a global language and its influence on sociopolitical ideologies at the global, national and local levels. In similar vein, Ushioda (2017: 471) posits that 'the globalization of English has a significant impact on socio-political ideologies and educational agendas at local, national, and transnational levels, and these ideologies and agendas, in turn, have inescapable repercussions for language learning motivation at individual level'. Hence, against this backdrop, there arises an interesting question: What motivates the learning of languages other than English (LOTEs)?

The conceptualization and understanding of the motivation to learn a language is highly situated due to the interplay between language learners and their social contexts: 'context and learners are inherently integrated' (Wang & Liu, 2020: 202). Nakamura (2019) demonstrates that a wide array of reasons might motivate language learners to learn LOTEs: for example, an internal drive to learn LOTEs (Ryan & Deci, 2017) or plain and pure enjoyment (de Burgh-Hirabe, 2019). Yet besides the 'specific and personalized reasons on the part of the learner' (Dörnyei & Al-Hoorie, 217: 462), learning a language also involves 'personal meaning-making' (Ushioda, 2009: 217), a process that is influenced by one's immediate and broader social context. This study explores the motivations of a group of Pakistani undergraduate university students for learning Chinese as a foreign language in Pakistan. While most research on language learning in Pakistan has focused on English language as the target language, only a small number of empirical studies has attempted to capture Pakistani individuals' experiences for learning LOTEs, including those of Iqbal and Masroor (2023), Khan et al. (2022) and Malik et al. (2020). The present qualitative study is thus expected to add to the current literature on LOTEs by sharing fresh insights from the relatively under-researched context of Pakistan.

Learning the Chinese Language in Pakistan

The National University of Modern Languages (NUML) in Islamabad, Pakistan was the first university to offer a crash course in Chinese language in 1971 (Azeem *et al.*, 2022). However, the spread and the rapid growth of Chinese learning in Pakistan is a relatively recent phenomenon, mainly due to the mega China–Pakistan Economic Corridor (CPEC) project. Scholarship regarding China–Pakistan relations shows that the relationship between the two countries has been largely strengthened in recent years (Ministry of Foreign Affairs, Government of Pakistan, 2018). This is evident in how the Senate of Pakistan, the Upper House of Parliament, 'passed a resolution "recommending" Chinese-language courses to be taught in Pakistan' (Jakhar, 2018: para. 1). Thus, many Pakistani students have increasingly become interested in learning Chinese.

The CPEC initiative has not only engendered a need to establish Confucius Institutes across the country, given their ability to meet the burgeoning demand for learning Chinese, but it has also led the provincial governments in Pakistan to announce that the Chinese language will be taught as a compulsory language in public education systems (Ali & David, 2022; Raza, 2020). The government of Sindh Province also signed a memorandum of understanding (MoU) with China in 2015. Indeed, a Pakistani daily English language paper reported:

> according to the accord, Chinese will be made a compulsory subject from Class VI in all of Sindh's schools within three years, while students learning the language will gain extra marks and scholarships. Students who pass the subject till matriculation and other higher classes shall also be given opportunities to visit China for education and skills training. (*The Express Tribune*, 2015)

However, there is still little evidence to show that the Chinese language has been introduced into the schools of Sindh province.

Gwadar is the central port city and the focal point of the CPEC projects in the Balochistan province of Pakistan. In 2018 the government of Balochistan ordered the Gwadar Development Authority (GDA) 'to start teaching the Chinese language to the local population' in Gwadar schools (*Arab News*, 2018). In this context of the CPEC in Balochistan province, the China Study Center was established in 2021 at the Balochistan University of Information Technology, Engineering & Management Sciences (BUITEMS), Quetta. BUITEMS is 'a member of the CPEC consortium of universities which pledges to enhance cooperation in business, science, and technologies between China and Pakistan' (BUITEMS, n.d.). Since its launch, the China Study Center at

BUITEMS, Quetta, has been offering crash courses in Chinese language learning to the students of Balochistan.

In considering the literature on learning languages other than English (LOTEs) in Pakistan, there are not many empirical studies to draw on. We find only a few studies related to the problems and policies of Chinese language teaching in Pakistan. Since the demand for Chinese may increase as the focus on the CPEC and its activities is maintained, it would be timely to understand the motives and perspectives of Pakistani students learning the Chinese language. We hold that Bourdieu (1977, 1986) offers an analytically critical lens to make sense of Pakistanis learning Chinese. Therefore, we draw upon his notions of *field*, *habitus*, and *capital* to make sense of Pakistani students' desires to learn Chinese. Taking the paucity of the literature and the present needs into account, we attempt to gain a qualitative understanding of Pakistani university students' motives and perspectives with regard to learning Chinese. We conducted the study in Quetta, Balochistan – the gateway of the CPEC in Pakistan – holding that the study was significant as it would help us understand how the Pakistani students viewed the role of Chinese for their future selves in a postcolonial context where English is a commonly sought after capital.

Conceptual Underpinnings

In his theory on social reproduction, Bourdieu (1977, 1986) coined the notions of field, habitus and capital to explain how social phenomena and human behavior are social products and are socially produced. Many scholars have held that these three concepts are inseparable because explaining one entails the others. For example, Bourdieu held that the field is a dynamic and evolving arena 'of production, circulation, and appropriation and exchange of goods, services, knowledge, or status, and the competitive positions held by actors in their struggle to accumulate, exchange, and monopolize different kinds of power resources (capitals)' (Swartz, 2016: para 1). Thus, every field has rules – referred to as doxa by Bourdieu in his theory of fields – that determine and drive the power struggle for its actors. In this context, Bourdieu (1977) has used higher education institutions, religion, law, literature etc., as examples of fields.

The term doxa refers to a set of beliefs, values and assumptions that is taken for granted within a particular social group or society. These beliefs and values are often so deeply ingrained that they go unquestioned and are perceived as natural or inevitable (Morillas & Romani, 2022). Doxa plays a crucial role in maintaining and reproducing power relations within a given field. It serves to legitimize the dominant positions within the field by defining what is considered legitimate or valuable knowledge, language, behavior and so on. Consequently, capital – cultural, social or economic – which according to Grenfell (2009) is the currency of the field, becomes capital when it is recognized as capital by the doxa of the field. Those who conform to the doxa are more likely to gain status and power within the field, while those who challenge the same can be at risk of being excluded or marginalized.

Bourdieu (1977: 82–83) explained habitus as 'a system of lasting, transposable dispositions which, integrating past experiences, functions at every moment as the matrix of perceptions, appreciations, and actions and makes possible the achievement of infinitely diversified tasks'. Thus, habitus is a subjective expected or probable way of being, thinking, behaving and acting to fit in and play in a particular field to accumulate value and power (capitals). Grenfell and James (1998: 15) held that habitus is 'subjective expectations of objective probabilities'. Malik (2012: 58) further posited that 'habitus includes the way a person uses his or her body' to achieve and/or accumulate resources, power and value (capitals). Bourdieu (1977, 1986) has called value, the power and power resources that an actor in any field expects to achieve, invest, accumulate, convert, expand and/or capitalize as capital, which can be symbolic, social, cultural and economic. An actor behaves in this way through their habitus – through different strategies and techniques of doing and being – because they want to achieve, 'maintain, or enhance' their position in the 'social hierarchy' (Malik, 2012: 52). These conceptual underpinnings offer us a valuable window to make sense of the participants' motives and opinions when learning Chinese in Pakistan.

Data and Methodology

This qualitative study aims to understand the motives and perspectives of those learning the Chinese language in Pakistan. Through the purposive sampling strategy (Creswell & Clark, 2017; Patton, 2002), the researchers recruited 10 male undergraduate students (aged between 18 and 24 years), who were enrolled in a Chinese language program at one of the universities of Quetta, Balochistan province, Pakistan. Six of the participants were enrolled in the HSK 1 course and the remaining four participants were enrolled in the HSK 2 course at the time of data collection. Hanyu Shuiping Kaoshi (HSK) is an international Chinese proficiency test which has six levels marking the different proficiency levels (China Education Center, n.d.). Besides their mother languages, all the participants were fluent in Urdu and the English language, the national and official languages of the country respectively. Table 10.1 provides demographic information about the participants of the study. However, to ensure confidentiality, participants were assigned pseudonyms.

At the time of the data collection – January 2023 – of the 10 participants, seven were enrolled on different undergraduate programs,

Table 10.1 Participant demographics

	Name	Gender	Department	Enrolment status HSK level
1.	Rizwan	Male	BS Economics	Enrolled HSK 1
2.	Kaleem	Male	BS Public Administration	Enrolled HSK 1
3.	Ali	Male	BS Computer Science	Enrolled HSK 1
4.	Sadiq	Male	BS Public Administration	Enrolled HSK 2
5.	Qasim	Male	BS Economics	Enrolled HSK 1
6.	Asif	Male	BS English	Graduated HSK 2
7.	Zameer	Male	BS English	Graduated HSK 2
8.	Salaar	Male	BS Mass Communication	Enrolled HSK 1
9.	Zain	Male	BS Public Administration	Enrolled HSK 1
10.	Muaz	Male	BS Mass communication	Graduated HSK 2

while the remaining three had graduated recently. Moreover, the data collection for the study coincided with the winter vacations of the university. Since Quetta falls within a region that is classified as having long cool winters (Khan et al., 2021), the winter vacations are longer than summer vacations and therefore the researchers could not reach out to female participants beyond university premises as most participants came from conservative societies.

Data were collected by conducting semi-structured interviews and a focus group discussion. Six participants were interviewed individually, and the other four participated in a focus group interview. The choice of the focus group was determined by time constraints since it facilitates collecting rich data in a brief time (Patton, 2002). All the interviews and the discussion were conducted in the Urdu language. Later, the interviews were translated into the English language by the principal author. Interviews ranged from 20 to 25 minutes, and the focus group discussion lasted for 45 minutes.

The collected responses throughout the interviews were thematically analyzed (Braun & Clarke, 2006) continuously. The 6-step thematic analysis proposed by Braun and Clarke (2006) comprises the following: (1) getting familiar with the data; (2) generating initial codes; (3) searching for themes; (4) reviewing themes; (5) defining those themes; and (6) writing them (Maguire & Delahunt, 2017). The interviews were conducted in the Urdu language to ensure active participation. Moreover, all recorded interviews were transcribed and translated into English and double-checked by the first author to ensure the trustworthiness of the study (Halai, 2007). To find the common thematic elements across the responses of the research participants, the researchers thematically analyzed the participants' responses using steps proposed by Braun and Clarke (2006). The participants were briefed about the purpose of the study and were informed of their right to withdraw at any point.

They signed informed consent letters before the interviews to show their willingness.

Findings

An analysis of the interviews reveals that most of the participants believed that learning the Chinese language was effective in furnishing opportunities for pursuing higher education in China. Mindful of the medium of instruction in most of the Chinese universities, they believed learning the Chinese language would facilitate their plans of pursuing Masters and PhD degrees in China. Besides paving new routes to higher education, many of them were of the opinion that learning the Chinese language could potentially make them eligible for an array of jobs opening up in the wake of the mega Chinese projects in Pakistan. Furthermore, many participants held that the growing influence of China in the form of heavy investment in Pakistan makes the Chinese language an important capital to possess. It was also reported that the different nature of the script, and its standing in the political landscape of the province of Balochistan, made learning Chinese a challenging endeavor. However, despite the challenges, many participants saw Chinese as one of the powerful languages around the globe now.

The next section elucidates the themes that emerged after analyzing the focus group discussion and individual interviews.

Chinese as an alternative road to higher education

All the participants in the study reported that they were learning Chinese to avail themselves of the Masters and PhD scholarships awarded by the Chinese government. The interviews highlighted the importance of learning the Chinese language for Pakistani students who wished to pursue higher education in China. Kaleem, a public administration undergraduate, said:

Excerpt 1

Learning Chinese is essential for availing of Chinese scholarships. The Chinese government offers fully-funded scholarships to Pakistani students for Masters and PhD programs.

Another participant, Muaaz, who was a mass communication graduate, stated:

Excerpt 2

The Chinese government is offering many scholarships for those Pakistanis who want to pursue their MS and PhD degrees in China. I am learning Chinese to do my MS and PhD in China. I believe learning the Chinese language would facilitate pursuing my educational career.

Learning Chinese can also help Pakistani students succeed in their academic and professional careers, enabling them to communicate effectively with Chinese colleagues and to build long-lasting relationships with them. Three participants, Asif, Salaar and Ali, were motivated by stories of their friends and teachers who had studied in China and shared their positive experiences of decent learning and living conditions for international students. Asif, one of the English department graduates, reported thus:

Excerpt 3

Hearing stories of friends and teachers who are studying/have studied in China motivates me to learn Chinese. The stories encourage me to pursue my higher education there. I have heard them say that they [the Chinese] provide decent learning and living conditions to international students.

This theme shows that the students interested in availing themselves of Chinese scholarships for higher education were learning the Chinese language to enhance their chances of getting selected for those scholarships. All the participants reiterated the fact that the Chinese language was crucial for Pakistani students who wished to pursue higher education in China. It facilitated communication between the two countries and offered various opportunities, including scholarships and exchange programs. However, it is evident from the responses of the participants that they were learning the language primarily for academic purposes.

Chinese projects as broadening vistas of job opportunities

The interviews highlighted the growing importance of Chinese in Balochistan. The Chinese government's involvement in mega copper and gold projects has motivated people in Pakistan to learn Chinese to communicate with those involved in those projects and take advantage of the opportunities they offer. Rizwan, a BS Economics student and an HSK Level 1 Chinese learner said:

Excerpt 4

China's influence in Balochistan, Pakistan, qualifies Chinese as a very prospective language regarding employability. Moreover, their involvement in mega projects such as a Saindak, Reko Diq, and CPEC motivates people to learn Chinese so that they can avail themselves of opportunities and communicate with people involved in those projects.

He further mentioned that 'Chinese companies prefer to recruit individuals who know their language'. In this vein, Qasim, a first-year BS Economics student, added the following comment:

Excerpt 5

Coming from a middle-class family, learning Chinese promises a bright career as it can help us find lucrative jobs.

The data analysis also showed that the importance of Chinese language proficiency extended beyond employment opportunities. Students who learned Chinese could also avail themselves of scholarships to study in China and potentially even start their businesses there. Additionally, it was important to know that the language was essential for building strong relationships with the local people in China, which could be beneficial for business and education collaborations. This point was clearly articulated by Salaar, as shown in Excerpt 6:

Excerpt 6

Whatever the nature of the venture that you want to start in China, learning Chinese is essential. Moreover, it is vital for bonding with the local people and such bonds are important for business and education collaborations.

The data analysis also suggests that the Chinese language has become a gateway to lucrative jobs and career opportunities in Balochistan, particularly within the context of the Chinese government's investment in the region. The ability to speak Chinese could not only provide a competitive edge in the job market but also create a bridge between the Chinese and Pakistani cultures. This is important for building trust and collaboration between the two nations. Overall, the participants collectively conveyed the view that the Chinese language has become a valuable skill in Pakistan in general, and in Balochistan in particular, owing to the significant Chinese investment in the region.

Learning Chinese amid society's disapproval

All the participants, apart from one, were vocal about the discouraging attitude of people towards learning the Chinese language. Many intimated that their friends, family, and people in their immediate social circles, openly disapproved of and criticized their learning of the language. According to the participants, this critique from the people around them was rooted in fears of a possible imperialist, colonizing future to which the Chinese language might be a precursor. Thus, the sentiments around equating learning the language with slavery resonate among the people. Ali, a computer science student, stated:

Excerpt 7

People around us discourage us from learning Chinese. Learning Chinese is stigmatized in Balochistan because it is associated with the exploitation of local resources. Many of my friends see its learning as a sign of a colonial mindset. They usually tell me that we used to be slaves of the British in the past. And, now, you are preparing yourselves to be ruled by the Chinese [people].

Kaleem, one of the participants in the focus group interview, further pointed out: 'I am discouraged by the people around me. They say learning Chinese is tantamount to preparing oneself for Chinese slavery'. The existing narrative of the association of the Chinese language with exploitation is due to the large-scale projects based around the natural resources of the province and its only port, Gwadar. However, all the participants articulated that despite being demotivated by people around them, they kept learning Chinese because the language had the potential to offer many social opportunities. Echoing this point, Zameer stated:

Excerpt 8

My friends usually demotivate me from learning the Chinese language. They usually say that by learning the Chinese language you are preparing yourself to be enslaved. I pay no heed to what they have to say. I believe that one should do anything that promises new opportunities.

Beyond our ken: An unfamiliar script for an unfamiliar language

All the participants found learning Chinese challenging at different levels. The difficulty was often attributed to its unique characters, pronunciation and grammar. Zameer elucidated this point:

Excerpt 9

Chinese is not a very common language in our context. Its writing system, its pronunciation, and grammar are very different from the languages known to us.

Moreover, a total lack of exposure to Chinese outside the classrooms was another factor that they considered might make learning this language difficult. Talking about the lack of exposure, Zain stated:

Excerpt 10

Learning the Chinese language is a real struggle. In the beginning, I was stuck in the basics. You don't hear the language outside the classrooms. In addition, one of the major difficulties in learning Chinese is its characters, which require persistence and practice.

The sheer number of characters is daunting, and being confused is common.

In a similar vein, Asif reported the difficulties he faced while learning Chinese, as may be seen from Excerpt 11:

Excerpt 11

In the beginning, I faced difficulty in learning Chinese. For the first few classes, everybody would find the mere sounds of Chinese funny. All of us would laugh. However, now I can have a basic conversation in Chinese. The most difficult thing about learning Chinese is its writing system, and the characters. There are 7000 characters in the Chinese language.

Despite these challenges, we can see from the analysis that some students found in-person classes helpful for gaining a better understanding of the language. Moreover, the complexity of the Chinese language and the scarcity of resources for it, made learning Chinese an overwhelming task for many. However, the participants found the language interesting and invested their time in learning it. The conversations also revealed that English was more accessible than Chinese in terms of resources and exposure to the language. Overall, the analysis indicated that learning Chinese was a challenging task due to its unique characters, pronunciation and grammar.

Chinese and China: An inevitable future

The data analysis indicates that all the participants believed that the dominance of Chinese around the world in general, and Pakistan in particular, was an inevitability even though they all differed in terms of the amount of time it might take. All the members of the focus group said: 'we see our future associated with the Chinese language and in China'. The participants' responses revolved around how and in what ways they can learn the Chinese language so that they can be included in the economy associated with it. None of the participants doubted the eventual spread and hegemony of China. To them, it was an irresistible and unavoidable future. As one of the participants (Asif) opined: 'We need to be prepared for these projects. Project vacancies openly mention that besides your other qualifications and credentials, they need Chinese language certification and diplomas too'. He added a rather dismal speculation:

Excerpt 12

Pakistanis must learn Chinese. The amount of debt and the money that Pakistan owes China – which Pakistan is unable to pay – indicates that soon the CPEC would be owned entirely by China and then they would need Pakistanis who can speak and understand the Chinese language.

Introduction of Chinese-language subjects at the provincial level

Upon asking about their views on the ongoing discussion around the introduction of the Chinese language in schools in the provinces of Balochistan and Sindh, most participants were positive about the idea of teaching Chinese at the school level. However, the participants differed in their opinions when it came to the particularities of implementation. Some suggested that Chinese language courses should not be made compulsory in schools and universities but, rather, offered as an optional subject. During the focus group discussion, Rizwan, a BS Economics student, added:

Excerpt 13

The introduction of Chinese language subjects at the primary level in Sindh and Balochistan seems to be a bit impossible. English is different. It was there before the partition. However, Chinese should be introduced as an optional subject in high schools and universities. If implemented in schools, this is going to help academically because the majority of scholarships available to Pakistanis are Chinese ones. Instead of doing IELTS, and GRE, which are expensive tests, we can avail ourselves of HSK Level 1 and Level 2 certificates and study in China.

During the focus group interview, Sadiq mentioned that 'it [the Chinese language] should not be introduced as a compulsory course in schools. Not everyone is interested in learning Chinese or going to China'. Others believed that the introduction of Chinese language courses would be academically advantageous as it would provide new career opportunities for students, broaden their horizons and prepare them for the global market. Moreover, the analysis reveals that many Pakistanis are currently working as translators in Chinese projects. This suggests that there is a need for Pakistanis who can understand and speak the Chinese language. Therefore, it would be wise for the provincial governments of Sindh and Balochistan to introduce Chinese language courses into schools and universities, as the number and scale of Chinese projects in Pakistan are increasing. Overall, in the group interview the difference of opinion regarding the introduction of Chinese as a subject was not about whether it should be introduced as a subject or not: rather, views differed regarding what would be an appropriate grade for introducing it.

The dominance of English: Is Chinese the tortoise of the race?

Participants were cognizant of the dominance of English as a global language and its role as the lingua franca for international communication and commerce. All of them, however, added that there were growing indications that the Chinese language was gaining influence in the world due to China's rapid economic growth and expanding presence in global affairs. Many participants believed that learning Chinese could open doors to opportunities, just as learning English does. The potential for Chinese to become a dominant language is reflected in China's growing economic influence and its investment in various countries around the world, such as the CPEC and One Belt, One Road initiatives. These projects often involve the use of the Chinese language, which can contribute to the spread of the language in those areas. The distribution of Chinese products worldwide also indicates the status of China as a superpower, with the future being Chinese. As Asif stated:

Excerpt 14

English has a far superior status to Chinese now. However, based on the increasing number of Chinese investments around the world, I believe Chinese can emerge as a more powerful and dominant language than English in the future [if God wills].

However, some argue that English still holds a dominant position. Indeed, the US, as a superpower, has promoted English worldwide to maintain its dominance. Nonetheless, the growing interest in learning Chinese reflects the country's increasing significance and power in global affairs, and the language is seen as a way to gain economic benefits and improve one's prospects. Others meanwhile stated that Chinese may take a long time to overtake English, given the latter's extensive use and dominance worldwide. Salaar shared his opinion (Excerpt 15) in this regard:

Excerpt 15

English is a dominant language. The US is on top of everything. It is a leading nation of the world not just in terms of economy but in every walk of life. It has promoted English a lot throughout the world. Similarly, China is the second most powerful emerging economy in the world. Sooner or later, it is going to become a superpower. Even if it doesn't replace the US, it is going to be the second most powerful country. Through their language, it wants other countries to rely on them. Learning Chinese ultimately benefits China.

In Pakistan, the dependence on Chinese products and the scale of Chinese projects have led some to believe that learning Chinese could shortly replace learning English. In this context, Muaaz shared his view:

English is a dominant language. However, in Pakistan, learning Chinese has more immediate economic benefits, which is why I believe everybody should learn the Chinese language. We can see the spread of Chinese influence not just in Pakistan but in the whole world. Half of the products used in Pakistan are Chinese.

Overall, the analysis reveals that the potential for Chinese to become a dominant language reflects China's growing economic and political influence. The participants pointed out the spread of the Chinese language through various projects and initiatives and they suggested that Chinese might eventually become a lingua franca, but it was not clear how much time this might take.

Discussion

In this section, we discuss the significance of the findings. We understand that globalization and the overall move towards a neoliberal orientation have had a great impact on the interpretation of what accounts for the purpose/s of education. According to Rizvi and Lingard (2010: 3), 'educational purposes have been redefined in terms of a narrower set of concerns about human capital development, and the role education must play to meet the needs of the global economy and to ensure the competitiveness of the national economy'. In sum, educational policies are reduced to a knee-jerk response to the needs of the global market and whatever qualifies as necessary for competition. The gravity of responding to global needs and competition has affected the authority of governments to develop their policies. 'The nature of this authority is no longer the same, affected significantly by imperatives of the global economy, shifts in global relations, and the changing patterns of global communication that are transforming people's sense of identity and belonging' (Rizvi & Lingard, 2010: 2).

By being exposed to such discourses, which have redefined the scope of education as a means to meet the needs of the global market and its being central to economic success, individuals have become what Foucault calls *self-contained enterprises* (McNay, 2009). It is evident from the responses of the Pakistani students that the way they want and expect their educational journeys and careers to unfold is directly influenced by the imperatives of the market. The participants' responses have shown how their decision to learn the Chinese language is, to a great extent, motivated by the increasing number of Chinese projects in Pakistan. Moreover, one of the most persistent themes across the responses is that competency in the Chinese language is seen as mandatory to access higher education scholarships in China. In Bourdieusian (1987) terms, participants perceived the Chinese language as an alternate capital that is acquiring currency in the field. Most importantly, recognition conferred by institutions 'makes it possible to establish conversion rates between cultural capital and economic capital by guaranteeing the monetary value of a given academic capital' (Bourdieu, 1987: 21).

Underpinned by the belief that 'economic capital is at the root of all other types of capital' (Bourdieu, 1987: 24), the penchant for learning Chinese among Pakistani students demonstrates that, besides economic uplift, they also see power and value in it: a chance at social uplift. This is quite evident in our analysis, which suggests that the participants see Chinese capital positively, despite the fact that they face criticism for learning Chinese and are considered as looking to secure Chinese colonial jobs. This perception and sense of possibility and agency shape one's preferences and dispositions with which one navigates the fields: this may be viewed as participants' habitus, the 'schemata or structures of perception, conception and action' (Bourdieu, 2002: 27). The decision to learn the language and the orientation towards it is the habitus that the Pakistani students want to traverse within the field, because, according to Edgerton and Roberts (2014: 195), 'it [habitus] entails perceptual schemes of which ends and means are reasonable given that individual's particular position in a stratified society'. Although habitus is interpreted as intrinsically immune to change and individuality, it is not immutable. Writing in this vein, Edgerton and Roberts stated:

> ... although the stability of perceptual and behavioral patterns of the habitus may be the default setting, and novel situations are first encountered in terms of past experiences, habitus is, in fact, adaptive and incrementally modifiable in the face of variant circumstances. That is, the dispositions of habitus are enduring but not unchanging. (2014: 199)

Learning Chinese within the Pakistani context is a manifestation of the mutability and malleability of habitus, which students see as an opportunity for economic and social uplift through the capital of Chinese language proficiency. Moreover, the growing spread of Chinese influence in Pakistan – where English is the official language and, predominantly, the language long affiliated with upward mobility – has begun to be seen as an alternate avenue. Although the participants acknowledged the strongly held monopoly of English in and outside Pakistan, they were optimistic that Chinese would reach a par with English if not replace it. This resonates with the observations of Duchêne and Heller (2012) regarding the increasing exchangeability of the Chinese language in the globalized market of the new economy and its growing symbolic and material value. This is similar to the context of Nepal, 'where English has traditionally occupied the status of the global language and often a colonial language as well ... The importance of Chinese is evident as more Nepalese learn it in order to benefit economically from tourism and other business' (Sharma, 2018). Interestingly, amid English-medium fever, all the participants of the study saw themselves and their futures as associated with the Chinese language. Associated with the increasing number of higher education opportunities, enhancing job prospects and promising business ventures, the Chinese language is considered to be an essential skill and resource in Pakistan (Iqbal & Masroor, 2023; Khan et al., 2022). This demonstrates how linguistic choices and the acquisition of knowledge are governed by the trends and mechanics of the market.

Implications and Limitations

The recognition of a certain language – the Chinese language in the context of this study – in the field as the capital, and the air of inevitability surrounding it, which is the doxa, can also potentially become a source of discontentment and contestation. The sentiments mounting due to the discredited capitals – the under-representation of indigenous languages – are also part of the field. As Bourdieu has rightly put it:

> Hidden behind the statistical relationships between educational capital or social origin and this or that type of knowledge or way of applying it, there are relationships between groups maintaining different, and even antagonistic, relations to culture, depending on the conditions in which they acquired their capital and the markets in which they can derive most profit from it. (Bourdieu, 1979: 4)

Neoliberal rationality, that is 'which governs without governing' (Rojo, 2018: 183), or what might be referred to as the 'reflexive habitus', and its never-ending necessitation for the adaptation on the part of individuals (Crossley, 2001; Sweetman, 2003) thus merits questioning with regard to its existential repercussions on linguistic diversity. Therefore, in seeing the findings of this study through a Bourdieusian understanding, one of the implications that we see is that the inroad of the Chinese language as the profitable capital in the linguistic ecology of Pakistan is adding another layer of diversity to the already linguistically diverse society. Yet Chinese linguistic capital seems to pose challenges not only for the English language but also for the weaker local languages in the field that are already struggling to be officially recognized, along with English and the Urdu language. Given the 'necessity, utility, advantage, social capital, power, advancement, mobility, migration, and cosmopolitanism' (Ushioda, 2017: 471) as the motivation of the language learners, LOTE in Pakistan predominantly means the learning of the Chinese language, which is evident in the growing number of universities and other institutes offering Chinese language courses. This promise of social upward mobility and economic uplift is also discursively capitalized by organizations, institutes and universities through their vision, mission and value statements. Iqbal and Masroor (2023: 17) argue that the 'vision/mission/value statements and ads of organizations involved in CPEC discourse show the underlying themes of a power structure where the potential stakeholders, customers, and Chinese language learners are pushed into an intended way of thinking'.

The emergence of Chinese as a language other than English in Pakistan seems to be quite far off, yet not impossible given its growing influence in the field and on the habitus of people in Pakistan. We admit, however, that this study has certain limitations. One of the main limitations is the representation of the participants. As the study recruited participants from only one of the four provinces of Pakistan, conducting further studies that explore the views and perspectives of students from across the country will prove to be essential in gaining a more holistic picture of the growing symbolic and capital value of Chinese in the region. Therefore, we recommend a countrywide study to gather further insights about the Chinese language and to understand the motives of the learners investing in the language.

References

Ali, A. and David, M.K. (2022) Challenges of teaching Chinese as a subject in an English-dominated region: Focus on Sindh, Pakistan. *IARS International Research Journal* 12 (01), 14–23.
Arab News (2018, 2 October) Schools in Gwadar are instructed to teach Mandarin. https://www.arabnews.com/node/1381331/pakistan.
Azeem, A., Naveed, T. and Jabbar, S. (2022) Chinese language teaching in Pakistan: Problems and solutions. *University of Wah Journal of Social Sciences* 5 (1), 55–80.
Braun, V. and Clarke, V. (2006) Using thematic analysis in psychology. *Qualitative Research in Psychology* 3 (2), 77–101.
Bourdieu, P. (1977) *Outline of a Theory of Practice*. Cambridge University Press.
Bourdieu, P. (1979) *Distinction* (trans. R. Nice). Routledge & Kegan Paul.
Bourdieu, P. (1986) The forms of capital. In J. Richardson (ed.) *Handbook of Theory and Research for the Sociology of Education* (pp. 241–259). Greenwood Press.
Bourdieu P (2002) Habitus. In J. Hillier and E. Rooksby (eds) *Habitus: A Sense of Place* (pp. 27–34). Ashgate.
China Education Center (n.d.) China education center – Study in China is now a lot closer than you think. Available at https://www.chinaeducenter.com/en/.
Creswell, J.W. and Plano Clark, V.L. (2017) *Designing and Conducting Mixed Methods Research*. Sage.
Crookes, G. and Schmidt, R. (1991) Motivation: Reopening the research agenda. *Language Learning* 41 (4), 469–512.
Crossley, N. (2001) The phenomenological habitus and its construction. *Theory and Society* 30, 81–120.
de Burgh-Hirabe, R. (2019) Motivation to learn Japanese as a foreign language in an English speaking country: An exploratory case study in New Zealand. *System* 80, 95–106.
Dörnyei, Z. (2009) The L2 motivational self system. In Z. Dörnyei ad E. Ushioda (eds) *Motivation, Language Identity and the L2 Self* (pp. 9–42). Multilingual Matters.
Dörnyei, Z. and Al-Hoorie, A.H. (2017) The motivational foundation of learning languages other than global English: Theoretical issues and research directions. *The Modern Language Journal* 101 (3), 456–468.
Duchêne, A. and Heller, M. (2012) *Language in Late Capitalism: Pride and Profit*. Routledge.
Edgerton, J.D. and Roberts, L.W. (2014) Cultural capital or habitus? Bourdieu and beyond in the explanation of enduring educational inequality. *Theory and Research in Education* 12 (2), 193–220.
Gardner, R.C. (1985) *Social Psychology and Second Language Learning: The Role of Attitudes and Motivation*. Edward Arnold.
Gardner, R.C. and Lambert, W.E. (1959) Motivational variables in second-language acquisition. *Canadian Journal of Psychology* 13 (4), 266–272.
Gardner, R.C. and MacIntyre, P.D. (1991) An instrumental motivation in language study: Who says it isn't effective? *Studies in Second Language Acquisition* 13 (1), 57–72.

Grenfell, M. (2009) Applying Bourdieu's field theory: The case of social capital and education. *Education, Knowledge and Economy* 3 (1), 17–34.
Grenfell, M. and James, D. (1998) *Bourdieu and Education*. Falmer Press.
Halai, N. (2007) Making use of bilingual interview data: Some experiences from the field. *The Qualitative Report* 12 (3), 344–355. https://doi.org/10.46743/2160-3715/2007.1621.
Heller, M. and Duchêne, A. (2012) Pride and profit: Changing discourses of language, capital and nation–state. In A. Duchêne and M. Heller (eds) *Language in Late Capitalism* (pp. 1–21). Routledge.
Iqbal, J. and Masroor, F. (2023) Projecting the Chinese language as a power tool in the discourse on the China–Pakistan Economic Corridor (CPEC). *International Journal of Strategic Communication*, 1–18. https://doi.org/10.1080/1553118x.2023.2204295.
Jakhar, P. (2018) Reality check: Is Chinese an official language in Pakistan? *BBC News*, 28 February. https://www.bbc.com/news/world-asia-43158523.
Khan, M.S., Zaki, S. and Memon, N. (2022) Chinese as a mandatory foreign language at a higher education institution in Pakistan. *South Asia Research* 43 (1), 49–67.
Khan, S., Shahab, S., Fani, M.I., Wahid, A., Hasan, M. and Khan, A. (2021) Climate and weather condition of Balochistan province, Pakistan. *International Journal of Economic and Environmental Geology* 12 (2), 65–71.
Kramsch, C. (2014) Teaching foreign languages in an era of globalization: Introduction. *The Modern Language Journal* 98 (1), 296–311.
Kubota, R. (2016) Neoliberal paradoxes of language learning: Xenophobia and international communication. *Journal of Multilingual and Multicultural Development* 37 (5), 467–480.
Lo Bianco, J. (2014) Domesticating the foreign: Globalization's effects on the place/s of languages. *The Modern Language Journal* 98 (1), 312–325.
Maguire, M. and Delahunt, B. (2017) Doing a thematic analysis: A practical, step-by-step guide for learning and teaching scholars. *All Ireland Journal of Teaching and Learning in Higher Education* 9 (3), 3351–3365.
Malik, A.H. (2012) A comparative study of elite-English-medium schools, public schools, and Islamic madaris in contemporary Pakistan: The use of Pierre Bourdieu's theory to understand 'Inequalities in educational and occupational Opportunities'. Unpublished doctoral dissertation, Department of Sociology and Equity Studies in Education, University of Toronto. Available at https://tspace.library.utoronto.ca/bitstream/1807/34798/1/Malik_Akhtar_H_201211_EdD_thesis.pdf.
Malik, S.N., Qin, H., Khan, S.G. and Ahmed, K. (2020) Quantitative analysis of the foreign language anxiety: Chinese and Pakistani postgraduates in focus. *Arab World English Journal* 11 (1), 315–330.
McNay, L. (2009) Self as enterprise. *Theory, Culture & Society* 26 (6), 55–77.
Ministry of Foreign Affairs, Government of Pakistan (2018) Pakistan and China diplomatic relations – Ministry of Foreign Affairs. Mofa.gov.pk. https://mofa.gov.pk/pakistan-and-china-diplomatic-relations/.
Morillas, M. and Romani, L. (2022) Ideology, doxa and critical reflexive learning: The possibilities and limits of thinking that 'diversity is good'. *Management Learning* 54 (4), 511–530. https://doi.org/10.1177/13505076221074632.
Nakamura, T. (2019) Understanding motivation for learning languages other than English: Life domains of L2 self. *System* 82, 111–121.
Patton. M.Q. (2002) *Qualitative Research and Evaluation Methods* (3rd edn). Sage.
Pavlenko, A. and Norton, B. (2007) Imagined communities, identity, and English language learning. In J. Cummins and C. Davison (eds) *International Handbook of Language Teaching* (pp. 669–680). Springer.
Raza, K. (2020) Language policy for China-Pakistan cooperation. *Language on the Move*, 20 July. www.languageonthemove.com/language-policy-for-china-pakistan-cooperation/.
Rizvi, F. and Lingard, B. (2010) *Globalizing Education Policy*. Routledge.

Rojo, L.M. (2018) Neoliberalism and linguistic governmentality. In J.W. Tollefson and M.P. Milans (eds) *The Oxford Handbook of Language Policy and Planning* (pp.544–567). Oxford University Press.

Ryan, R.M. and Deci. E.L. (2017) *Self-Determination Theory: Basic Psychological Needs in Motivation, Development, and Wellness*. Guilford Press.

Sharma, B.K. (2018) Non-English lingua franca? Mobility, market and ideologies of the Chinese language in Nepal. *Global Chinese* 4 (1), 63–88. Available at https://doi.org/10.1515/glochi-2018-0004.

Swartz, D.L. (2016) *Bourdieu's Concept of Field*. Oxford Bibliographies (online). Oxford University Press.

Sweetman, P. (2003) Twenty-first century dis-ease? Habitual reflexivity or the reflexive habitus. *The Sociological Review* 51 (4), 528–549.

The Express Tribune (2015, 25 March) MoU signed to teach Chinese in Sindh schools. Available at www.tribune.com.pk/story/858704/mou-signed-to-teach-chinese-in-sindh-schools.

Ushioda, E. (2009) A person-in-context relational view of emergent motivation, self and identity. In Z. Dörnyei and E. Ushioda (eds) *Motivation, Language Identity and the L2 Self* (pp. 215–228). Multilingual Matters.

Ushioda, E. (2017) The impact of global English on motivation to learn other languages: Toward an ideal multilingual self. *The Modern Language Journal* 101 (3), 469–482.

Wang, T. and Liu, Y. (2020) Dynamic L3 selves: A longitudinal study of five university L3 learners' motivational trajectories in China. *The Language Learning Journal* 48 (2), 201–212.

Yashima, T. (2009) International posture and the ideal L2 self in the Japanese EFL context. In Z. Dörnyei and E. Ushioda (eds) *Motivation, Language Identity and the L2 Self* (pp. 144–163). Multilingual Matters.

11 Understanding Challenges, Strategy Use and the Ideal Multilingual Self of Internally Displaced Syrians on the Syria–Turkey Border

Anas Hajar

Introduction

The Arab Spring refers to a wave of pro-democracy protests that began in late 2010 in Tunisia and involved associated uprisings in the Middle East and North Africa. It had a transformative impact on the region, resulting in the downfall of regimes in Tunisia, Egypt, Libya and Yemen. The wave of uprisings reached Syria but had a different outcome. Syria's uprising turned into the prolonged quagmire of a civil war that remains unresolved to this day. Bombing raids and intense clashes between armed opposition groups and the government have also led to the displacement of millions of Syrians, both internally and externally, affecting all aspects of daily life, including education.

One area with an influx of many internally displaced Syrians is the Afrin district of Aleppo governorate in northwest Syria, the context of the present study. ACAPS estimates that there are 442,000 Syrians living in Afrin (ACAPS, 2021). Since March 2018, Turkish Armed Forces have maintained control of the district and adopted a Turkification policy in parts of northwestern Syria to 'influence and control, not just support' (Yüksel & Veen, 2019: 6). This is evidenced through the introduction of the Turkish language as a compulsory subject in the primary school curriculum. Syrians have also been compelled to obtain new ID cards issued by the Turkish authority to gain access to basic social services like education and healthcare (Yüksel & Veen, 2019). In addition, Turkish is used instead of Arabic in the linguistic landscape of areas under Turkey's control (Yüksel & Veen, 2019). As a result of these developments, many internally displaced Syrians in Afrin have become motivated to learn Turkish for various purposes.

Research into L2 motivation has predominately focused on English as the target language due to its 'necessity, utility, advantage, social capital, power, advancement, mobility, migration, and cosmopolitanism' (Ushioda, 2017: 471). In a review of journal articles and book chapters published between 2005 and 2014 (N = 416) concerning L2 motivation, Boo *et al.* (2015: 151) found that almost 73% of empirical studies investigated the motives for English language learning. Ortega (2022: 237) points out that there has been an increase in studies using a *multilingual lens* to understand the L2 motivation of multilingual students in learning languages other than English (LOTEs) in both Anglophone and non-Anglophone contexts, especially after Ushioda and Dörnyei's (2017) special issue of *The Modern Language Journal*. Takahashi (2023: 31), however, argues that there is 'a geographical skewness' to previous studies of LOTEs because most have been conducted in European and Anglophone contexts.

In a similar vein, Ortega (2022) asserts the importance of the *social justice lens* by investigating the L2 motivation of multilinguals living in non-affluent geographical contexts, like those suffering in, or fleeing from, war. In line with this perspective, the present qualitative study explores six internally displaced Syrians' experiences of learning Turkish as L3 or L4 while geographically situated in Afrin. The study considers their underlying language learning motivation and the learners' strategic efforts. In what follows, the *social turn* in language learning strategies (LLSs) and previous LOTE motivation studies in Asia are explained. The chapter then describes the theoretical framework adopted in this study, before providing an analysis of the responses of the study participants. It concludes by illustrating the pedagogical implications and limitations of the study.

Advancing a Sociocultural Perspective of LOTE Motivation and LLS Research

Following the 'social turn' in language education (Block, 2003), sociocultural perspectives have recently become more established in language learning research (Hajar *et al.*, 2023). From social perspectives, we understand a variety of approaches to learning that stress the importance of social, political and cultural processes in mediating language learners' cognitive and metacognitive processes. Some researchers have adopted socially oriented theoretical models (e.g. Hajar, 2021; Norton,

2013; Thomas & Rose, 2019; Ushioda, 2020), emphasising the research value of focusing on 'real persons situated in particularized social realities, rather than on language learners as idealized theoretical abstractions' (Ushioda 2020: 42). In this sense, from a sociocultural perspective, language learners are perceived as socially constrained but also as agents in active pursuit of both linguistic and non-linguistic objectives, mainly related to identity construction and development. That is, they interact with the outside world to gain a foothold in the contexts in which they find themselves, and use different social, cultural and material resources, such as siblings, textbooks, media, technology and language itself (Thomas *et al.*, 2022).

Research on individual differences in language learning and use has increasingly used a sociocultural lens to capture the dynamics and context sensitivity of individuals' language learning experiences according to their particular situation or task (Li *et al.*, 2022). The social turn has been associated with a methodologically qualitative approach to research (Takahashi, 2023). In this regard, May (2014: 2) underlines the need to 'resituate the issue of multilingualism more centrally in applied linguistics' and focus on individuals' holistic linguistic repertoires and the interconnections between L1, L2, L3 and Lx. Understanding a person's experience of language learning is not only about their strategic efforts to learn a specific language but also about their multilingual orientation and their sense of self in relation to the larger social world that underlies their multiple identities as 'student', 'immigrant', 'actor', 'university lecturer' etc. The concept of the *ideal multilingual self* (Henry, 2017; Ushioda, 2017) has thus been proposed to delineate individuals' motivation for multiple language learning in a globalised world where multilingualism is the norm in many societies.

Takahashi (2023) points out that LOTE motivation is sometimes called L3 motivation due to the dominance of English in the globalised world, which means that most multilingual individuals in non-English speaking countries study English as their first L2. Takahashi (2023) further argues that most studies of LOTE motivation have been conducted in European and Anglophone contexts (e.g. Busse, 2017; Henry, 2020; Oakes & Howard, 2022; Thompson, 2020), while the bulk of language learning motivation research comes from Asia, largely investigating motivation to learn English as a foreign language. An increasing number of LOTE motivation studies has recently been noted in Asia, however, and especially in China (e.g. Teo *et al.*, 2019; Wang & Zheng, 2021; Zheng *et al.*, 2020), Japan (e.g. Fukui & Yashima, 2021; Takahashi, 2023; Umino & Benson, 2016) and, to a lesser extent, in other Asian countries such as Iran (e.g. Nourzadeh *et al.*, 2020), Malaysia (e.g. Nikitina & Furuoka, 2019), Saudi Arabia (e.g. Al-Nofaie, 2018) and Vietnam (e.g. Han, 2021). Almost all these studies have been carried out in stable or peaceful states, with Dörnyei's (2009) L2 motivational self system (L2MSS) as the theoretical framework, originally developed to understand language learner motivation for studying English (e.g. the 30 studies synthesised by Mendoza & Phung, 2019).

Dörnyei's (2009) L2MSS identifies two kinds of possible self: the *ought-to* and *ideal* selves. The *ought-to language self* encapsulates the pressures from significant others or external factors that learners are aware of throughout the language learning process and which makes them attempt to avoid any possible negative consequences (Dörnyei, 2009). Takahashi (2023: 17) indicates that the goals or visions of the *ought-to self* are likely to be 'for a shorter period of time and anxiety-provoking' because they are less internalised within the self and entail responsibilities or duties. Conversely, *the ideal language self* is an idealised self-image that captures how much an individual is willing to invest in language learning to achieve their personal hopes, dreams and wishes for their vocational or social purposes (Dörnyei, 2009). An individual's ideal self-vision can be prompted by specific motivational language orientations; *integrativeness* (Gardner, 1985) and *international posture* (i.e. an interest in intercultural friendship and international affairs along with openness to other cultures) (Yashima, 2002).

Achieving the ideal language self, as Dörnyei and Kubanyiova (2014: 11) point out, should be accompanied by 'relevant and effective procedural strategies that act as a roadmap towards the goal', similar to an elite athlete's training plan. Otherwise, one's future vision turns into having 'the character more of fantasy rather than concrete ambition' (Lamb, 2013: 24). The sociocultural view of LLSs does not seek to eliminate the individual from the picture but, rather, focuses on the interaction 'between the individual and the social; between the human agency of these learners and the social practices of their communities' (Norton & Toohey, 2001: 308). The present study adopts Hajar's (2019) definition of LLSs, which stresses the dynamism and context-sensitivity of LLSs. Hajar (2019) claims that LLSs are an individual's active engagement in the learning process in a particular setting in order to achieve their proximal learning goals – for instance, getting high grades – and/or ultimate ones like mastering the target language for academic, professional and/or national advancement.

Study Details

This qualitative study is the first empirical study to explore a group of internally displaced Syrians' multilingual selves and their strategic language learning of a LOTE in a conflict-affected situation. The study was guided by the following research questions:

(1) What motivated the participants to learn Turkish as an L3 or L4 in Afrin, Syria?
(2) What strategies did they use to achieve their learning goals?

The participants were three females and three males aged between 18 and 34 years. Given that the information to be disclosed was likely to be sensitive, the researcher was particularly conscious of the need for anonymity. The participants are referred to by the pseudonyms Jamal, Dina, Mazen, Nawal, Rula and Zaid. All were Syrian and had moved from their homes of Aleppo or Damascus – two Syrian cities – to Afrin in 2018 or 2019. Arabic was their native language, although two participants – Jamal and Nawal – were bilingual (Kurdish and Arabic). They had begun to learn the English language in Grade 5 of a public primary school when they were 10 years old. None of the participants was known to the researcher prior to data collection. The participants were recruited with the help of the director of a tutorial centre in Afrin after the researcher had arranged an online meeting with her on WhatsApp to explain the aims and procedures of the study. All the participants had willingly agreed to participate in this study and all were at pre-intermediate or intermediate level in Turkish. The participants' profiles are shown in Table 11.1.

Two semi-structured, in-depth interviews with each participant were conducted online via WhatsApp, the only online platform all the participants were familiar with. Each interview lasted approximately one hour. All the interviews were conducted in Arabic to help the participants express their ideas clearly and confidently. With the participants' permission, all the interviews were audiotaped and transcribed. The researcher conducted member checks, by which he gave the participants the transcripts of their interviews to review and asked them to indicate if the transcripts accurately represented the perceptions, views and experiences they had given.

The data were analysed using Braun and Clarke's (2013) guidelines for conducting thematic analysis, to identify themes and interpret them in rich detail. First, the data were transcribed verbatim in Arabic and then translated into English by an expert translator to ensure meaning was preserved. The researcher familiarised himself with the data by reading and re-reading the interview transcripts critically to generate initial codes in the light of the research questions. Codes that shared common features were grouped to generate themes and sub-themes. The final thematic map of the data was then produced (Figure 11.1). The next section offers excerpts under each theme to illustrate the participants' in-depth accounts of their experiences.

Table 11.1 Demographic data of the participants

Name	Gender	Age	Birthplace	Education	Family background notes	Job	Marital status
Rula	Female	33	Rural Damascus	BA in chemistry	Father was a farmer, mother a housewife	Housewife	Married
Dina	Female	18	Rural Aleppo	Preparing for the baccalaureate examination	Parents separated	Secondary school student	Engaged (to a Turkish man)
Nawal	Female	18	Aleppo	Preparing for the baccalaureate examination	Father was an architect, mother a physics teacher	Secondary school student	Single
Jamal	Male	34	Rural Aleppo	MA in English language and literature	Parents were farmers	Private tutor of English	Married
Zaid	Male	26	Damascus	BA in Arabic literature	Father was a government clerk, mother a housewife	Clerk in a humanitarian organisation in Afrin	Single
Mazen	Male	25	Rural Damascus	BA in biology	Parents were farmers	Private tutor of Arabic	Single

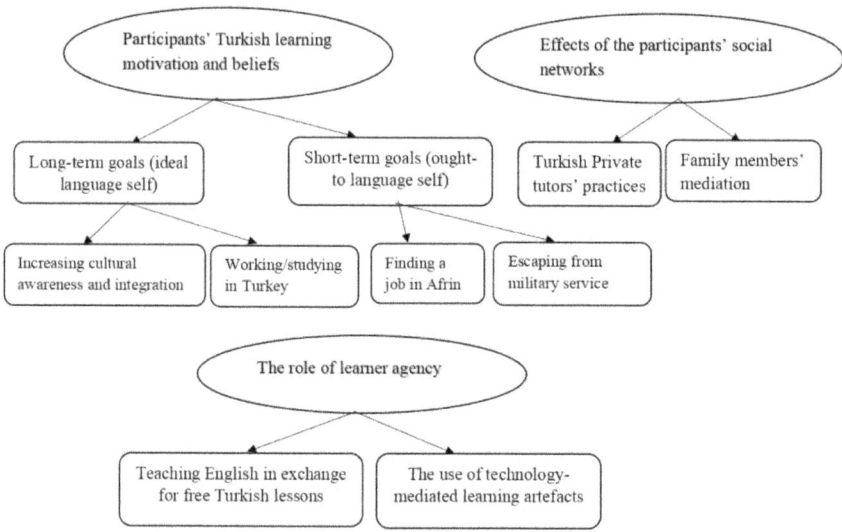

Figure 11.1 The final thematic map

Findings

This section examines the three main themes that emerged from the analysis of the interview data: the *participants' motivation for learning Turkish and their beliefs*; the *mediating role of social actors*; and the *role of learner agency*. Notably, these emergent themes, which influenced the participants' strategic language learning efforts and future vision, operated together, as revealed in the next sub-sections.

Participants' motivation for learning Turkish and their beliefs

The data analysis showed that the ought-to language self originated from a sense of duty and that the avoidance of possible negative future outcomes (e.g. being afraid of being conscripted for military service and being jobless) dominated Mazen's motivational discourse. Such motivation tended to have a short-term effect and made Mazen confine his LLSs largely to those regulated by his Turkish private tutor. Such strategies, as Hajar (2021) describes, are *compulsory strategies* because they are employed by an individual to achieve proximal learning goals and are in response to the direct involvement or coercion of some influential actors, principally teachers and parents. Excerpt 1 elucidates this point.

Excerpt 1

Before the Civil war in Syria, my focus was only on improving my English level. I never thought of learning Turkish. I moved to Afrin in 2019 to escape from military service. I gradually recognised the importance of learning Turkish to find a job in Afrin. Having an adequate level of Turkish is essential to work in any humanitarian organisation here ... I'm currently teaching Arabic in a tutorial centre, but I'm unhappy because my salary is poor ... I depend almost only on the teaching materials provided by a tutor to improve my Turkish because I couldn't find Turkish people here. (Zaid, first interview)

The experiential account of another participant, Jamal, indicates that he had dual goals for learning Turkish: (1) his short-term goal was to secure an additional income to support his family in Afrin, and (2) his long-term goal was to learn more about Turkish culture and to obtain the required score on the TÖMER test as a prerequisite for working as an English instructor at one of the Turkish colleges. The TÖMER test measures an applicant's Turkish language proficiency, and is a condition for entry into Turkish universities for foreigners to obtain a government position, as elucidated in Excerpt 2:

Excerpt 2

Thousands of Syrians moved to Afrin, which made the town more densely populated. Many newcomers were university graduates and many started teaching English like me ... As Turkish is now taught from Grade 1 at schools in Afrin, I decided to learn Turkish to find an additional job to support my family. I'm interested in learning about Turkish culture, especially since it is similar to Syria. Further, I want to get a good score on the TÖMER test to be able to teach English at one of the Turkish universities in the future. (Jamal, first interview)

Two participants (Mazen and Rula) articulated long-term goals for learning Turkish. Both were interested in expanding their knowledge of Turkish culture. In addition, after moving to Turkey with her husband, Rula aspired to help her two children's education without the need to hire a private tutor. In Excerpt 3, Mazen asserts that learning Turkish would be essential to finding a job in Turkey:

Excerpt 3

I decided to learn Turkish because I had free time. Also, my older brother living in Turkey encouraged me to learn Turkish to find a job if I move there ... I recently discovered that there are large cultural similarities between Turkey and Syria in terms of lifestyle and religious practices ... I know English is an international language, but Turkish is now more important to me. (Mazen, first interview)

An integrative motivation was particularly evident in Dina's case because she was engaged to a Turkish man living in Afrin and intended to move to Turkey after getting married (Excerpt 4):

Excerpt 4

As I am engaged to a Turkish man living in Afrin, I must learn and master Turkish. I will settle down in Tukey after marriage. I also plan to study at one of the Turkish Universities. I can say that Turkish is now more important than English to me … Turkish has some similarities with Kurdish. (Dina, first interview)

The mediating role of social actors

By examining the data related to the mediating role of social actors on the participants' motivation and future vision while learning Turkish, two kinds of fundamental agents emerged: namely *family members* and *private tutors*. Apart from Nawal, all the other participants had experienced a noticeable lack of almost any kind of support from their immediate family members for their Turkish language learning (or even their education). They ascribed this limited family involvement in their language learning and development to the low income and education levels of their parents. That is, their parents, as internally displaced figures, were unable to offer an appropriate language learning environment for their children – for instance, by purchasing Turkish learning material or creating opportunities for practising Turkish. As a result, most participants found themselves in a less favorable position because they could afford little or no private Turkish tutoring courses, even with poorly qualified tutors, thus adding to their social disadvantage.

Nevertheless, one participant, Nawal, reported that her father was well educated and financially stable, and that he was both directly and indirectly involved in Nawal's strategic Turkish efforts, especially since he had completed his Bachelor's degree in Turkey before the Syrian civil war in 2011. After moving to Afrin in 2019, Nawal's father realised that mastering Turkish would be essential for his daughter's academic studies and future job prospects. Therefore, he attempted to instil a positive attitude and motivate her to learn Turkish by practising oral Turkish at home, watching Turkish programmes together, sending her on a private Turkish course and intentionally purchasing some Turkish resources (e.g. Turkish movies and novels) for her. Nawal made the following comment (Excerpt 5):

Excerpt 5

My father can speak Turkish. Before moving to Afrin, he used to communicate in Arabic and Kurdish with us. In Afrin, my father taught me the basics of Turkish and verb tenses … We sometimes watch Turkish programs or movies together and I ask him about the meaning of some words. Interestingly, I discovered how some Kurdish words are very similar to Turkish such as *masa* [table], *hafta* [week], *renk* [colour], *pencere* [window] and *peynir* [cheese] … My father purchased interesting novels for me, such as *Sadako and the Thousand Paper Cranes* and *Eroinle Dans*. They were translated into Turkish … I also like to record my speech and listen to it. This is an effective strategy for me to improve my pronunciation. (Nawal, second interview)

Excerpt 5 reveals that Nawal displayed a balance between the use of compulsory and voluntary strategies while learning Turkish. Another participant, Rula, described how her husband encouraged her to attend a Turkish language course with him and practise Turkish together (i.e. affective and social strategies), as described in Excerpt 6:

Excerpt 6

Some of my relatives told me that Turkish was difficult and that there was no point in learning it. However, my husband motivated me to register for a Turkish course with him. He also sometimes uses Turkish with me in our daily communication. We decided to use Turkish when we texted each other on WhatsApp. (Rula, second interview)

One participant, Dina, also reported (Excerpt 7) that her Turkish fiancé had encouraged her to learn Turkish and try out some metacognitive and social strategies (e.g. by asking questions in Turkish for clarification or correction and by learning new vocabulary in context):

Excerpt 7

I was shy talking to my fiancé because I knew only some Turkish vocabulary, so I used to rely on a translation program I downloaded on my smartphone when I talked to him. He always encouraged me to use Turkish with him and practise what I had learnt on the course with him so he could clarify anything I didn't understand. (Dina, second interview)

In this study, all the participants indicated that they had attended private tutoring in Turkish at a tutorial centre in Afrin. These courses did not meet their expectations, mainly because the tutors were Syrian and lacked the appropriate experience in teaching Turkish. As shown in Excerpt 8, they still regarded them as useful for obtaining some of the knowledge necessary to search for jobs in Afrin and/or to prepare themselves for the TÖMER test as a prerequisite for applying for academic jobs or applying to universities in Turkey.

Excerpt 8

After I moved to Afrin, I attended two Turkish courses at a tutorial centre for seven months. The cost of each course was almost 40$. I currently cannot afford other courses. The tutor was Syrian. Although he sometimes mispronounced some words and had little experience in teaching Turkish, I learnt from him many useful grammar rules and vocabulary. For example, the most important element in Turkish is the verb, which comes at the end of the sentence. Also, there's a similarity in pronouncing some Arabic and Turkish words, for instance, *adalet* [justice], *basit* [simple], *beyit* [house], *cezire* [island], *dakika* [minute] and *devlet* [government] ... The language certificate I got from this institute could be beneficial when I apply for jobs. (Mazen, second interview)

Excerpt 8 reveals how private tutors – despite their insufficient teaching experience and Turkish language proficiency – helped the participants to access some effective LLSs. Examples of these strategies were memory and cognitive strategies such as grouping and associating the new vocabulary with other known words with similar pronunciations.

The role of learner agency

All the participants recognised that the input they obtained from their private tutors to learn and improve their level in Turkish was not sufficient, so, to varying degrees, they exercised their agentive power by capitalising on the language opportunities offered by informal social actors and investing more time in learning and practising Turkish in out-of-class contexts. Learner agency implies that learners should not only be perceived as 'reactive to context but also as complex human beings ... [who] make sense of and engage with contexts and can also change and influence contexts' (Mercer, 2012: 43). Almost all participants highlighted the role of technology-mediated learning artefacts (e.g. TV movies and series, music, WhatsApp and the internet) in mediating their strategic language learning efforts. For example, three participants (Dina, Nawal and Rula) reported that they used to watch Turkish drama series dubbed in spoken Syrian before moving to Afrin. However, after the move, they started watching these series on TV channels or YouTube in their original versions with Turkish and sometimes Arabic subtitles. Excerpt 9 clarifies this point:

Excerpt 9

After coming to Afrin, I started watching Turkish drama series on TV channels or YouTube that had subtitles in Turkish and sometimes in Arabic. Watching Turkish series such as *El-Ahd* and *Miracle Doctor* helped me to learn new vocabulary in context and to know more about Turkish culture and people ... If I don't understand something while I am watching a series, I play it again and sometimes jot down new words and phrases in my notebook to lodge them in my memory. (Rula, first interview)

Excerpt 9 illustrates how watching TV series in Turkish as a purposeful LLS led some participants to expand their exposure to Turkish input and accumulate a repository of vocabulary items and phrases, along with developing their cultural understanding (i.e. cognitive and social strategies).

Three participants (Rula, Jamal, Mazen) shared their reflections on the experience of joining a WhatsApp group created by some Syrians to improve their Turkish language learning and exchange ideas. Referring to this point, Mazen says (Excerpt 10):

Excerpt 10

My Syrian friend learning Turkish advised me to join a WhatsApp group, especially since most people in Afrin cannot afford to pay for Turkish courses … it is run by a teacher from Turkistan, a minority group in Syria. … He and some other members of the group post new Turkish vocabulary, proverbs, and grammatical rules daily on the WhatsApp group. There is one condition in this group: anything one posts should be in both Arabic and Turkish. (Mazen, second interview)

Interestingly, Jamal reported that he developed his oral skills and preparation for the TÖMER test with the help of a Turkish man who was working in one of the humanitarian organisations in Afrin. Given that Jamal was unable to afford other private Turkish tutoring courses, he exercised his agency by suggesting he teach this Turkish man some English in exchange (Excerpt 11):

Excerpt 11

One Turkish man working in a humanitarian organisation was having private English tutoring at the institute where I teach. He accepted my offer to teach him English, and he trained me for the TÖMER test since he holds a Bachelor's degree in Turkish literature … He provided me with written feedback on my essays and I also practised Turkish with him. (Jamal, second interview)

In this sense, most participants acted as proactive agents by displaying their capability in terms of thinking, wishing and acting when recognising the significance of a specific activity to overcome certain contextual constraints and accomplish their ultimate goals (see Hajar, 2021).

Discussion and Implications

The findings presented illustrate how the positive benefits of exercising agency were not confined to participants reinforcing and expanding their multilingual repertoires during the civil wars in their countries. In addition to the likelihood of helping them professionally by finding a job in Afrin or Turkey, learning Turkish has led them to have a certain level of cultural enrichment, as testified by Dina's ability to communicate with her fiancé in Turkish and most participants' increasing interest in building meaningful friendships with Turkish citizens and watching Turkish drama series on TV channels or YouTube. There has thus been a degree of cultural as well as vocational enrichment, and this is related to the orientations of travel, knowledge and friendship identified by Kruidenier and Clement (1986).

Related to this, Teo *et al.* (2019) investigated what motivated a group of Chinese University students to learn Japanese despite unfavourable sociopolitical conditions between China and Japan. The study found that most participants showed an interest in Japan's cultural products, such as comics and popular culture, in addition to the employment opportunities associated with learning Japanese. It also revealed how learning Japanese contributed to all participants' positive attitudes to Japan, without being influenced by the negative image portrayed of the two countries in the media. In this sense, learning a language can promote cross-cultural exchanges, mutual understanding, and peace between people of different communities, regardless of their religious or political beliefs. This point was echoed in the present study, which demonstrated the participants' positive perceptions of, and attitudes to, Turkish society and culture, in spite of the escalating diplomatic tensions between the governments of Syria and Turkey and increased negative media coverage over the last decade.

The findings of this study align with the call of some researchers (e.g. Gkonou *et al.*, 2021; Ortega & Oxford, 2023; Oxford *et al.*, 2021; Teo *et al.*, 2019) to foreground the encouragement of language educators to minimise the negative impact of wider contextual processes, such as rising tensions between the two countries, on language learners and bring the world together through language learning. Gkonou *et al.* (2021), for instance, have highlighted the significance of training prospective second language teachers to become peacebuilders, and to enable them to promote a peaceful environment in the classroom when they begin teaching and to have a positive impact on future generations of language learners. In this regard, language teacher preparation programmes should incorporate fundamental concepts of peace and provide strategic activities for teachers of English/LOTEs to integrate peacebuilding competencies gradually and consciously into their knowledge base (Gkonou *et al.*, 2021). The competencies for peacebuilding mainly involve language teachers' willingness to learn about, relate to and respect other cultures, acknowledging similarities and differences between their native culture and others (Gkonou *et al.*, 2021). Further research on LOTE motivation needs to explore the nexus between motivations for learning/teaching LOTEs and peacebuilding.

As shown in the present study, the participants displayed a sense of agency to varying degrees according to their different contextual constraints and affordances and their learning goals. They mainly adopted a variety of LLSs mediated by social actors and invested more time in learning and practising Turkish across different settings. As Mercer (2012: 55–56) points out, learner agency is not 'readily quantifiable and is perhaps best discussed in terms of degrees of agency on a continuum from highly agentic to moderately or weakly agentic'. To illustrate, Jamal exercised a higher degree of agency than other participants in relation to the use of LLSs by, for example, recognising that attending low-quality private tutoring courses in Turkish would not enable him to master Turkish and achieve his ideal desired future self-image. In addition to the use of technology-mediated language learning artefacts outside the tutorial sessions, he approached a Turkish man working in Afrin to teach him Turkish, especially because he could not afford high-quality tutoring in Turkish.

The study also revealed that all the participants had attended fee-paying private courses in Turkish, which in turn, directly or indirectly, caused them to employ certain LLSs. Despite its popularity and its implications for theories, practices and policies, research on private tutoring in languages is still in its infancy (Yung & Hajar, 2023), particularly in LOTEs. This is arguably a fruitful area for further research that can link the fields of applied linguistics and comparative education and assist language practitioners, researchers and policymakers in capturing a comprehensive picture of an individual's language learning experiences across different settings, without missing 'alternative perspectives on the meaning of, and social and cognitive processes involved in, language learning and teaching' (Benson & Reinders, 2011: 1).

Conclusion

This qualitative study is one of the few empirical studies, if not the only one, that has examined the language learning experiences and future vision of internally displaced Syrians while learning Turkish as their third or fourth language. The study highlights the significance of conducting empirical research on LOTE motivation in non-affluent geographies to serve the language learning needs of all multilingual individuals, not just the privileged. This demonstrates the importance of SLA research for all, regardless of their socioeconomic status, and emphasises the focal role currently assigned to languages to bring people together by speaking the language of peace. In this regard, future language teachers should receive sufficient training to develop ethnocultural empathy and intercultural understanding and to contribute to creating a peaceful world, both during their pre-service teaching practices and throughout their professional lives.

Although the results of this research provide key information on internally displaced Syrians' strategic language learning efforts and their interactions with different contextual conditions while learning Turkish, it has limitations that should be acknowledged. In particular, this study relied on a limited number of internally displaced Syrians as its research participants. In addition to exploring individuals' motivations for learning a LOTE in war-related situations, as in the present study, it would also be useful to conduct longitudinal, qualitative studies taking into account the perceptions and actions of respondents' significant others (e.g. language teachers and tutors, family members) who may have influenced the participants' LOTE motivations, LLS choices and their endeavours to gain entry into their desired community and accomplish their desired possible self-images.

References

ACAPS (2021) Syria humanitarian needs in Afrin. https://www.acaps.org/fileadmin/Data_Product/Main_media/20200302_acaps_short_note_syria_huamitarian_needs_in_afrin.pdf (Accessed 9 February 2023).

Al-Nofaie, H. (2018) The attitudes and motivation of children towards learning rarely spoken foreign languages: A case study from Saudi Arabia. *International Journal of Bilingual Education and Bilingualism* 21 (4), 451–464.

Benson, P. and Reinders, H. (2011) Introduction. In P. Benson and H. Reinders (eds) *Beyond the Language Classroom* (pp. 1–6). Palgrave Macmillan.

Block, D. (2003) *The Social Turn in Second Language Acquisition*. Edinburgh University Press.

Boo, Z., Dörnyei, Z. and Ryan, S. (2015) L2 motivation research 2005–2014: Understanding a publication surge and a changing landscape. *System* 55, 145–157.

Braun, V. and Clarke, V. (2013) *Successful Qualitative Research: A Practical Guide for Beginners*. Sage.

Busse, V. (2017) Plurilingualism in Europe: Exploring attitudes toward English and other European languages among adolescents in Bulgaria, Germany, the Netherlands, and Spain. *The Modern Language Journal* 101 (3), 566–582.

Dörnyei, Z. (2009) The L2 motivational self system. In Z. Dörnyei and E. Ushioda (eds) *Motivation, Language Identity and the L2 Self* (pp. 9–42). Multilingual Matters.

Dörnyei, Z. and Kubanyiova, M. (2014) *Motivating Learners, Motivating Teachers: Building Vision in the Language Classroom*. Cambridge University Press.

Fukui, H. and Yashima, T. (2021) Exploring evolving motivation to learn two languages simultaneously in a study-abroad context. *The Modern Language Journal* 105 (1), 267–293.

Gardner, R.C. (1985) *Social Psychology and Second Language Learning: The Role of Attitudes and Motivation*. Edward Arnold.

Gknou, C., Oliverao, M.M. and Oxford, R.L. (2021) Empowering language teachers to be influential peacebuilders: Knowledge, competencies and activities. In R.L. Oxford, M.M. Olivero, M. Harrison and T. Gregersen (eds) *Peacebuilding in Language Education: Innovations in Theory and Practice* (pp. 29–42). Multilingual Matters.

Hajar, A. (2019) *International Students' Challenges, Strategies and Future Vision: A Socio-Dynamic Perspective*. Multilingual Matters.

Hajar, A. (2021) Shifting learning strategies and future selves of Arab postgraduate students in Britain: A qualitative inquiry. *Innovation in Language Learning and Teaching* 15 (1), 233–246.

Hajar, A., Batyrkhanova, G. and Manan, S.A. (2023) Understanding challenges, investment, and strategic language use of postgraduate students in an English-medium university in Kazakhstan. *Asian Englishes*. https://10.1080/13488678.2023.2216868.

Han, Y. (2021) Motivations for learning Korean in Vietnam: L2 selves and regulatory focus perspectives. *Journal of Language, Identity & Education*, 1–15.

Henry, A. (2017) L2 motivation and multilingual identities. *The Modern Language Journal* 101 (3), 548–565.

Henry, A. (2020) Learner–environment adaptations in multiple language learning: Casing the ideal multilingual self as a system functioning in context. *International Journal of Multilingualism* 20 (2), 97–114.

Kruidenier, B. and Clement, R. (1986) The effect of context on the composition and role of orientations in second language acquisition. Dissertation, International Centre for Research on Bilingualism (Québec).

Lamb, M. (2013) Your mum and dad can't teach you! Constraints on agency among rural learners of English in Indonesia. *Journal of Multilingual and Multicultural Development* 34 (1), 14–29.

Li, S., Hiver, P. and Papi, M. (eds) (2022) *The Routledge Handbook of Second Language Acquisition and Individual Differences*. Routledge.

May, S. (2014) *The Multilingual Turn: Implications for SLA, TESOL and Bilingual Education*. Routledge.

Mendoza, A. and Phung, H. (2019) Motivation to learn languages other than English: A critical research synthesis. *Foreign Language Annals* 52 (1), 121–140.

Mercer, S. (2012) The complexity of learner agency. *Apples – Journal of Applied Language Studies* 6 (2), 41–59.

Nikitina, L. and Furuoka, F. (2019) Language learners' mental images of Korea: Insights for the teaching of culture in the language classroom. *Journal of Multilingual and Multicultural Development* 40 (9), 774–786.

Norton, B. (2013) *Identity and Language Learning: Extending the Conversation* (2nd edn). Multilingual Matters.

Norton, B. and Toohey, K. (2001) Changing perspectives on good language learners. *TESOL Quarterly* 35 (2), 307–322.

Nourzadeh, S., Fathi, J. and Davari, H. (2023) An examination of Iranian learners' motivation for and experience in learning Korean as an additional language. *International Journal of Multilingualism* 20 (2), 115–129.

Oakes, L. and Howard, M. (2022) Learning French as a foreign language in a globalised world: An empirical critique of the L2 motivational self system. *International Journal of Bilingual Education and Bilingualism* 25 (1), 166–182.

Ortega, L. (2022) Afterword. In A.H. Al-Hoorie and F. Szabó (eds) *Researching Language Learning Motivation: A Concise Guide* (pp. 235–240). Bloomsbury.

Ortega, Y. and Oxford, R. (2023) Immigrants' and refugees' 'funds of knowledge(s)' on the path to intercultural competence. *Journal of Multilingual and Multicultural Development*, 1–12.

Oxford, R.L., Olivero, M.M., Harrison, M. and Gregersen, T. (eds) (2021) *Peacebuilding in Language Education: Innovations in Theory and Practice*. Multilingual Matters.

Takahashi, C. (2023) *Motivation to Learn Multiple Languages in Japan: A Longitudinal Perspective*. Multilingual Matters.

Teo, T., Weng, C., Gao, X. and Lv, L. (2019) What motivates Chinese university students to learn Japanese? Understanding their motivation in terms of 'posture'. *The Modern Language Journal* 103 (1), 327–342.

Thomas, N. and Rose, H. (2019) Do language learning strategies need to be self-directed? Disentangling strategies from self-regulated learning, *TESOL Quarterly* 53 (1), 248–257.

Thomas, N., Rose, H., Cohen, A.D., Gao, X.A., Sasaki, A. and Hernandez-Gonzalez, T. (2022) The third wind of language learning strategies research. *Language Teaching* 55 (3), 417–421.

Thompson, A.S. (2020) My many selves are still me: Motivation and multilingualism. *Studies in Second Language Learning and Teaching* 10 (1), 159–176.

Umino, T. and Benson, P. (2016) Communities of practice in study abroad: A four-year study of an Indonesian student's experience in Japan. *The Modern Language Journal* 100 (4), 757–774.

Ushioda, E. (2017) The impact of global English on motivation to learn other languages: Toward an ideal multilingual self. *The Modern Language Journal* 101 (3), 469–482.

Ushioda, E. (2020) *Language Learning Motivation*. Oxford University Press.

Ushioda, E. and Dörnyei, Z. (2017) Beyond global English: Motivation to learn languages in a multicultural world: Introduction to the special issue. *The Modern Language Journal* 101 (3), 451–454.

Wang, Z. and Zheng, Y. (2021) Chinese university students' multilingual learning motivation under contextual influences: A multi-case study of Japanese majors. *International Journal of Multilingualism* 18 (3), 384–401.

Yashima, T. (2002) Willingness to communicate in a second language: The Japanese EFL context. *The Modern Language Journal* 86 (1), 54–66.

Yüksel, E. and Veen, E.V. (2019) Turkey in northwestern Syria: Rebuilding empire at the margins. CRU Policy Brief, Clingendael Institute – the Netherlands Institute of International Relations, 1–10.

Yung, K. and Hajar, A. (eds) (2023) *International Perspectives on English Private Tutoring: Theories, Practices, and Policies*. Palgrave Macmillan.

Zheng, Y., Lu, X. and Ren, W. (2020) Tracking the evolution of Chinese learners' multilingual motivation through a longitudinal Q methodology. *The Modern Language Journal* 104 (4), 781–803.

12 L2 Selves as a Source of Emotional Discomfort: A Self-Discrepancy Perspective

Yeji Han

Introduction

It is widely acknowledged that language learning entails intense emotional experiences, potentially due to the significant involvement of 'self'. However, it is difficult to grasp the precise role of emotional experiences in L2 (second language) learning due to its momentary nature and conceptual complexity. Unfortunately, negative emotions can be commonly experienced during the L2 learning process (e.g. anxiety), but they are often taken for granted and left to individual learners to overcome. The neglect of negative emotions may be due to the lack of understanding and theory-driven explanation of their impact on L2 learning.

This study aims to elucidate negative emotional experiences during L2 learning within the theoretical framework of the self-discrepancy theory and L2 motivational self system (L2MSS). The ideal L2 self and ought-to L2 self have been extensively studied in L2 motivation research in the last decade. With regards to the emotional dimensions of the L2 selves, however, little is understood.

Concerning LOTEs learning, negative emotions have not received much scholarly attention. Recent studies on motivation for LOTEs learning showed that learners tend to have a strong positive emotional attachment to the target culture and personal reasons for studying LOTEs (Dörnyei & Al-Hoorie, 2017). The patterns were extracted from studies on LOTEs in various contexts, including Europe, North America, and East and Southeast Asia. Therefore, it is risky to generalise the patterns of LOTEs motivation without taking into consideration the learning context. For example, motivation for learning LOTEs among Anglophone learners in the UK involves the anti ought-to L2 self as a rebellious reaction against a societal view of undermining language learning (Lanvers, 2016). The monoglot culture in the UK may be applicable to other Anglophone countries but is not relevant to non-Anglophone contexts, such as Asia.

The research population in this study is students enrolled in a Korean degree programme in Vietnam. The Korean programme is mainly designed as a training programme for language-specialists, such as a Vietnamese–Korean professional interpreter/translator or a Korean language instructor in Vietnam. The heavy focus on language proficiency creates a highly intensive learning environment, and the consequence of learning the language is high stakes in terms of career prospects and exams. Many students choose to enter the programme due to a love of Korean pop culture and the promising career opportunities expected from a high proficiency in Korean, but they often experience emotional turbulence during the intensive learning process. This study focuses on dejection and anxiety, which are commonly experienced among language learners.

Self-discrepancy: The Current and the Future

A few empirical studies have investigated the relationship between L2 selves and emotional regulation. For example, Csizér and Kormos (2014) conducted a correlation study between emotional regulation and L2 selves. The ideal L2 self was not significantly correlated with emotional control and only marginally correlated with satiation control (i.e. overcoming boredom). In other words, even if learners can vividly visualise their future selves, they may not be efficient in emotional regulation during the L2 learning process. Since the ideal L2 self is 'future', learners may not carry over their future selves in the 'current' L2 learning context.

Emotional experience may be intertwined with learners' perception of their L2 selves and their perceived capacity to fulfil them. In Garrett and Young's (2009) case study with a student of the Portuguese language, a majority of emotional comments was related to self-efficacy to cope with learning tasks and self-image that the participant wanted to project to her peers in the class. Negative comments, such as *overwhelming* and *embarrassing*, were found when the desired self and perceived view of the current self were mismatched, whilst positive comments were often coupled with episodes of managing learning tasks successfully.

Bown and White (2010) investigated the types of emotions that emerged from open-ended interviews and participant journals with Russian language learners. Not surprisingly, negative emotions were twice as frequent as positive emotions. Learners frequently experienced *frustration, disappointment* and *nervousness*. They also mentioned *feeling stupid* or *unsuccessful* as a reason for quitting the language programme. In terms of the themes related to emotions, cognitive appraisal was found to be most frequent in both positive and negative emotions. In other words, emotional experience during the L2 learning process is often influenced by external situation-related assessment (e.g. a teacher's praise) or internal appraisal of self. Similarly, Aragão (2011) found a close relationship between self-concept and learners' emotional experience in class. Although the author did not use the term the ideal L2 self, the qualitative data showed that *fear*, *shame* and *inhibition* were strongly associated with the mismatch between their current capacity to use L2 and the desired goal, i.e. 'idealized model' (Aragão, 2011: 307).

The qualitative findings from the previous studies are particularly relevant to this study investigating the perceived discrepancy between the current and future L2 selves within the framework of self-discrepancy theory. The qualitative results imply that negative emotional experience is closely linked to self-doubt or failure in maintaining desirable L2 selves, whereas positive emotion is often mentioned as an outcome of the successful management of learning tasks. There needs to be a systematic approach with a relevant theory to understand why and how negative emotional experience is involved with the L2 selves, while positive emotion is not.

According to L2MSS, language learners' perceptions of themselves related to L2 learning are the central component of motivation as they make motivational efforts to become the person they want to be as a result of successful L2 learning. The initial L2MSS model proposed by Dörnyei (2005, 2009) consisted of three components: (1) the ideal L2 self; (2) the ought-to L2 self; and (3) the L2 learning experience. The ideal L2 self represents L2-specific attributes that learners would like to possess in the future, thereby reflecting hopes and aspirations. The ought-to L2 self refers to L2-related attributes they believe they should possess or that others (i.e. parents, teachers, society) expect them to have in the future, and is thereby related to responsibilities or duties. The third component, the L2 learning experience, concerns situated and temporary motives influenced by the immediate learning environment, such as a teacher, peers or learning materials.

A key assumption of the L2MSS is that motivation arises from acknowledging the discrepancy between the future selves and the current state. Learners put effort into reducing the discrepancy to reach their desirable L2 selves. Dörnyei (2005) claimed that adequate distance between the current state and the L2 selves is one of the prerequisite conditions in order to exert motivational effort. On the one hand, the L2 selves must not be comfortably attainable without increasing effort because, if a learner believes that their future selves will be fulfilled, they may not try to achieve their goals. On the other hand, the L2 selves should be plausible and realistic, anchored within possible expectations. If the L2 selves are far beyond their capacity, it is understandable that learners would not try to achieve them.

In psychology, self-discrepancy theory primarily concerns the negative emotional consequences of the discrepancy between the current and future ideal and ought selves. Chronic discrepancy between the current and ideal self evokes dejection-related feelings, and discrepancy between the current and ought self evokes agitation-related feelings (Higgins, 1987). Feelings of dejection and agitation are commonly experienced during the process of L2 learning, although agitation arousal has been studied more extensively due in part to the noticeability of the feelings. When students are anxious, they tend to notice the feeling more easily than dejection-related feelings, such as boredom, frustration or disappointment.

In applied linguistics, adequate discrepancy between the current and future L2 self has been favoured for motivated efforts, despite a lack of empirical support. A few exceptional studies have found that close distance between the current and future L2 self leads to motivational effort. For example, Hessel (2015) tested the predictive power of properties of the ideal L2 self (i.e. desirability, accessibility, discrepancy, plausibility) on intended effort and reported that lower discrepancy led to more effort. MacIntyre et al. (2009) found similar results with a possible selves scale developed based on Gardner's Attitude/Motivation Test Battery (AMTB; Gardner, 1985) and the concept of possible selves in psychology (Markus & Nurius, 1986). Eighteen items were adapted from Gardner's AMTB and five follow-up questions were generated for each item. The first two follow-up questions were about current and future selves, asking whether the participants have the characteristics of the prompt now and in the future: '1) Describe me now (yes/no) and 2) Describe possible future (yes/no)' (MacIntyre et al., 2009: 198). A series of ANOVAs was run for each of the 18 AMTB questionnaire items based on the responses to the two follow-up questions. The yes/no dichotomous questions generated three possible groups for each item: Group 1 – those who perceive that the prompt questionnaire item describes the individual now and in the future (yes/yes); Group 2 – those who perceive they do not possess the prompt characteristics now but expect or desire to have them in future (no/yes); and Group 3 – those who think they do not possess the prompt characteristics now and will not in the future (no/no). The results of the ANOVAs showed that Group 1 displayed the highest motivation, followed by Group 2 and Group 3. Although the motivational construct was based on Gardner's AMTB, the results may still be relevant to clarify the key assumption of L2MSS: that discrepancy between the current and future L2 self is the precondition for exerting motivation to reduce the discrepancy.

L2 motivation literature suggests that a key approach to the L2 future self is 'not too close' and 'not too far'. It may be a fair assumption that attainable goals without effort would not trigger motivated behaviour, but within such a broad range of perceived plausibility, the role of the discrepancy needs to be clarified. This study investigates empirically the emotional aspects of the distance between the current and future L2 selves within the framework of self-discrepancy theory.

The Emotional Properties of L2MSS

Recently, there have been several studies that investigated learners' emotional experience using the L2MSS framework within the component of the L2 learning experience, which was originally defined as 'situation-specific motives related to the immediate learning environment' (Dörnyei, 2009: 106). However, the recent conceptualisation of the L2 learning experience goes beyond the momentary, external stimuli experienced in classroom settings such as peer interaction or learning materials (Csizér & Kálmán, 2019). This broader conceptualisation may better capture emotional experience which occurs concurrently and retrospectively, based on the cognitive appraisal of ongoing and past learning experiences and situations.

Pavelescu (2019) investigated qualitatively the L2 learning experience of two teenage EFL (English as a foreign language) learners in Romania and identified the types of emotion linked to motivation. The theme-based analysis of data (i.e. journal reflection, a semi-structured interview with students and a teacher, class observation) showed two themes related to positive emotions: (1) *love*, defined as generic positive attitudes towards the target language, not necessarily tied to the learning context; (2) *like*, defined as positive emotions linked to specific learning contexts such as classroom, culture-related aspects of English, and English usage outside the classroom. Both generic *love* and situation-specific *like* are linked to motivation (i.e. a driving force to learn English) in idiosyncratic ways. The findings suggest that both the generic and the situation-specific scope of emotional experiences emerge organically where L2 learning takes place, and they shape motivation in behavioural terms.

Hiver *et al.* (2019) explored the L2 learning experience using narrative methods from the complex dynamic systems perspective. The most salient theme emerging from the data was '*emotional loading or emotional tone*, ranging from extreme positivity to extreme negativity' (2019: 99; emphasis added). The narrative analysis revealed a mixture of positive (e.g. enjoyment, enthusiasm, excitement) and negative experiences (e.g. frustration, fear, embarrassment, discouragement), and a transition of emotional experience from negative to positive emotions that corresponds with overcoming learning difficulties. The finding supported the salience of emotional experience in L2 learning and its interaction with engagement.

As reported in past studies, L2 learning involves intense emotional loads. While past studies on the emotional dimension of the L2 learning experience have taken an exploratory and qualitative approach, this study takes a theory-driven approach to clarify the emotional dimension of the L2 learning experience about the ideal and ought-to L2 selves within the framework of self-discrepancy theory.

Asian Learners of Asian LOTEs

In recent L2 motivation literature, East Asian learners became the majority of the research population within the L2MSS framework (Boo et al., 2015). The previous research with East Asian learners has yielded some context- and culture-specific dimensions of L2 motivation – for example, the strong ought-to L2 self, family influence, or exam pressure (Apple et al., 2017). Not surprisingly, global English is often the target language in Asian countries due to the strong career prospects and international opportunities expected to be gained from this L2. Unlike global English, learning other Asian languages in Asian countries is a marked choice due to the lack of societal support and low instrumental values of the target languages. However, a few studies reported advantages of learning LOTEs as L3 in Asian countries, including gaining competitiveness in job markets, developing general intelligence and cultural understanding, and appreciating cultural and language similarities between the mother tongue and the target L3 Asian language (Huang, 2019).

The unique status of LOTEs in Asian countries is likely to trigger ambivalent motivation for learning them. In general, there is an absence of societal support for LOTEs learning, due to the low instrumental value of language proficiency (Dörnyei & Al-Hoorie, 2017), and Asian countries that have been influenced by Confucianism tend to value societal harmony and family approval on important life decisions (Chen et al., 2005). Therefore, congruence between one's desire to learn LOTEs and family and societal support is likely to be important. When learners encounter societal objections against their choice of learning LOTEs, they may need stronger motivation for LOTEs to compensate for the lack of societal support. The previous research found that cultural interests towards the target LOTEs are often a strong factor that predicts motivational behaviour in various LOTEs learning contexts, including Asian countries.

In the case of the Korean language, which is the target LOTE in this study, there has been a sharp increase in the number of language learners in the world over the last two decades due to the popularity of Korean pop culture and media (Yang & Yu, 2020). The fondness for Korean pop culture can be an initial attractor for Korean language learning. However, in Vietnam, which is the research site of this study, students enrolled in Korean degree programmes at university tend to have strong economic reasons for studying Korean. Korean language instructors commented that graduates from the Korean degree programmes can earn a high salary from working in the Korean business sector located in Vietnam (Kim, 2022). In this context, Korean language learning at university can be highly intensive and competitive, causing stress and negative emotional reactions among students.

The Focal Setting

The target population for this research is Vietnamese learners of the Korean language in Hanoi, Vietnam. They are enrolled in a four-year Korean degree programme whose curriculum consists of Korean language and culture. The Korean language is the core subject area, whereas Korean studies such as Korean literature, history and linguistics are only marginal. Most contact hours are assigned to Korean language reading, writing, speaking, listening, grammar and Korean–Vietnamese translation. Graduation requirements include passing the Test of Proficiency in Korean Level 5. The description of the required level is:

> The individual can use the language skills professionally or for research in a specialized field to a certain extent and understand and express him/herself regarding unfamiliar topics concerning politics, the economy, culture, and so on. He/she can appropriately use different forms of language according to the context and situation (e.g. formal/informal and colloquial/literary). (National Institute for International Education, 2021)

In addition to exam pressure, the expected proficiency in Korean is high because most graduates work as professional translators/interpreters at Korean organisations or pursue graduate studies in South Korea. In recent years, the Korean degree programmes in Vietnam have become extremely popular, attracting students with strong academic backgrounds. The entry requirement for the programme is the highest among modern language programmes, followed by global English, Chinese and Japanese (Lee, 2020). Due to the popularity of the language and to the career prospects, admission to the programme is considered prestigious. The student retention rate is high even though the proficiency level varies between students, which may cause stress to those who do not progress at the same rate as others.

The purpose of this study is to test the following hypotheses.

(1) Greater discrepancy between the current and the ideal L2 self is associated with dejection-related feelings compared to modest discrepancy.
(2) Greater discrepancy between the current and the ought-to L2 self imposed by others is associated with anxiety-related feelings compared to modest discrepancy.

Methodology

The participants

A total of 533 Vietnamese learners of Korean participated in this study (age *mean* = 20.05, *SD* = 1.46; female *n* = 495, male *n* = 20, unidentified *n* = 18). The participants were enrolled in an undergraduate degree programme in Korean language and culture in Hanoi, Vietnam. All participants spoke Vietnamese as their first language.

Instrument development and materials

A paper-and-pencil questionnaire was employed, consisting of two parts. The first part was the L2 selves measures and the second part was 5-point Likert-type items of dejection and anxiety in L2 learning. The first part of the questionnaire consisted of open-ended questions for the ideal L2 self and the ought-to L2 self adopted from *Selves Questionnaire* (Higgins *et al.*, 1985). The ideal L2 self was measured by asking the participants to list four attributes that they would like to have as a result of achieving L2 learning goals, and the ought-to L2 self was operationalised as four expectations that others (i.e. parents, a teacher or peers) have on their L2 learning. Because the L2 selves are highly personal and idiosyncratic, the open-ended responses to the L2 selves would allow identification of the domains of the L2 selves (e.g. careers, living abroad, test scores) that are personally important to individual learners. The responses were written in Vietnamese or Korean by the participants and translated into English by two professional translators.

The responses for the ideal L2 self and the ought-to L2 self consisted of four open-ended answers, respectively (e.g. *I want to be successful in my career*; *I ought to make good money when I graduate from university*). Under each open-ended response to the ideal L2 self and the ought-to L2 self, three follow-up questions were asked in order to measure: (1) the importance of the L2 selves; (2) the distance between the current and the ideal L2 self or the ought-to L2 self, adopted from the *Inclusion of Other in the Self (IOS)* scale (Aron *et al.*, 1992); and (3) plausibility of the ideal L2 self or the ought-to L2 self (see Appendix A).

For the Likert-scale items of L2 dejection and L2 anxiety, previous literature on measures of L2 emotions (e.g. anxiety) was examined, following the guidelines for the development of questionnaires in the field of applied linguistics (Dörnyei & Taguchi, 2009). However, since it has been rare to study L2 dejection-related feelings as a quantitative measure, the questionnaire items for this study were adopted from social psychology, in particular the *Subjective Vitality Scale* (Ryan & Frederick, 1997), and some items were newly developed for the L2 learning context. L2 anxiety items were adopted from the *Foreign Language Classroom Anxiety Scale* (Horwitz *et al.*, 1986).

The questionnaire was originally designed in English and then translated into Vietnamese. The initial translation was back-translated into English in order to validate the Vietnamese translation. Some phrasings were changed after back-translation. After the revisions, the Vietnamese version of the questionnaire was compared with the original English version by a Vietnamese native speaker and piloted for readability by four Vietnamese undergraduate students in Hanoi, Vietnam. The questionnaire items used in this study were part of a larger questionnaire on L2 motivation (item $k = 83$). The participants completed all items in the questionnaire but, for the purpose of this study, only emotion-related items (item $k = 45$) and the L2 selves measure were analysed.

The procedure

After obtaining permission to carry out the research from the ethics board of a Canadian university and the head of the department at a Vietnamese university, the pen-and-pencil questionnaire was administered during in-person Korean classes in Vietnam. The participants were informed of the general purpose of the research and their right to disagree or discontinue participating in the study was made clear. They were also reminded that their instructors would not have access to the data and that taking part in the questionnaire would not affect their grades. The consent form and the questionnaire were written in Vietnamese. The participants were not rewarded for completing the questionnaire. The survey data were collected in 2016.

Data Analysis

Testing the hypotheses through statistical analyses involved two steps: prior analysis and main analysis.

Prior analysis: L2-dejection and L2-anxiety scales

The questionnaire items for dejection and anxiety in the L2 context were developed and validated with principal component analysis (PCA) and confirmatory factor analysis (CFA). For all analyses, missing values were excluded listwise. Among the total of 533 participants, 276 participants were randomly selected for PCA and the other 257 participants were assigned for CFA. With the validated items of L2 dejection and L2 anxiety using the 5-point Likert scale, the sums of the L2-dejection scale and the L2-anxiety scale were computed respectively for t-test analysis (for final items, see Appendix B and Appendix C).

Main analysis: L2 self-discrepancy (distance * plausibility)

The L2 self-discrepancy was computed using the following steps. First, out of the four open-ended responses to the ideal L2 self, the response with the highest score of importance was selected (i.e. *How much does each answer matter to you? Circle the level of importance of each of your answers. 1 = not important; 5 = very important*). Second, L2 self-discrepancy was computed by multiplying the distance between the current and the ideal L2 self and the plausibility of the ideal L2 self upon the 5-point Likert scale. The same procedure was applied to the open-ended responses to the ought-to L2 self and the subsequent questions regarding the importance, distance and plausibility of the open-ended responses to the ought-to L2 self. Thus, two values were computed for self-discrepancy of the ideal L2 self and the ought-to L2 self ($min = 1, max = 25$).

In some cases, the participants assigned an equal rate of importance to multiple open-responses to the ideal L2 self or the ought-to L2 self. For example, the highest value of the importance of the ideal L2 self could be given to multiple items (e.g. 5 = *very important* on the Likert scale for *studying aboard for graduate studies* and *getting a well-paid job*), indicating the most important ideal L2 self lies in multiple life domains. In this case, the L2 self-discrepancy was computed by averaging the values of the L2 self-discrepancy for each response that was highest rated on importance.

The hypotheses were tested by dividing the participants into quartiles on the L2 self-discrepancy scores on the ideal L2 self and the ought-to L2 self (i.e. the distance score multiplied by the plausibility score of the most important ideal L2 self and the ought-to L2 self). The upper and the lower quartiles of the participants were selected for t-test analysis of L2-dejection and L2-anxiety scales to test if the two groups of participants were significantly and sizeably different on the scores for L2 dejection and anxiety.

Results

The overall results partially supported the hypotheses that the discrepancy of the ideal L2 self would be associated with L2 dejection and the discrepancy of the ought-to L2 self would be associated with L2 anxiety. The groups with the greatest discrepancies in both ideal and ought-to L2 self tended to experience both L2 dejection-related and L2 anxiety-related feelings more intensely than those who perceived the least discrepancies. No specific links between the ideal L2 self and dejection or the ought-to L2 self and anxiety were found.

Prior analysis for L2 dejection and L2 anxiety

Prior to the comparison-based statistic (i.e. t-test), the PCA and CFA tests were run with the L2-dejection and L2-anxiety items as noted above. The tests validated the L2-dejection scale with three subconstructs

Table 12.1 Component correlations of L2 dejection

	Lack of L2 self-efficacy	Disappointment in L2 use	Learning fatigue
Lack of L2 self-efficacy		.48	.37
Disappointment in L2 use			.13

$p < .001$

Table 12.2 Component correlations of L2 anxiety

	Fear of negative evaluation	Test anxiety	Communication apprehension
Fear of negative evaluation		.47	.51
Test anxiety			.41

$p < .001$

of (1) *lack of L2 self-efficacy* (initial $\lambda = 4.17$, explained variance = 34.72%); (2) *disappointment in L2 use* (initial $\lambda = 1.75$, explained variance = 14.57%); and (3) *learning fatigue* (initial $\lambda = 1.11$, explained variance = 9.21%). For the L2-anxiety scale the three subconstructs were: (1) *fear of negative evaluation* (initial $\lambda = 4.46$, explained variance = 44.59%); (2) *test anxiety* (initial $\lambda = 1.34$, explained variance = 13.40%); and (3) *communication apprehension* (initial $\lambda = 1.10$, explained variance = 10.96%). This is consistent with the *Foreign Language Classroom Anxiety Scale* devised by Horwitz et al. (1986).

CFA with maximum likelihood was conducted to estimate the L2-dejection and L2-anxiety constructs respectively ($n = 257$). The goodness of fit indices were excellent: for L2 dejection, χ^2 (51, $n = 255$) = 73.22, $p = 0.02$, comparative fix index (CFI) = .98, root mean square error of approximation (RMSEA) = 0.04, $p = 0.74$; for L2 anxiety, χ^2 (32, $n = 255$) = 38.95, $p = 0.02$, comparative fix index (CFI) = .99, root mean square error of approximation (RMSEA) = 0.03, $p = 0.87$.

As shown in Tables 12.1 and 12.2, respectively, the overall L2-dejection and L2-anxiety components showed small to moderate correlations; the highest correlation was found between fear of negative evaluation and communication apprehension ($r = .51$). The final items with the factor loadings and Cohen's alpha are given in the Appendix B and Appendix C.

Main analysis for t-test between the groups with the greatest and least discrepancies

In order to test the two hypotheses, two separate t-tests were conducted with the upper and the lower quartiles of the ideal L2 self discrepancy (i.e. distance * plausibility, $n = 113$ for the least discrepancy group, $n = 129$ for the greatest discrepancy group) and the ought-to L2 self discrepancy ($n = 116$ for the least discrepancy group, $n = 105$ for the

Table 12.3 Descriptive statistics of upper and lower quartiles of the ideal L2 self discrepancy (distance * plausibility) and the ought-to L2 self discrepancy (distance * plausibility) on the constructs of L2 dejection and L2 anxiety

The ideal L2 self discrepancy

	Group	Mean	SD
Lack of L2 self-efficacy	Least discrepancy ($n = 116$)	2.47	.82
	Greatest discrepancy ($n = 105$)	3.09	.77
Disappointment in L2 use	Least discrepancy	2.90	.88
	Greatest discrepancy	3.29	.87
Learning fatigue	Least discrepancy	2.25	.63
	Greatest discrepancy	2.55	.57
Communication apprehension	Least discrepancy	3.12	.84
	Greatest discrepancy	3.58	.79
Test anxiety	Least discrepancy	2.69	.96
	Greatest discrepancy	3.06	.97
Fear of negative evaluation	Least discrepancy	3.27	.90
	Greatest discrepancy	3.59	.75

The ought-to L2 self discrepancy

	Group	Mean	SD
Lack of L2 self-efficacy	Least discrepancy ($n = 113$)	2.45	.78
	Greatest discrepancy ($n = 129$)	2.98	.73
Disappointment in L2 use	Least discrepancy	2.82	.81
	Greatest discrepancy	3.07	.83
Learning fatigue	Least discrepancy	2.30	.61
	Greatest discrepancy	2.51	.58
Communication apprehension	Least discrepancy	3.09	.82
	Greatest discrepancy	3.45	.77
Test anxiety	Least discrepancy	2.54	.92
	Greatest discrepancy	2.99	.83
Fear of negative evaluation	Least discrepancy	3.24	.87
	Greatest discrepancy	3.53	.76

greatest discrepancy group) based on the means of the constructs of the L2 dejection and L2 anxiety. The t-test results showed that the upper and lower quartiles for both ideal and ought-to L2 self discrepancies were significantly different on all subscales with medium to large effect-sizes.

As shown in Table 12.3, the groups with the greatest discrepancy in both ideal and ought-to L2 self showed significantly higher scores on L2 dejection and anxiety. For the ideal L2 self, the significant and sizeable differences of the greatest and least discrepancy groups were found in the lack of L2 self-efficacy with a large effect size, $t(219) = -5.776$, $p < .001$, $d = .78$ and communication apprehension with a medium-to-large effect size $t(219) = -3.602$, $p < .001$, $d = .56$. For the ought-to L2 self, the significant and sizeable differences between the greatest and least discrepancy groups were found on the lack of L2 self-efficacy with a large effect size, $t(240) = -5.45$, $p < .001$, $d = .70$, and test anxiety with a medium-to-large effect size, $t(240) = -4.04$, $p < .001$, $d = .51$.

The size of the effect sizes was judged based on the field-specific benchmark proposed by Plonsky and Oswald (2014).

Discussion

Self-perception of the current state in relation to the ideal L2 self and the ought-to L2 self is one of the important assumptions in the L2MSS theory. However, the current aspect has been under-investigated thus far, whereas the importance of having vivid images of the ideal L2 self has been extensively discussed as a source of generating willpower (e.g. You & Chan, 2015). Substantiating the vision of the ideal L2 self may enhance the perceived plausibility of the ideal L2 self, as claimed by Dörnyei (2009). Imagining the desired future is a way of activating the future self, and bringing the future self to the current working self triggers motivational action (Markus & Kunda, 1986; Markus & Wurf, 1987). The perceived plausibility of the ideal L2 self is consistent with the central tenet in expectancy-value theories in psychology; however, there have been untested properties of the L2 selves regarding the current perception of the ideal and the ought-to L2 self.

The results of this study strongly suggest that learners who perceive their ideal and ought-to L2 self as being more distant and less plausible are likely to experience dejection and anxiety more intensely compared to those who perceive lower discrepancies. The findings further confirmed previous studies by MacIntyre *et al.* (2009) and Hessel (2015) in that learners who perceive themselves as possessing desired attributes (i.e. possible self) now and in the future are better motivated than those who do not have a connection between the desired attributes and the current state.

With regards to the relationship between the L2 selves and negative emotions, the first hypothesis – that ideal L2 self discrepancy would be associated with L2 dejection – was partially supported. Both ideal L2 self discrepancy and ought-to L2 self discrepancy were associated with the lack of L2 self-efficacy with large effect sizes. The lack of L2 self-efficacy is a cognitive dimension of dejection-related feelings – that is, the appraisal of one's capacity to fulfil the desired learning outcomes. It is perhaps not surprising that those who perceive the greatest self-discrepancy in either ideal or ought-to L2 self tend to experience the cognitive dimension of dejection the most. The large effect sizes from the comparison of learner groups of the greatest and least self-discrepancy imply that the appraisal of the self-discrepancy in the L2 self is closely linked to evaluating one's efficacy in L2 learning.

The ideal and ought-to L2 self discrepancy differed in the experience of anxiety-related emotions. The ideal L2 self discrepancy was associated with communication apprehension, and the ought-to L2 self discrepancy was associated with test anxiety, both with medium effect sizes. Communication apprehension derives from one's perception of L2 capacity, and test anxiety refers to anxious feelings aroused from the fear of failure (Horwitz *et al.*, 1986). Interestingly, both communication apprehension and test anxiety are state-based anxieties, whereas fear of negative evaluation represents prolonged anxiety from the L2 learning process (e.g. *I feel anxious about a large number of grammar rules and vocabulary I have to study*) or from undesired consequences in the long term (e.g. *I worry about experiencing failure in learning Korean*). In other words, the ideal and ought-to L2 self discrepancies have an impact on temporarily experienced anxiety in L2 communication and test settings. On a temporary basis, a student may feel anxious when they notice errors in L2 speaking, and these anxious feelings may lead to self-doubt in achieving their ideal L2 self. On the other hand, it is also possible that a student who is unsure about their capacity to achieve the ideal L2 self may be more anxious when carrying out L2 conversation. Therefore, self-perceptions of the L2 selves and emotions are likely to have bidirectional relationships.

The results showed that self-discrepancy has a detrimental influence on emotional experiences in general, but the fine-tuned links between the ideal L2 self discrepancy and L2 dejection, and between the ought-to L2 self discrepancy and L2 anxiety, were not supported. L2 emotional experience is likely to be dynamically mixed, whereas dejection and anxiety in clinical psychology are characterised by a chronic nature. Therefore, the original self-discrepancy theory from psychology is, to some extent, applicable to the L2 context in the sense that prolonged self-discrepancy is linked to negative emotions. However, the core aspect of the original self-discrepancy theory – an exclusive link between ideal self discrepancy and depression and ought self discrepancy and anxiety – is harder to apply to the context of L2 learning.

L2 learners experience emotions intensely because the learning process involves constant cognitive appraisal of one's learning capacity and progress. It is widely considered that L2 learning is a process to overcome some kind of deficiency in L2; thus, the learning process can be mentally and emotionally draining, especially among adult learners who have mastered at least one language – usually their mother tongue. The significant divergence of L1 and L2 proficiency is a constant reminder of the self-discrepancy between the current state and the desirable future of L2 selves. Research attention thus far has been directed to the motivational dimension of self-discrepancy, assuming that efforts to reduce the gap between the current and desired future are the key source of motivation. However, as MacIntyre and Vincze (2017: 67) noted: 'although Dörnyei emphasizes discrepancies in cognition about the present and the future, there is a role to be played by emotional reactions that emerge from perceived discrepancies and the prior experience of positive and negative emotions associated with language learning contexts'. The findings from the present study highlight the detrimental emotional reaction from discrepancy, consistent with previous research (e.g. MacIntyre *et al.*, 2009). In addition to the cognitive dimension of self-discrepancy, emotional reactions from discrepancy are worth considering for future investigation in L2 motivation research.

Conclusion and Implications

During the last two decades, the L2 motivation research population has been highly skewed towards learners of global English in East Asia, Europe and North America (Boo *et al.*, 2015). This bias of research populations and locations may be problematic for generalising research findings to non-English learning contexts or other geographical locations. This study, along with other chapters in this book, contributes to diversifying the research population with a focus on Asian learners learning an Asian language. More specifically, the study reported in this chapter focused on Vietnamese learners of the Korean language in an intensive degree programme in Hanoi, Vietnam. The sociocultural context of Korean language learning is worth taking into consideration. It has been repeatedly reported that the Korean language learning context in Vietnam has strong integrative and instrumental purposes (Han, 2021; Han & McDonough, 2018, 2021). Korean pop culture has become popular in Vietnam as well as in other countries worldwide, thereby attracting a large number of Korean language learners. In addition to the initial attraction and desire to assimilate the target culture as a consumer of Korean media, students expect to work in the Korean community in Vietnam. Due to the close ties with the target language community and expected monetary rewards related to Korean language learning, Vietnamese learners of the Korean language can be strongly motivated but, at the same time, frustrated and anxious if they perceive that their desired outcomes are unlikely to be attained. The intensive language learning environment in this study is somewhat unique compared to the previous studies on LOTEs motivation (Dörnyei & Al-Hoorie, 2017). The findings cast doubts on the key assumption of the self discrepancy between the present and future, which can be applied to other intensive L2 learning contexts.

A geographical location cannot decide 'culture', and it is controversial to decide factors that constitute 'Asia'. However, there should be some commonalities across so-called Asian learners of Asian languages, such as crafting the edge for the job market, philological similarities between the target language and the mother tongue, and exam pressures (Apple *et al.*, 2017). Aligned with previous research in the Asian context, this study provides a new perspective on emotional experiences, which need further scholarly attention in other LOTEs contexts.

This study, however, is not without limitations. First of all, the learning context may have changed since the data were collected in 2016. For example, Korean studies have been added to the degree programme in which the participants were enrolled, potentially reducing the perceived importance of language proficiency. With regard to career prospects, the COVID-19 pandemic may have affected motivation and emotional experience due to economic uncertainty and the shrinking of the job market for Korean businesses in Vietnam. Also, the participants were highly skewed towards females, reflecting the student population learning Korean. The gender influence lurking in the data, as well as the contextual change from the data collection point, may limit the scope of generalisation of the findings.

Appendix A: L2 Selves Questionnaire

Ideal L2 self

Imagine yourself reaching your goals as an L2 speaker in 10 years. What would you like to do with the language proficiency? And who would you like to be? Please fill in the following table.

I would like to ...	I would like to be a person who...
	A)
	B)
	C)
	D)

<Follow-up questions>

- *Significance of L2 self*

How much does each answer from A) to D) matter to you? Circle the appropriate numbers from 1 (slightly important) to 5 (extremely important).
(5-point Likert scale

- *Distance of L2 self*

How close do you think the person you are currently is to the person in the future? Circle the picture that best represents the distance.

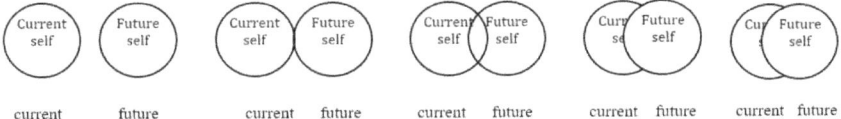

- *Plausibility of L2 self*

How likely are your answers from A) to D) to happen in future? Circle the closest number that best represents the plausibility.
(5-point Likert scale, 1 = 10%, 2 = 30%, 3 = 50%, 4 = 70%, 5 = 90%)

Ought-to L2 self

During and after you learn L2, what expectations do people around you have about you? List <u>4 expectations they have about your L2 learning</u> and <u>the people who have these expectations</u>.

Expectation	People
A)	
B)	
C)	
D)	

<Follow-up questions>

226 Multilingual Selves and Motivations for Learning Languages other than English

- *Significance of L2 self*

    How much does each answer from A) to D) matter to you? Circle the appropriate numbers from 1 (slightly important) to 5 (extremely important).
    (5-point Likert scale)

- *Distance of L2 self*

    How close do you think the person you are currently is to the person in the future? Circle the picture that best represents the distance.

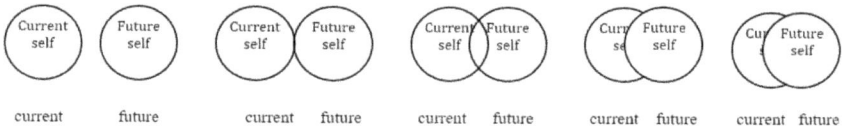

- *Plausibility of L2 self*

    How likely are your answers from A) to D) to happen in future? Circle the closest number that best represents the plausibility.
    (5-point Likert scale, 1 = 10%, 2 = 30%, 3 = 50%, 4 = 70%, 5 = 90%)

Appendix B

Table Appendix B.1 Principal component analysis of the items constituting the L2 dejection scale. (Promax oblique rotation, pattern matrix; three-factor solution. Lack of L2 learning self-efficacy, $\alpha = .81$; Disappointment in L2 use, $\alpha = .77$, learning fatigue, $\alpha = .65$; factor loadings under .3 are not shown in the table for reasons of readability)

	Lack of L2 learning self-efficacy	Disappointment in L2 use	Learning fatigue
Learning Korean is not interesting to me.			.73
I feel unmotivated in Korean classes.			.74
I don't feel very energetic in Korean classes.			.72
*I feel alert in Korean classes.			.57
I don't make any progress in Korean learning.	.84		
I don't think I have the capacity to learn Korean.	.71		
So far, my Korean results have been unsatisfactory.	.73		
I am getting behind my peers in Korean class.	.75		
Being fluent in Korean is beyond my capacity.	.70		
I feel disappointed in myself if I don't understand Korean conversations.		.74	
I feel disappointed in myself if people don't understand my Korean.		.89	
I feel disappointed in myself if I make mistakes in Korean conversations.		.85	

*reversed order scale (Likert scale 1 to 5 is reversed for the analysis, i.e. higher scale means less fatigue)

Appendix C

Table Appendix C.1 Principal component analysis of the items constituting the L2 anxiety scales
(Promax oblique rotation, pattern matrix; three-factor solution. Fear of negative evaluation, $\alpha = .80$; test anxiety, $\alpha = .84$; communication apprehension, $\alpha = .76$; factor loadings under .3 are not shown in the table for reason s of readability)

	Fear of negative evaluation	Test anxiety	Communication apprehension
I am afraid of making mistakes when speaking Korean.			.88
I don't feel confident in speaking Korean.			.85
I feel anxious when I don't understand what Korean people say.			.75
I am afraid of getting low marks on the Korean test.	.88		
I worry about experiencing failure in learning Korean.	.88		
I feel anxious because of the large number of grammar rules and vocabulary I have to study.	.65		
I am afraid that I will disappoint my parents.	.70		
In the Korean test, I get so nervous that I forget things I know.		.81	
I can't concentrate on Korean tests because I am so anxious.		.90	
I can't handle my anxiety while taking a Korean test.		.90	

References

Apple, M.T., Da Silva, D. and Fellner, T. (eds) (2017) *L2 Selves and Motivations in Asian Contexts*. Multilingual Matters.
Aragão, R. (2011) Beliefs and emotions in foreign language learning. *System* 39 (3), 302–313.
Aron, A., Aron, E.N. and Smollan, D. (1992) Inclusion of other in the self scale and the structure of interpersonal closeness. *Journal of Personality and Social Psychology* 63 (4), 596–612.
Boo, Z., Dörnyei, Z. and Ryan, S. (2015) L2 motivation research 2005–2014: Understanding a publication surge and a changing landscape. *System* 55, 145–157.
Bown, J. and White, C.J. (2010) Affect in a self-regulatory framework for language learning. *System* 38 (3), 432–443.
Chen, J.F., Warden, C.A. and Chang, H.-T. (2005) Motivators that do not motivate: The case of Chinese EFL learners and the influence of culture on motivation. *TESOL Quarterly* 39 (4), 609–633.
Csizér, K. and Kormos, J. (2014) The ideal L2 self, self-regulatory strategies and autonomous learning: A comparison of different groups of English language learners. In K. Csizér and M. Magid (eds) *The Impact of Self-Concept on Language Learning* (pp. 73–86). Multilingual Matters.

Csizér, K. and Kálmán, C. (2019) A study of retrospective and concurrent foreign language learning experiences: A comparative interview study in Hungary. *Studies in Second Language Learning and Teaching* 9 (1), 225–246.

Dörnyei, Z. (2005) *The Psychology of the Language Learner: Individual Differences in Second Language Acquisition*. Lawrence Erlbaum.

Dörnyei, Z. (2009) The motivational self system. In Z. Dörnyei and E. Ushioda (eds) *Motivation, Language Identity and the L2 Self* (pp. 9–42). Multilingual Matters.

Dörnyei, Z. and Taguchi, T. (2009) *Questionnaires in Second Language Research: Construction, Administration, and Processing* (2nd edn). Routledge.

Dörnyei, Z. and Al-Hoorie, A.H. (2017) The motivational foundation of learning languages other than global English: Theoretical issues and research directions. *The Modern Language Journal* 101 (3), 455–468.

Gardner, R.C. (1985) *Social Psychology and Second Language Learning: The Role of Attitudes and Motivation*. Edward Arnold.

Garrett, P. and Young, R.F. (2009) Theorizing affect in foreign language learning: An analysis of one learner's responses to a communicative Portuguese course. *The Modern Language Journal* 93 (2), 209–226.

Han, Y. (2021) Motivations for learning Korean in Vietnam: L2 selves and regulatory focus perspectives. *Journal of Language, Identity & Education*, 1–15.

Han, Y. and McDonough, K. (2018) Korean L2 speakers' regulatory focus and oral task performance. *International Review of Applied Linguistics in Language Teaching* 56 (2), 181–203.

Han, Y. and McDonough, K. (2021) Motivation as individual differences and task conditions from a regulatory focus perspective: Their effects on L2 Korean speech performance. *Innovation in Language Learning and Teaching* 15 (1), 1–12.

Hessel, G. (2015) From vision to action: Inquiring into the conditions for the motivational capacity of ideal second language selves. *System* 52, 103–114.

Higgins, E.T. (1987) Self-discrepancy: A theory relating self and affect. *Psychological Review* 94, 319–340.

Higgins, E.T., Klein, R. and Strauman, T. (1985) Self-concept discrepancy theory: A psychological model for distinguishing among different aspects of depression and anxiety. *Social Cognition* 3, 51–76.

Hiver, P., Obando, G., Sang, Y., Tahmouresi, S., Zhou, A. and Zhou, Y. (2019) Reframing the L2 learning experience as narrative reconstructions of classroom learning. *Studies in Second Language Learning and Teaching* 9 (1), 83–116.

Horwitz, E.K., Horwitz, M.B. and Cope, J. (1986) Foreign language classroom anxiety. *The Modern Language Journal* 70 (2), 125–132.

Huang, S.C. (2019) Learning experience reigns: Taiwanese learners' motivation in learning eight additional languages as compared to English. *Journal of Multilingual and Multicultural Development* 40 (7), 576–589.

Kim, S. (2022) I get a good job, I get a good treatment, I am popular ... Lack of teachers and teaching materials is a problem. *Kyunghyun Newspaper*, 23 November. https://m.khan.co.kr/world/asia-australia/article/202211231647001.

Lanvers, U. (2016) Lots of selves, some rebellious: Developing the self discrepancy model for language learners. *System* 60, 79–92.

Lee, H.S. (2020) The highest score in the prestigious Hanoi University entrance exam is the Korean Language Department. *Inside Vina,* 6 October. http://www.insidevina.com/news/articleView.html?idxno=14534.

MacIntyre, P.D. and Vincze, L. (2017) Positive and negative emotions underlie motivation for L2 learning. *Studies in Second Language Learning and Teaching* 7 (1), 61–88.

Macintyre, P.D., Mackinnon, S.P. and Clément, R. (2009) Toward the development of a scale to assess possible selves as a source of language learning motivation. In Z. Dörnyei and E. Ushioda (eds) *Motivation, Language Identity and the L2 Self* (pp. 193–214). Multilingual Matters.

Markus, H.R. and Kunda, Z. (1986) Stability and malleability of the self-concept. *Journal of Personality and Social Psychology* 51 (4), 63–78.
Markus, H.R. and Nurius, P. (1986) Possible selves. *American Psychologist* 41 (9), 954–969.
Markus, H.R. and Wurf, E. (1987) The dynamic self-concept: A social psychological perspective. *Annual Review of Psychology* 38, 299–337.
National Institute for International Education (2021) Test of Proficiency in Korean. https://www.topik.go.kr/HMENU0/HMENU00018.do.
Pavelescu, L.M. (2019) Motivation and emotion in the EFL learning experience of Romanian adolescent students: Two contrasting cases. *Studies in Second Language Learning and Teaching* 9 (1), 55–82.
Plonsky, L. and Oswald, F.L. (2014) How big is 'big'? Interpreting effect sizes in L2 research. *Language Learning* 64 (4), 878–912.
Ryan, R.M. and Frederick, C.M. (1997) On energy, personality and health: Subjective vitality as a dynamic reflection of well-being. *Journal of Personality* 65 (3), 529–565.
Yang, K. and Yu, S. (2020) 국제 언어로서 한국어의 위상 [The status of Korean as an international language]. *Korea Foundation for International Cultural Exchange*, 23 January. https://kofice.or.kr/b20industry/b20_industry_03_view.asp?seq=8009.
You, C. and Chan, L. (2015) The dynamics of L2 imagery in future motivational self-guides. In Z. Dörnyei, P.D. MacIntyre and A. Henry (eds) *Motivational Dynamics in Language Learning* (pp. 397–418). Multilingual Matters.

13 Current Understandings and Future Directions in L2 Motivation Research

Amy S. Thompson

When the editors of this volume, Anas Hajar and Syed Abdul Manan, asked me to write the concluding chapter to address 'ways forward' for motivation research, I was delighted to see that this whole volume, in essence, addresses many of the needed 'ways forward' in the field. The empirical studies included in this volume fill a gap in the motivation research in terms of the contexts studied, the languages involved and, by and large, the multilingual profiles of the learners. One of the crucial aspects of motivation research is not only addressing, but also highlighting and analyzing, multilingual profiles of language learners. The symbiotic nature of motivation and multilingualism is an area oft ignored; Henry (Chapter 2) summarizes the multilingual turn in motivation research, highlighting articles by Thompson (2017a, 2017b) and Henry (2017) that are described as 'cornerstones of an emerging body of ontologically non-essentialist research that explores motivation in contexts of multiple learning/acquisition' (p. 16). Thompson (2017b) operationalized Perceived Positive Language Interaction (PPLI), which is a framework used to investigate learners' perceptions of intertwined language systems to facilitate subsequent language learning, using Herdina and Jessner's Dynamic Model of Multilingualism (DMM). Henry and Thorsen (2018) operationalized the concept of the multilingual self, which is a framework describing the activation and utilization of a multilingual self guide, rather than self guides for individual languages of study. Indeed, many of the chapters in this volume not only describe but also include, as part of the analysis, the multilingual profiles of the language learners involved, effectively combatting what Ortega (2014) first argued as two reasons contributing to the erasure of multilingualism in SLA – the monolingual bias and nativespeakerism:

I have argued (Ortega, 2014) that SLA erased bilingualism and multilingualism from the object of inquiry because of two unexamined deleterious ideologies. The first one is the monolingual bias associated with the nation state project, just described. Inadvertently augmenting it and intertwined with it is the second ideology: the native speaker bias (or nativespeakerism, Holliday, 2006), which holds that owning a language from birth results in a form of linguistic competence superior to the competencies that may develop through any other means over the life trajectory. Both biases work together to cast a deficit light on the object of study, portraying language learners as doomed to failure. (Ortega, 2019: 24)

In terms of context, Henrich *et al.* (2010) coined the term WEIRD (Western, Educated, Industrialized, Rich, and Democratic societies) to describe the types of participants that predominantly populate social science (including second language acquisition) research, and criticize the fact that theories of learning have consistently been formed based on this small subset of the global population. Most of the contexts highlighted in this volume are wonderfully unique in the research: Kazakhstan, Indonesia, Malaysia, Pakistan, the Syrian/Turkish border and Vietnam, along with the inclusion of two contexts that have been more frequently represented in the literature – China and Japan. As addressed in Serafini (2020: 13), context is not monolithic but refers to 'multiple levels of contexts stretching from micro-level interactional contexts to macro-level cultures'. What is especially compelling in this volume is the juxtaposition of varied aspects of these under-studied contexts with languages other than English (LOTEs), which are underrepresented in the language learning motivation research, largely in part due to the large number of English language learners worldwide. Indeed, the authors talk about learners of Arabic, German, Japanese, Korean, Portuguese, French, Spanish, Chinese and Turkish in contexts in which learning these languages is perhaps unexpected with the current status of global English.

But how can the role of context be integrated into motivation research, specifically considering the L2 Motivational Self System (L2MSS; Dörnyei, 2009)? The selves aspects of the L2MSS have taken priority in the literature, leaving the learning experience aspect of the L2MSS largely untheorized. As Dörnyei states:

It was felt right from the beginning that the label L2 Learning Experience was hardly more than a broad, place-holding umbrella term that would need to be fine-tuned at one point, but it appears that the interest in the potentials of the new self-approach has overshadowed this research need, thereby leaving the L2 Learning Experience the Cinderella of the L2 Motivational Self System. (Dörnyei, 2009: 22)

In some of my recent work (i.e. Thompson, 2017b, 2021a), I have operationalized the learning experience aspect of the L2MSS as the sociopolitical context in which the learning takes place:

> The learning experience is the aspect of the L2MSS that looks at the context of the language learning process and the effect of the context on the psychological aspects of self. Target language exchanges are comprised of interactions both in and out of the classroom and include both successful and unsuccessful experiences. As such, there are effects of instructional context and peers, and it is important to note that the language learners themselves can also have an effect on their context (i.e., the influence of context is bidirectional). In the current study, the learning experience aspect of the model specifically relates to the linguistic landscape of the United States and the target language choice. (Thompson, 2017b: 484)

While examining contexts, it is imperative to understand the variability of the contexts involved and how individuals interact with a similar context in a different way; as Mercer (2016: 12) indicates: 'acknowledging the role of contexts is only a first step'. Intricacies of the learner/context interactions need to be operationalized and scrutinized.

As such, carefully examining the context as an influence for self development is an important direction for future motivation research. Also within the scope of context, Ushioda (2011) states:

> In short, there is no doubt that context matters in SLA, yet what matters just as much is the individual agency of L2 learners, inherently part of and actively shaping the developing contexts of learning, input and interaction in which they are situated. (Ushioda, 2011: 189)

Two of the chapters in this volume focus on aspects of learner agency. An and Zheng (Chapter 3) analyze past, present and imagined agentive actions for L1 Chinese, L2 English learners of Arabic. The authors emphasize the importance of examining agency for language learners for languages other than global English. Hajar (Chapter 11) writes about the unique context of internally displaced Syrians learning Turkish on the Syrian–Turkish border. The participants' multilingual selves were examined, as Turkish was an L3 or L4, and how political conflict interacted with their Turkish learning. Multilingual selves and their strategic language learning of a LOTE in a conflict-affected situation were examined. Their learner agency supported their language learning process, not only linguistically but culturally as well. These chapters are both examples of the importance of learner agency in the language acquisition process and highlight a potential future area of future research.

Also related to context and an area ripe for future research is the concept of intercultural citizenship, i.e. creating a sense of belonging (i.e. citizenship) that transcends national borders through shared values, which is addressed in Hajar and Manan's chapter (Chapter 7). These authors call for further research on this concept, particularly in the context of learning LOTEs via cultures with potentially similar values. I agree that this is an important aspect of motivation research, with the caveat of care taken not to be reductive in terms of discussions involving different contexts and cultures. As Mercer (2016: 12) states:

> At times, cultures and contexts appear to be presented as static, monolithic, external entities which affect individual characteristics in a simple unidirectional manner. Such simplistic views of cultures or contexts risk distorting the nature of an individual's relationship with them and potentially leading to unintended stereotyping and over-generalisations

and that

> generalisable simplistic understandings of contexts cannot be assumed to be the same for everyone.

If learners have a strong sense of intercultural citizenship, this could potentially lead to a stronger ideal self; however, when looking at concepts such as intercultural citizenship, care needs to be taken not to oversimplify the concept of culture or context.

Another area ripe for exploration is the anti-ought-to self (Thompson & Vásquez, 2015; Thompson, 2017a), which is similar to the rebellious self (Lanvers, 2016). The core idea for these selves is when learners are motivated to learn a language, despite external pressure to the contrary. The theoretical underpinnings for the anti-ought-to self stem from Reactance Theory (Brehm, 1966), which outlines the desire in some individuals to resist authority if they perceive a threat to personal freedom or do not want to adhere to a particular set of social norms. This sentiment can arise in learners both with more commonly taught languages, such as English (e.g. pressure to obtain a business degree, rather than an English degree) or with less commonly studied languages (i.e. learning Arabic in an Anglophone country). Khan, Channa and Khan (Chapter 10) illustrate such an anti-ought-to self with Chinese language learners in Pakistan. The students were learning Chinese for a number of reasons: availing themselves of scholarships awarded by the Chinese government and enhanced job opportunities. However, some participants who chose to study Chinese indicated external pressure not to study Chinese: 'I am discouraged by the people around me. They say learning Chinese is tantamount to preparing oneself for Chinese slavery' (p. 182). Sentiments such as these are examples of the anti-ought-to self by studying a specific language despite external pressure not to do so.

In fact, the authors in this volume seem to have sought out unique learners in largely under-represented contexts – perhaps these authors have a bit of anti-ought-to self characteristics themselves! The authors have shed light on not only under-studied contexts, but also learners in these contexts who are studying languages other than English.

To further explore selves such as the anti-ought-to or rebellious self, populations that have not been often explored should be considered. Hajar's chapter (Chapter 11) about the internally displaced refugees in Syria who are learning Turkish is one example. Although refugees in this context, as well as other contexts, must learn the language of the context for survival, those who thrive may have the propensity to flourish in challenging situations. Although quite a different situation because of the agency involved, aspects of the anti-ought-to self may also be present in international students, especially when choosing a country of study in a place very different from the country of origin. I have been thinking about the connection between anti-ought-to self and success in studies while working with a current group of Fulbright grantees on a six-week pre-academic program through the English Language Learning Institute in the Department of World Languages, Literatures, and Linguistics at West Virginia University. These students have undergone fierce competition to win a graduate studies scholarship; as we are working with them in this pre-academic program, I am (anecdotally) noticing differences in academic success based on the willingness to embrace challenges. It would be fascinating to study groups like this longitudinally to measure specific aspects of self, including the anti-ought-to self, to see how their language learning and scholastic motivation change over time. And certainly, relating aspects of the L2MSS to other constructs such as grit, buoyancy and perseverance, to name a few, would also shed light on the intricacies of motivational selves and the relation to selves and context (Thompson, 2021b).

In sum, this edited volume does an outstanding job of highlighting aspects of motivation research that are often under-studied: multilingualism, LOTEs and contexts, with other complexities interwoven. This volume will certainly be a valuable resource for any scholar who works in this area, particularly those who wish to push the boundaries of what has traditionally been done in this field.

References

Brehm, J.W. (1966) *A Theory of Psychological Reactance*. Academic Press.
Dörnyei, Z. (2009) The L2 motivational self system. In Z. Dörnyei and E. Ushioda (eds) *Motivation, Language Identity and the L2 Self* (pp. 9–42). Multilingual Matters.
Henrich, J., Heine, S.J. and Norenzayan, A. (2010) The weirdest people in the world? *Behavioral and Brain Sciences* 33 (2–3), 61–135.
Henry, A. (2017) L2 motivation and multilingual identities. *The Modern Language Journal* 101 (3), 548–565.

Henry, A. and Thorsen, C. (2018) The ideal multilingual self: Validity, influences on motivation, and role in a multilingual education. *International Journal of Multilingualism* 15 (4), 349–364.
Holliday, A. (2006) Native-speakerism. *ELT Journal* 60 (4), 385–387.
Lanvers, U. (2016) Lots of selves, some rebellious: Developing the self discrepancy model for language learners. *System* 60, 79–92.
Mercer, S. (2016) The contexts within me: L2 self as a complex dynamic system. In J. King (ed.) *The Dynamic Interplay Between Context and the Language Learner* (pp. 11–28). Palgrave Macmillan.
Ortega, L. (2014) Ways forward for a bi/multilingual turn in SLA. In S. May (ed.) *The Multilingual Turn: Implications for SLA, TESOL, and Bilingual Education* (pp. 32–53). Routledge.
Ortega, L. (2019) SLA and the study of equitable multilingualism. *The Modern Language Journal* 103 (S1), 23–38.
Serafini, E.J. (2020) Further exploring the dynamicity, situatedness, and emergence of the self: The key role of context. *Studies in Second Language Learning and Teaching* 10 (1), 133–157.
Thompson, A.S. (2017a) Don't tell me what to do! The anti-ought-to self and language learning motivation. *System* 67, 38–49.
Thompson, A.S. (2017b) Language learning motivation in the United States: An examination of language choice and multilingualism. *The Modern Language Journal* 101 (3), 483–500.
Thompson, A.S. (2021a) *The Role of Context in Language Teachers' Self Development and Motivation: Perspectives from Multilingual Settings*. Multilingual Matters.
Thompson, A.S. (2021b) Conceptualizing the anti-ought-to self: Background and new directions. *Revue TDFLE* 78, 1–21.
Thompson, A.S. and Vásquez, C. (2015) Exploring motivational profiles through language learning narratives. *The Modern Language Journal* 99 (1), 158–174.
Ushioda, E. (2011) Why autonomy? Insights from motivation theory and research. *Innovation in Language Learning and Teaching* 5 (2), 221–232.

Index

Al-Hoorie, A. 2, 10, 72, 84, 86, 109, 124, 174, 189, 207, 209, 214, 223, 228
Anti-ought-to self 209, 233–235
Arabic v, viii, xvii, 3, 5, 34–51, 108, 112, 124, 130, 144, 152–153, 193, 196–197, 199–200, 202–203, 231–233

Block, D. 14, 30, 90, 105, 111, 124, 193, 206
Bourdieusian vi, 7, 173, 186, 188

China xvi, xvii, xviii, 3, 7, 9, 28, 32, 35, 37, 40–41, 47, 50–51, 55–57, 59, 60, 64, 68–69, 74, 88, 110, 112, 117, 122, 172, 175, 177, 179–181, 1831–86, 189–191, 194, 204, 231
Chinese v, vi, vii, xvi, xvii, 3, 5, 7, 11, 33–38, 40, 42, 45–46, 49–53, 56–58, 69–70, 74–75, 93, 95–95, 108, 112, 116–118, 124–125, 130, 143, 145, 148–149, 151–152, 157, 160, 162, 167, 171–177, 179–191, 204, 207–208, 215, 227, 231–233
Civil war 4, 192, 198, 200, 203
Contentedly bilingual self 5, 16, 21, 23–26, 72–73, 76, 78, 83–85
COVID-19 pandemic 76, 79, 224
Csizér, K. 11–12, 32, 106, 129, 141, 171, 210, 213, 227–228

Dörnyei, Z. 2, 10–12, 15–17, 31, 33, 35–36, 50–51, 53–55, 58, 67–69, 72, 77–78, 84, 86–88, 91, 93, 105–107, 109, 112, 121–125, 141, 147, 165, 170, 173–174, 189, 191, 195, 206, 208–209, 211, 213–214, 216, 221–223, 227–229, 231, 234

Emotional discomfort vi, 8, 209
Emotional experience 8, 171, 209–211, 213, 222–224
Emotional reactions 215, 222–223

England xvi, xviii, 68, 112, 139
English as a global language 6, 72, 74, 78, 81, 84–85, 174, 184
English as a foreign language (EFL) xv, 68–69, 86, 88, 105–106, 191, 208, 213, 227, 229
Europe; European 3, 74, 84, 86, 127–129, 134–135, 139–140, 193–194, 206, 209, 223
Extrinsic motivation 84, 92, 94, 100, 103, 106

French 3, 22–23, 25, 28–29, 31, 37–38, 41, 74–75, 87, 105, 109, 122, 127, 130, 144, 148–149, 153, 156, 165–170, 207, 231
Future self/selves 19, 22, 32, 69, 113, 176, 205–206, 210–212, 221

Gao, A. v, xvi, xvii, xviii, 2, 8–9, 11, 34, 50–51, 56, 68–69, 124, 207
Gardner, R.C. 1, 11, 72, 77, 86, 91, 105, 131, 141–142, 147, 165, 170, 173, 189, 195, 206, 212, 228
German 3, 5–6, 23, 28–29, 37, 41, 56–57, 59–67, 74–86, 105, 116, 127, 130, 144, 148–149, 153, 165, 167, 169, 231
Germany 78–82, 86, 90, 106, 206

Higher-order Self-guides 16, 20–21
Henry, A. v, x, 1, 2, 4–5, 10–13, 15–17, 20–21, 23–32, 34–35, 48, 51, 53–54, 58, 68–69, 72–74, 77, 83–84, 87, 92, 105, 109, 124, 146–147, 163, 165, 170–171, 194, 206–207, 229–230, 234–235
Higgins, E.T. 17, 26–27, 30–32, 72, 87, 146, 170, 212, 216, 228

Ideal (L2) self viii, 10, 22, 69, 88, 91, 146, 191, 209–212, 215–222, 225, 227

236

Ideal multilingual self 4, 5, 9–10, 12, 16, 21, 25–26, 28–29, 31, 33–34, 51, 53–54, 66–67, 69, 73, 76–78, 83, 85, 87–88, 109, 123, 125, 146–147, 165, 170, 191–192, 194, 207–208, 235
Indonesia; Indonesian v, xvii, 3–4, 7, 9, 93, 124, 126–127, 129–132, 134, 136, 139–140, 142, 145, 170, 207, 231
Integrativeness 72, 77, 83–84, 195
Intercultural citizen(ship) 7, 108, 123–124, 232–233
Internally Displaced Syrians vi, xvii, 8, 192–193, 195, 205, 232
International posture 77, 84, 88, 173, 191, 195, 207
Intrinsic motivation 72, 79–81, 84, 92, 100, 103–105
International English Language Testing System (IELTS) 113, 184
International students 6, 9, 11, 89–91, 93, 95, 100–101, 124–125, 180, 206, 234
Invest; investment v, 14, 50, 66, 109, 111–113, 120, 122, 177, 195

Japan v, xvii, xviii, 3, 6, 9, 11–12, 55, 69, 71–75, 82–89, 91, 93–94, 98, 101, 104–106, 125, 147–148, 194, 204, 207, 231
Japanese v, vii, xvi, 3, 6, 37, 41, 69–70, 32, 73–76, 81–95, 97–106, 110, 144, 147–149, 152–153, 167, 172, 189, 191, 204, 207–208, 215, 231

Kazakhstan xvii, 3, 6, 9, 108–110, 113, 115–117, 119–121, 123, 125, 206, 231
Korean v, vii, xv, xvii, 3, 6, 8, 37, 50, 75–78, 83, 85, 93, 95, 97–98, 102, 108–125, 144, 147, 152–153, 170–171, 206–207, 210, 214–217, 223–224, 226–229, 231

L2 motivational self system (L2MSS) 17, 54, 58, 69, 91, 195, 209, 211–214, 221, 231–232, 234
Lamb, M. 1, 11–12, 29, 32, 55, 67, 69, 123–124, 171, 195, 207
Language learning strategy(ies) (LLS); strategic language learning 3, 6, 9, 11, 89, 108, 109, 111–113, 116, 120–125, 165, 192–196, 198, 200–202, 204–207, 227, 232
Learner agency 9, 120, 198, 202, 204, 207, 232
Likert scale 149–150, 153, 155–156, 159, 161, 216–218, 225–226
long-term motivation, 66, 90, 92, 106

MacIntyre, P. 30, 32, 87, 104, 106, 147, 165, 170–171, 173, 189, 212, 221–223, 228–229
Malaysia xvii, 3, 7, 9, 127, 139, 141–145, 147–148, 157, 163–165, 170–172, 194, 231
May, S. 2–4, 11, 13, 32, 34, 51, 194, 207, 235
Mental images xvii, 7, 126–133, 139–142, 207
Mercer, S. xiv, 4, 9–12, 202, 204, 207, 231–233, 235
Mixed methods 32, 122–123, 130, 132, 189
Monolingual self 5, 16, 21–23, 26
Multilingual agentive selves (MASs) 5, 36, 39–40, 44, 46–50
Multilingual turn (in SLA) xvii, 2, 4–5, 11, 13–15, 29–30, 32, 34, 44, 51, 53–54, 105, 207, 230, 235
Multilingualism xvi, xviii, 2–3, 5, 8–14, 21, 27, 30–33, 50–51, 54, 66, 68–70, 74, 87, 105, 144, 146, 169, 171–172, 194, 207, 230–231, 234–235
Multimodal language learning histories (MLLHs) viii, 6, 89–91, 93–100, 103–104

Near peer role models (NPRMs) 7, 111, 119–120, 121–122, 125
Norton, B. 14, 32, 34, 51, 109, 111, 124–125, 173, 190, 193, 195, 207

Ortega, L. 2–3, 9, 11, 13–15, 29, 32–33, 193, 204, 207, 230–231, 235
Ought-to (L2) self viii, 8, 69, 91, 209, 211, 214–216, 218–222, 225
Ought-to multilingual self 5, 16, 27–29, 53, 56–68

Pakistan xvii, 3–4, 7, 9, 11, 125, 173–177, 179–181, 183–190, 233
Peace 47, 204–205
Persistence v, 6, 9, 11, 66, 68, 71, 75, 78, 84–85–87, 182
Person-in-context relational view of motivation 92, 107, 191
Politics; Political xvi, 19, 27, 38, 42–44, 71, 85, 87, 115, 117, 119, 124, 127, 174, 179, 185, 193, 204, 215, 232
Portugal; Portuguese vii, viii, xvii, 3, 7, 37, 126–142, 144–145, 171, 210, 228, 231

Qualitative 5, 8, 28, 50–51, 56–57, 68–69, 86, 92, 104, 110–111, 113–114, 124, 129–133, 142, 174, 176–177, 190, 193–195, 205–206, 211, 213

Quantitative 5, 8, 28, 68, 92, 130–133, 190, 216
Questionnaire 7, 75, 130–132, 136–137, 144, 148–150, 154, 165–167, 212, 216–217, 225, 228

Refugees 207, 234
Ryan, S. xiv, 1, 10–12, 32, 50, 55, 69, 72, 79, 84, 86–87, 91–92, 94, 105–106, 124, 171, 174, 191, 206, 216, 227, 229

Self-discrepancy theory 8, 17, 72, 209, 211–214, 222
Self-determination theory 87, 91, 106, 191
Self-efficacy 124, 147, 210, 219–221, 226
Social turn (in SLA) 14, 30, 124, 193–194, 206
South Korea 76–77, 110, 113, 115–120, 124, 215
Sweden 21, 23, 25, 28, 31, 74
Swedish 22–25, 30–31, 37, 72, 109
Syria; Syrian xvii, 3–4, 8–9, 124, 192, 196, 198–199, 203–204, 206, 208, 234

Test of proficiency in Korean (TOPIK) 76, 115–117, 121, 229
Third language 23, 31, 57, 108, 143

Thompson, A.S. vi, 4, 8–9, 12, 15–16, 33, 53, 55, 69, 172, 194, 207, 230, 232–235
Turkey 8, 192, 199–201, 203–204, 208
Turkish xvii, 3, 8, 192–193, 196–205, 231–232, 234

Umino, T. v, 6, 89, 91, 94, 106, 194, 207
Ushioda, E. 2, 4, 10, 12, 15, 31, 33–36, 48, 51, 53–54, 67–69, 72, 83, 88, 92–93, 103, 105, 107–109, 111, 125, 172–174, 188–189, 191, 193–194, 206, 208, 228, 232, 234–235

Vietnam xvii, 3–4, 8–9, 124, 195, 206, 210, 214–217, 223–224, 228, 231
Vietnamese 8, 210, 215–217, 223

WEIRD (Western, Educated, Industrialized, Rich, and Democratic societies) 231, 234
Willingness to communicate 31, 104, 106, 208

Yashima, T. 77, 88, 173, 191, 194–195, 206, 208

Zheng, Y. xvi, xvii, xviii, 5, 34–37, 41, 45, 48–54, 56, 68, 70, 74, 88, 124, 146, 165, 172, 194, 208, 232

Milton Keynes UK
Ingram Content Group UK Ltd.
UKHW020842310524
443451UK00007B/467